Table of Contents

Publisher's note

The views and opinions expressed in this book are those of the author entirely and are not necessarily shared by the publisher. Readers should draw their own conclusions about all claims made or any facts or opinions stated in the book concerning which the possibility of alternative interpretations, narratives, terminology or descriptions should be borne in mind.

Acknowledgements

Many people have helped me with writing this book. I thank them all. At the forefront are two old friends and colleagues, Professor Terence Walters BL, LLM, LLB, and Phil Huxley LLM, LLB. Their knowledge of police powers, criminal law, evidence and procedure is truly immense, and their expertise in these areas was invaluable as I trod through the minefield of facts and law applicable to this case. My most grateful thanks also to Dr Edward Tierney and Dr David Anderson for granting me access to their notes and sharing their recollection of a case in which they had direct involvement in events and formidable insight into their meaning.

The views on the law expressed in this book, and the interpretation of the facts as disclosed in the evidence are, however, mine alone.

I owe an immense debt to the law firm of Stephensons, Solicitors LLP for allowing me access to the original papers in this case and above all to their litigation partner, Campbell Malone. He and his colleagues at Stephensons enjoy an international reputation for their splendid and courageous work, righting the wrongs of many miscarriages of justice in the criminal justice system in England and Wales. They prove that those who search for the truth with determination and dedication, even in the face of great public hostility, will frequently prevail.

Campbell Malone promised Stefan Kiszko's mother Charlotte, just before she died, that he would do his best to ensure that Stefan's case was never forgotten. If this book helps in the keeping of that promise then all the time and effort involved in its writing will be worthwhile.

When I asked Campbell who he thought had wounded Charlotte Kiszko the most — the Nazis who invaded her native Yugoslavia when she was a young girl or the criminal justice system in her adopted country to which she fled seeking safety — he replied with her amazing story; she arrived in this country and started work in the cotton mills of Rochdale, was struck down by byssinosis, then lost her son to a monstrous miscarriage of justice. Nevertheless, he said, becoming the inaugural Rochdale Woman of the Year was the proudest day of her life, after Stefan's successful appeal. She was 'a truly indomitable woman'. I trust that few who read this book will disagree with that. She died in May 1994, aged 70, some 20 weeks after Stefan's sudden and unexpected death at the family home. The inscription on her tombstone reads 'A loving wife and a very devoted mother'. She died as she lived, for Charlotte Kiszko remains forever a shining example of a mother's love for her son.

Michael O'Connell
June 2017

About the Author

Michael O'Connell was called to the Bar of England and Wales in 1966 and to that of the Republic of Ireland in 1977. He was a pupil in 1 Temple Gardens in London where the head of chambers was one of the UK's most famous advocates and prosecutors, Christmas Humphreys. He was for a number of years honorary legal adviser to the Catholic Social Services for Prisoners, a charitable organization that helps serving prisoners and their families. He has a Masters Degree for his research in the area of arrest, interrogation and detention powers of the Irish Police, *An Garda Siochana*. He retired from criminal practice in 2006.

He wrote, jointly with Professor Terence Walters, *A Guide to the Police & Criminal Evidence Act 1984* (Financial Training, 1985), and was joint editor, with Phil Huxley, of the first nine editions of *Blackstone's Statutes on Evidence* (Oxford University Press). His book, *In Search of the Truth* (2017), about British injustice and collusion in Northern Ireland during The Troubles was published by Collins Press of Cork, Republic of Ireland.

The author of the Foreword

Campbell Malone was admitted as a solicitor in 1969 and initially worked as a legal aid practitioner in the North West of England, principally in his own small practices. In 1999 he was invited to join the leading firm of Stephensons, where he remained as a partner until 2010, and then consultant until his retirement in 2013. During his time at Stephensons, two separate partner-led departments were established, one specialising in Criminal Appeals, the other in Human Rights. Working mainly as a criminal defence lawyer, one of his notable early cases was that of the Shrewsbury Pickets (building workers Des Warren and now actor Ricky Tomlinson) in 1973/74. After the successful appeal of Stefan Kiszko (who he represented) appeals and applications to the Criminal Cases Review Commission played an increasing part of his work, with well over a dozen serious cases being referred back to the Court of Appeal. These included two successful appeals against murder convictions involving a confession. He was the solicitor in three out of the four conjoined appeals in *R v Harris* ([2005] EWCA Crim 1980) the leading case on Shaken Baby Syndrome. In 2002, Campbell Malone helped establish the Criminal Appeal Lawyers Association which he chaired from its inception until his retirement. He was also a founder member of the Inside Justice panel. He now 'delights in being a fond grandfather ... and a struggling artist!'

This book is dedicated with love to my wife Eileen, and to my two sisters Mary and Patricia, my brother Charles and to the memory of my parents James and Mary O'Connell, to whom I owe so much.

Foreword

Campbell Malone

The story of the appalling and savage murder of the young Lesley Molseed and the subsequent arrest, trial and conviction for murder of Stefan Kiszko is both tragic and compelling. It is the perfect illustration of how a serious miscarriage of justice can arise and the devastation that can be caused, not just to the wrongly accused and his family but to the victim and the family of the victim.

As Michael O'Connell, the author of this powerful and comprehensive analysis of the case, points out I would have been ready to welcome another look at this case because I promised Charlotte Kiszko in the final months of her life (and shortly after the premature death of her son, Stefan) that I would do whatever was in my power to keep alive the memory of her son and what the deficiencies of our legal system did to him. I have been happy to assist Michael wherever I could in the way of access to papers and to my recollections as to what happened in the progress to a successful appeal but I must emphasise that this is very much Michael's book to which he brings not only obvious diligence and time-consuming research but his own passion, perception and trenchant critique.

So I have an obvious interest in the story having been approached by Charlotte to assist her son in attempting to overturn his conviction and been lucky enough to have assisted in clearing his name but why should the modern reader be concerned with the story of a murder and a wrongful conviction now over 40-years-old. The first reason is that the case of Stefan Kiszko is the story of a classic miscarriage of justice, of a vulnerable young man convicted of murder following a confession to that crime when he could not have possibly committed it; and also to two offences of indecent exposure, one of which almost certainly never happened.

I have always believed that for a miscarriage of justice to occur there has to be a defective police investigation, an inadequate defence and a flawed trial. All of those things certainly applied to Stefan Kiszko and that is putting it mildly. Michael, in his book, is more trenchant and readers, faced with the evidence he puts before them, will decide for themselves whether, for example, the police officers in the case were incompetent or something more sinister. So Stefan's case is a classic miscarriage of justice but it is also unusual in that in clearing his name it was established, on the basis of overwhelming scientific evidence, that he was not merely not guilty but totally innocent. It is also relatively unusual that, albeit some 30 years after the murder, another man, Ronald Castree, was tried to conviction for killing Lesley.

Of course it is undoubtedly true that many things that may have contributed to Stefan's ordeal have changed. Stefan was interviewed and made his damaging confession unrepresented and without the protection of the Police and Criminal Evidence Act 1984. Dr James McKeith and Professor Gisli Gudjonsson were yet to join forces to carry out their pioneering research into suggestibility in relation to confessions. Although DNA evidence led to the conviction of Ronald Castree it was not available to either the police or the defence of the time of Stefan's trial. I am conscious of the penetrating criticism of the defence lawyers by Michael in this book but my own recollection as a criminal lawyer practising at that time is that forensic scientists were rarely challenged and that defence lawyers were, in any event, ill-equipped so to do.

Things are of course different now and in many ways better but my second reason for welcoming this book as being important and relevant is that there are many reasons to believe that miscarriages of justice are just as likely to occur nowadays, if not more! Stefan's conviction was overturned at a time when a number of other wrongful convictions were coming to light. The successful appeals of Judith Ward, the Birmingham six, etc. led for a time to a feeling that things would be different from then on and the setting up of the Criminal Cases Review Commission was widely welcomed but the pendulum has long since swung back. The pressure on legal aid funding is a time bomb ticking away. Solicitors are poorly paid for criminal defence work and it is often done by inexperienced and overworked unqualified staff. Far from there being a financial incentive to prepare a case for trial properly the reverse is in fact true. Of course there are many diligent and committed lawyers working on behalf of defendants but I am aware that even in complex cases counsel will receive the papers where absolutely no preparation has been done. When attempts are made to prepare a case properly there is constant resistance and downward pressure on expenditure on such things as expert witnesses who may well be absolutely vital in those cases where it is necessary to challenge scientific evidence. This book demonstrates only too clearly why it is vital that defence lawyers do their jobs in a thorough and competent manner.

My concern is that not only are wrongful convictions just as likely to occur (albeit in different circumstances to those that applied to Stefan) but that there are not going to be experienced defence lawyers willing and able to take on the investigation required to overturn them. Legal aid is reluctantly made available but at uneconomic rates. The decision to close the Forensic Science Service some years ago was foolish in the extreme and already problems are occurring. Those still involved in trying to bring justice to the wrongly convicted are sometimes experiencing difficulty in tracing exhibits. As well as the age-old problem of trying to get disclosure of key items and documents out of a reluctant public body there is now the problem of who actually is responsible for maintaining and preserving them. As I am writing this Foreword there is an investigation into apparent manipulation of scientific data in criminal cases at Randox with possible implications in many cases. The CCRC is overwhelmed with applications but is consistently underfunded with the result that it is taking longer and longer to complete complex enquiries and may well be unable to investigate as extensively as might be required. They are open to the criticism that they are too cautious in referring cases back to the Court of Appeal

Stefan's case is in so many ways the benchmark for what can go wrong in the criminal process and how lives can be ruined and in some cases cut short. This book reminds us of why we should care and seek to ensure that it never happens again.

An Overview of the Case

Sunday 5 October 1975 was a cool and quiet early autumn day but one that was marked by the tragic murder of a little girl. The victim was Lesley Susan Molseed, then aged eleven. She lived on Delamere Road on the Turf Hill Estate in Rochdale, Greater Manchester with her mother April and stepfather Danny, her two sisters, 16-year-old Julie and 13-year old Laura, and their brother, 12-year-old Freddie. As well as being the youngest member of the family, Lesley, known as Lel, was especially treasured because she was so tiny, weighing only three stone (19 kilogrammes) and standing just four feet tall (1.2 metres). She had been born with heart and breathing difficulties and in fact spent the first year of her life in hospital. She later attended a school for children with special needs. Around 1 pm on that Sunday Lesley was told by her mother April that she wanted a loaf of bread and an air freshener from a local shop. The younger children of the family, that is her 12-year-old brother Freddie as well as Lesley herself, took it in turns to run these errands for which there was a small cash payment. On this Sunday it was really Freddie's turn to go to the shop, either the Spar shop on Ansdell Road or Margaret's shop on Broad Lane, both only a short distance away, but he was off kicking a football, so Lesley went instead. It is clear that for the remainder of his life Freddie was unforgiving in his sense of guilt and self-criticism that, 'if only, if only' he had gone to the shop instead of Lesley, she would not have been abducted and murdered on that terrible day.

On 19 March 2005, after 30 years of unrelenting grief and in a state of deep depression, Freddie took his own life by cutting his throat with a kitchen knife. His body was found at his home in Wardle Edge, Smallbridge, Rochdale. He was married, with a wife and three children.

At the subsequent inquest the coroner was told that he was deeply affected by his sister's death.

When Lesley left the house around lunchtime her sister Julie watched as the little girl skipped down the path onto the pavement, setting off towards the shops. She was wearing a blue coat with a hood and carrying a blue lined shopping bag. Julie also noticed Lesley was wearing her Bay City Rollers socks—they were her favourite pop group. Julie could not have realised that Lesley was leaving home for the last time. She would never see her little sister alive again, for this dearly loved little girl had only a few hours to live. A sexual predator armed with a knife, a lustful man with a propensity for ferocious violence against children was trawling the area in a motor car seeking a suitable victim. He saw Lesley and somehow or other lured her into his vehicle. She was to become a victim of a vicious paedophilic psychopathic killer

Her mutilated body, lying face down, was found three days later, at about 7 am on Wednesday 8 October 1975 on Rishworth Moor above the A672 Oldham to Halifax Road. It was on an elevated area of moorland about 15 feet higher than the carriageway of the A672 leading to the motorway intersection number 22. There was a lay-by immediately below on the right hand side of the road from the direction of Ripponden. She had been brutally stabbed 12 times. Her murderer had ejaculated over her body and clothing. The police officers involved in the subsequent murder inquiry, many of them with young children of their own, were fiercely determined that Lesley's killer should be arrested, charged, convicted and imprisoned for so long that he would be completely removed from society and never kill again.

Near to the body was a small purse and a blue shopping bag, and on a rock some yards away was found a felt-tipped pen. The man who found the body was a shop fitter and joiner from Nottingham. He had spent the night sleeping in his motor vehicle parked in the lay-by. Lesley had been stabbed 12 times in a sustained and frenzied attack. The cause of death was multiple stab wounds in the heart, the aorta and the left lung. It appeared that she was attacked where she was found and probably on the day she was abducted. The most likely weapon was a knife, the blade of which was around 2.5 inches long and the blows to her chest appeared to be targeted, not random.

The first police officer arrived at the murder scene at 8.25 am. Detective Superintendent Richard Holland arrived there at 9 am He was the second most senior officer on the inquiry team, which was headed by Detective Chief Superintendent Jack Dibb, the head of the West Yorkshire No. 1 Crime Area. It was agreed at the outset that there would be a joint inquiry into the murder carried out by officers from the Greater Manchester Police and the West Yorkshire Police. At a very early stage in this inquiry, Dibb was appointed to investigate another murder, this time in the Bradford area. Although he remained in overall charge, the main ongoing responsibility rested with Superintendent Holland.

A pathologist, Professor David Gee, and Mr Ronald Outteridge, a principal scientific officer in charge of biology based at the Home Office Forensic Science Laboratory in Harrogate and on occasions at Wetherby, attended the scene. They arrived at about 10.30 am, examined the body and took samples. At first sight it did not seem to be a murder with a sexual motive, for Lesley's underclothing seemed undisturbed. But later analysis of her clothing in the laboratory showed light staining of semen on her skirt and knickers. There was insufficient to enable a blood grouping to be established, but the semen was shown to contain sperm heads, albeit in limited numbers. A forensic scientist, Peter Guise, made up microscope slides from the semen stains and carried out a test to record the level of sperm heads. It was the lowest available, +H. His results were communicated to the police the next day, 9 October 1975. Ronald Outteridge was informed of them at 5 pm that same day as well. There was, however, no reference in the preliminary report to the existence of sperm in the semen. Most such specimens would contain sperm and at this early stage of the police investigation in October 1975 this would not be regarded as being of great importance.

By December 1975 this had changed. It is now known that when the police detained Stefan Kiszko and induced him to confess to murder they subsequently searched his home, on 21 December 1975. Police Constable Booth, who may have known that semen had been found upon the dead girl's clothing, found a handkerchief under a pillow on

Stefan's bed and this was sent to the forensic science laboratory the next day. An examination carried out on that handkerchief by a scientist Mr Brian Damper revealed the presence of semen that contained no sperm whatsoever. He conveyed the results to Chief Superintendent Dibb and Ronald Outteridge that same afternoon. That was, of course, before Dr Edward Tierney had obtained the sample from Stefan Kiszko. The whole object of that exercise was to establish whether or not the semen on the murdered victim's underclothing had been left there by Stefan Kiszko. The one person who would be most interested, one would think, would be the very person who had written out the confession statement, that is Detective Superintendent Holland. The analysis of the sample would undoubtedly corroborate the confession, but only, of course, if it was a true confession.

In a statement dated 22 December 1992, after Stefan's conviction had been quashed by the Appeal Court the then retired former Superintendent Dick Holland wrote: 'I have never received a report or statement to the effect that the semen on Molseed's knickers did not match the ejaculation of Kiszko, or he would not have been charged'. Much depends on whether that statement is true

On 22 February 1992 Dr Tierney was interviewed by a journalist, Margarette Driscoll of the *Sunday Times*, who recorded him as saying,

> 'My physical examination confirmed a diagnosis of hypogonadism. It was explained to Dibb that if indeed Stefan was suffering from hypogonadism then he would be sterile. If he was sterile, there would be no sperm heads present.'

Detective Superintendent Holland was interviewed by the same journalist. She describes him as 'the other principal investigating officer'. He told her,

> '…had there been any discrepancy between the sample on the girl and the sample produced by Kiszko, then I would have expected the forensic scientist to come back to us and say categorically they don't match. That would have thrown an entirely different light on the matter.'

I simply don't believe him. I think he was told and realised exactly the difficulty he had created for himself. He maintained that Stefan Kiszko had provided, openly and voluntarily, three vitally important pieces of information known only to the murderer and a limited number of other people, including Holland himself.

First, it was claimed in cross-examination at the trial that only five police officers, none of them lower than the rank of chief inspector, knew that the killer had ejaculated over the body of the little girl. (That answer may not be entirely accurate or truthful. We know that PC Booth had removed a handkerchief from under a pillow in Stefan's bedroom for the express purpose of forensic examination. I consider that constable knew for what purpose he took possession of that object). Second, it was never publicly disclosed that the killer had not removed the child's knickers. Third, the forensic evidence supported Stefan's purported claim about wiping the blade of the murder weapon on the body or the clothes of the little murdered girl.

Since these detailed facts were set out in Stefan's confession statement, and he was not the killer, that information must have been fed to him by someone, probably Holland, either before or during the making of the statement. That is what Stefan claimed while giving evidence at his trial. The words were not his, they were those of the police officer who wrote them.

If the Director of Public Prosecutions had been told that the forensic scientists were stating that Stefan Kiszko's semen did not match that on the child's underclothing and accordingly he was not the murderer, how could these facts in the so-called voluntary confession be explained away by Holland? I believe that someone decided that the scientific evidence should be suppressed, simply because of the complete and utter conviction held by some, including Superintendent Holland, once Stefan became a suspect because of the young girls' allegations of indecency and the testosterone injections he had been having (see particularly *Chapter Ten*), that he was Lesley Molseed's killer. Nothing was going to change that view. In any event, once the confession came into existence, it was too late to change it anyway.

The man who abducted and murdered Lesley was Ronald Charles Edward Castree, a 21-year-old part-time taxi driver who later became a market trader and then a shop owner selling comics, an occupation which would have given him easy and ready access to children if he so wished. Only he knows how he lured Lesley from the pavement into his car and to her death on that first Sunday in October. According to Robert Lindsay Whittaker, Lesley's teacher at High Birch School, she would have gone off with someone if they had approached her in a manner that suited her. It is now very unlikely that Ronald Castree will ever say how he enticed her into his vehicle. The probability is that he will continue to maintain his innocence, as he did at his trial in 2007, pointing to the fact that a completely innocent man, Stefan Kiszko, had previously been convicted of Lesley's murder, and now here he is, another innocent man, serving a life sentence for a crime he did not commit either. This approach disregards the weight and nature of the evidence against him.

Ronald Castree was born on 19 October 1953 in Littleborough, some three miles from Rochdale but within its Metropolitan borough. He was not even a suspect in the murder in 1975. He stood and watched as Stefan Kiszko was detained by the police in December 1975 and following six interviews whilst in the police station Stefan confessed in detail to killing Lesley Molseed. After making a written confession statement, written for him of course by a police officer for notwithstanding the fact Stefan worked as a clerk for the Inland Revenue, he like so many others seemed to lose the capacity to write whilst in a police station, he was then allowed access to a solicitor. Immediately after seeing the solicitor he retracted that confession indicating it was involuntary and untrue, That solicitor then left his client at the police station without even bothering to check his status. If he had, he would have discovered that Stefan was a volunteer, and not under arrest. He should have been told, both by the police and by his own solicitor that he was free to leave the police station anytime he wished. The solicitor also failed to call for and examine the Detained Person's Register (otherwise and elsewhere described as 'the detention sheet') which recorded relevant details of his treatment by the police including the reason for him being in that police station in the first instance. In fact because Stefan had not been arrested but had been invited to the police station to help with enquires no Detained Person's Register would have been opened; that was only required for those under arrest. Access to legal advice was also only available at that time to arrested persons. A competent and experienced solicitor would also have asked the police first: 'What was the status of my client when he arrived at the police station and where is the written record of his treatment here?' And second, at the later stage, 'When, if at all, is my client to be charged with any criminal offence, more especially the offence of murder which you claim he voluntarily admitted?' No such questions were ever asked.

Stefan was being questioned about allegations of indecent exposure all of which he at first denied. Initially there was no mention by the police of Lesley's murder. I consider he was being unlawfully detained when he was put into a cell and kept all night at that police station. That unlawful detention continued whilst Stefan confessed twice, once orally and then in writing, in considerable detail, to murdering Lesley Molseed. He was at that time 23-years-of-age. He had led a solitary life with virtually no friends, even as a schoolboy, and certainly no enemies. His asthmatic condition had prevented him from starting school until he was seven-years-old. In his late teens he was grossly overweight, weighing in at over 17 stone. He was a person of good character, with no criminal convictions of any kind and with no propensity for violence. He would never hurt anyone. He was quietly spoken and spent most of his free time outside of working hours at the family home with his mother Charlotte and frequently her sister Alfreda as well. He became even closer to them following the sudden and unexpected death of his father, who collapsed and died in the street in September 1970, when Stefan was only 18 years of age. The following year his mother bought him as new Hillman Avenger motor car. It became his pride and joy. Nothing pleased him more than for him to be able to take his mother to and from work and to bring her, and her sister Alfreda, to the shops for the weekly grocery shopping.

Neither of these elderly ladies wavered in their support for Stefan, they never accepted his guilt and together they bravely fought to establish his innocence. No one would listen to his and their claims that he had not committed a terrible murder to which he had confessed while detained in police custody. Protestations of innocence by the convicted in what some claim to be the finest criminal justice system in the World are commonplace. Those protestations are seldom believed and are frequently disregarded. Often, perhaps too often, they turn out to be true.

Stefan's case has been described as one of the greatest miscarriages of justice of all time. He had a medical condition known as male hypogonadism. Forensic evidence conclusively proving he could not have killed Lesley Molseed was suppressed by the police.

Stefan was moved from prison to prison after his conviction. From Leed's Armley Gaol to Wakefield in the north of England to Gloucester and Bristol in the south-west. His mother and her sister travelled thousands of miles by train and bus to visit him in an effort to support him in the fight to clear his name. They watched helplessly as Stefan's mind began to disintegrate. His fellow prisoners constantly ridiculed him because of his appearance and demeanour, and followed that by seriously assaulting him, claiming they were extracting vengeance for Lesley and her family. The prison staff did not hurry to intervene in the punching and kicking to which Stefan was subjected to on several occasions. Convicted child killers, even those who maintain their innocence, have no friends within the confines of the prison wall. By 1983, Stefan's mental condition had deteriorated so much that it was recommended that he should be transferred to Broadmoor, a high security psychiatric hospital at Crowthorne in Berkshire, which houses Britain's most dangerous criminals. In the event Stefan was not sent there, but moved back to Wakefield Prison where he was nearer his family.

Stefan's mother eventually enlisted the help of a highly experienced criminal solicitor Campbell Malone, whose drive and determination eventually got Stefan's case referred back to the Appeal Court for a second time. His conviction was then set aside when his total innocence was established. Following his release from prison he returned home on 17 March 1992. There Stefan spoke lovingly of the care and devotion heaped upon him by his mother and his aunt, and of his wish to travel, to marry and to settle down and lead a normal life. It was not to be. He collapsed and died at his family home in December 1993. A friend told the *Guardian* newspaper on 24 December:

'[A]fter being released Stefan could not rouse himself and never recovered from what had happened…he could not face the World'.

Although it was a medical opinion that considered Stefan suffered from delusions of innocence, in reality he was wrongly convicted simply because, as I strongly believe, a ruthless and corrupt senior police officer, former Superintendent Richard Holland, now deceased, was suffering from 'delusions of guilt'. He had totally convinced himself and others that Stefan had murdered Lesley; it is my view that he falsified evidence in order to prove it. Later Stefan was to claim that at the start of an interview in the police station the superintendent was very aggressive and threatening in his manner. He assaulted Stefan, it is claimed by the latter, by poking him on the shoulder, repeatedly saying, 'I'll get the fucking truth out of you one way or the other'. On that ground alone, in my view, the defence ought to have challenged and sought a ruling from the trial judge on the admissibility of the confession evidence, for without that confession there was no proof from anyone or anything that Stefan was guilty of the murder of Lesley Molseed. No such challenge was ever put forward.

Stefan's trial for murder began at Leeds Crown Court on Wednesday 7 July 1976. Four days prior to that, on the Saturday, the brutal child killer Ronald Castree was trawling the streets of Rochdale looking for another vulnerable victim. He was driving a taxi, which he did on a part-time basis during the evenings and at weekends, when he spotted a nine-year-old girl playing in the area of Vavasour Street. That little girl lived on the Turf Hill Estate, as Lesley did; in fact her house was only some ten minutes walk away from Lesley's family home. She was about the same size and weight as Lesley and she too had learning difficulties and attended a special school. She was playing a game of 'tig' with a friend when she was grabbed by the driver of the red taxi and pulled into the car. She was able to describe her assailant as having ginger hair with as bald patch. 'He just grabbed me and shut the door of the car,' she later said, 'I just said I wanted to go home now. "Let me go"'.

In spite of her protests Castree took her to a derelict house not far from her home. There he subjected her to a serious sexual assault, recreating no doubt some of the dreadful activities to which he had subjected Lesley Molseed. She later said that he gave her some foreign coins but she kicked him on the leg and managed to break free. She ran home and complained to her mother that a man had done things to her. The local police were contacted. The mother and daughter took part in a sweeping search of the area from inside a police vehicle. The little girl spotted Castree; he was still in the red taxi. He was arrested and charged with two offences: indecent assault and incitement to commit an act of gross indecency.

His wife, Beverley Castree, later related that he had arrived at their home and told her, 'You can divorce me now'. When she asked him why he replied, 'The police have had me in. I'm in trouble. I have interfered with a little girl'. She later described him as a vile monster who forced her into degrading acts of bondage. She said he was cruel with his mouth and cruel with his fists. She knew of his interest in young girls but did not think for a moment he would sink to the depths of depravity and murder a small child. Speaking on the *Granada Reports* programme on television she described how, sitting side-by-side, they had both watched news items about Lesley Molseed's murder. She recalled saying words like, 'That is awful, God, I hope they catch the person who did it, that is dreadful'. She had not even a slight suspicion that Lesley's killer was sitting right beside her.

On Monday 12 July 1976, only nine days after the offences, Ronald Castree pleaded guilty to both offences against the nine-year-old little girl. A medical report from a psychiatrist described him as 'immature'. Others with lesser medical qualifications might have described him as dangerous. He was fined the sum of 25 pounds on each charge. Some may regard that as derisory and not meeting the justice of the case. I regard the decision of the prosecution to seek summary trial on these offences to be entirely wrong in principle. Castree should instead have been sent to the Crown Court to be dealt with there. That court has much greater powers of sentencing compared to the magistrates. Any magistrate who considers that a small fine, less than that often imposed upon a motorist who exceeds the speed limit, is the proper level of sentence for indecent assault on a nine-year-old child, and inciting her to commit an act of gross indecency, is unfit to hold judicial office and ought to my mind to be removed from the bench. Even in the 1970s when sexual offences against children had yet to assume their present-day heightened focus for all sentencers.

How ironic it was that at this very same time and date an entirely innocent man, Stefan Kiszko, was on the trial at Leeds Crown Court for a crime for which he bore no responsibility, when in nearby Rochdale the real killer of Lesley Molseed was walking free from a magistrates' court punished only with a derisory fine.

One is bound to ask why did no-one, either in the Rochdale police or the police prosecutions department, notice Castree's vile sexual activity with that little nine-year-old girl in Rochdale in July 1976 and tie it in with the strikingly similar method of getting Lesley into a motor car in October 1975, committing a serious sexual offence against her, and then savagely killing her? A check would soon have established that in October 1975 when Lesley was murdered, Castree lived only a miles away from her home and he knew the town of Rochdale well, not only because he was a part-time taxi driver, but also because he had been born and bred in its immediate vicinity. The answer is of course that, once the police have obtained a confession to a crime, they do not look for anyone else, anywhere, at any time.

It should not be though by anyone that Castree's despicable conduct ended with his conviction and fine in 1976. It is now known that some two years after Stefan Kiszko's wrongful conviction for murder, Castree struck again. On this occasion he forcibly abducted a seven-year -old boy and took him to a disused garage. That child was playing near some garages in Rochdale when Castree approached. The other children who had been playing with that child ran away. Castree was seen to raise his hand to strike the little boy's bottom. The abduction took place only about a mile from Lesley Molseed's family home. According to a report in the *Daily Mirror* newspaper he stripped the little boy naked and told him to keep quiet. That child did not really understand what was going on and what was happening to him. Was Castree about to subject that little boy to the same ghastly ritual to which he had already subjected two little girls? Years afterwards the victim recalled Castree being totally calm, but the little boy did not remain silent as ordered. He screamed as if his life depended on it. Someone walking nearby bravely came to his assistance. He said if he had not screamed, 'I don't think I would be here today if I hadn't'.

Ronald Castree was arrested and charged with assaulting that boy, causing him harm. I find that unusual in the sense that the assault was committed in circumstances of indecency by stripping the child of his clothing but in any event after his plea of guilty was entered Castree was fined the sum of £50 after the prosecution and the magistrates consented to the case being tried summarily. That was on 17 July 1978. It is presumed that his previous conviction for strikingly similar conduct against the young girl in 1976 was disclosed to the magistrates who heard his case. If and when that was disclosed, did no-one consider whether this man was a danger to young children and treat him accordingly? He was not a first offender. He had been caught a second time. I would have regarded his conduct as evidence that he was a danger to children and deserving of severe punishment. I criticise severely the prosecuting authorities and the police for not taking the same view. On any view the imposition of a fine for a second similar serious offence is nothing short of a disgrace. The magistrates, of course, could not have known at that time that they were dealing with an undetected brutal child murderer. However, if the police had arrested Lesley Molseed's real killer instead of an innocent man in 1975, neither of the two serious assaults against these two young children would ever have taken place.

Stefan Kiszko was convicted of murder at Leeds Crown Court on 21 July 1976 and sentenced to life imprisonment. Did Castree breath of sigh of relief when he heard the news of that conviction and sentence and think he had got away with murder?

As innocent men and woman so often do, betrayed by the criminal justice system, Stefan began a descent into perhaps the most cruel of all mental illnesses, that of paranoid schizophrenia, faced as he was with the probability of never being released, since he would never admit that he had killed Lesley, and therefore in the language of the Home Office, he failed to address his offending.[1] While in Wakefield Prison he was kept

---

1. This responsibility has now passed to the Ministry of Justice.

in isolation, which involved remaining in a cell for 23 hours a day; that lasted for some five years. The purpose may have been for his own safety. It helped not just to demean him, but also to destroy him.

When Stefan was eventually granted legal aid for his trial, by Rochdale Magistrates' Court, it was granted for a solicitor and two counsel, one a Queen's Counsel, the second a junior counsel. The solicitor instructed in the case was Albert Wright, a partner in a firm based in Rochdale. He briefed David Waddington QC, a Conservative politician who had lost his Parliamentary seat in the second General Election in October 1974, and as junior counsel, Philip Clegg. Clegg later became a Circuit Judge.

At no stage in this case, from beginning to end, did Stefan ever admit killing Lesley Molseed. He denied doing so in the most forceful and vehement terms. When his defence leading counsel, David Waddington QC, in the course of the subsequent murder trial, fought hard for a verdict of not guilty of murder but canvassed, impliedly if not expressly, the possibility of a verdict of guilty of manslaughter on the ground of diminished responsibility, he must have surely realised that, even in the event of a conviction for the lesser offence, Stefan was likely to face a discretionary life sentence for the brutal killing of a defenceless little girl. If it was imposed, and Stefan failed or refused to admit his guilt, as he would not have done because he knew the truth, that he was innocent, the Parole Board would not have recommended his release until he did, on the ground he had not 'addressed his offending'. Figures published by the Home Office in March 1980 show that a breakdown of 259 life sentence prisoners who, on 31 December 1978, had been detained for nine years or more. They continued to serve their sentences at that date. No less than 184 men and two women had been convicted of murder. For those who received a life sentence for manslaughter on the ground of diminished responsibility, eight had served nine to ten years; three, including one woman had served ten to eleven years; five had served 11 to 12 years; four had served 12 to 13 years; one had served 13 to 14 years; three had served 14 to 15 years; four more had served 16 to 20 years. If convicted, Stefan Kiszko faced a very long prison sentence. It was however the practice at the time that if a psychiatric report recommended and justified it, and there were no contrary indications, the trial judge was likely to make a hospital order. That meant confinement in a special hospital such as Rampton in Nottinghamshire or Broadmoor in Berkshire, without limitation of time. No such psychiatric report was made in this case. Where no such hospital order was recommended, or not appropriate, and the defendant constituted a danger to the public for an unpredictable length of time, the right sentence was, in all probability, one of life imprisonment.

Because of his illness, Stefan was later examined in prison after his conviction, by a psychiatrist, who concluded that Stefan was suffering from 'delusions of innocence'. Poor Stefan. Could anything have been further from the truth? He placed his faith and trust in a system that totally failed him. It has long been my view that those who know the criminal justice system best admire it least. It is a system littered with the wrongful and repetitive conviction of the innocent.

There were two people who never accepted Stefan's guilt and fought an unrelenting battle to establish his innocence. They were his mother Charlotte and her sister Alfreda Tosic. They never lost hope and believed that truth would prevail and justice would be done. Charlotte Kiszko was greatly fortunate that she had the help of the solicitor, Campbell Malone, who came to share her belief in her son's innocence. In the event, as will be described, Stefan's conviction for murder was quashed by the Criminal Division of the Court of Appeal on 18 February 1992. Material evidence that established his innocence was always available but carefully concealed. Those responsible for that have escaped punishment. That scientific evidence proved that seminal staining on Lesley's clothing could not have been his. It was that of Ronald Charles Edward Castree.

Following Stefan's release, a cold case review was undertaken by the West Yorkshire Police in 2001. The senior investigating officer told the media that the police were in regular contact with Lesley's family who were still desperate to bring her killer to justice. Until that happened there would be no closure for them. However, little progress seemed to be made. Then there was a breakthrough.

On 1 October 2005, Ronald Castree, now 52 years-of-age, was arrested in Oldham. A woman who worked as a prostitute claimed that she met Castree by arrangement in a room at a local hotel. She further claimed that he assaulted her, something he always denied. He was arrested. A DNA sample was taken from him. Tests on that sample led to his arrest on 5 November 2006. As he was taken into custody he was alleged to have said, 'I've been expecting this for years'.

On 23 October 2007 he appeared at Bradford Crown Court on a charge of murdering Lesley Molseed. He denied that charge. The jury did not believe his denials and found him guilty of murder. He was sentenced to imprisonment for life.

The police officer who led the last inquiry into the case, Detective Chief Superintendant Max McLean of the West Yorkshire Police, made a statement on television saying, 'We are very, very sorry for what happened. It was a dreadful miscarriage of justice'. There are some who continue to maintain that Castree is innocent, convicted on unreliable and untrue evidence in the same way as Stefan Kiszko was.

At the outset, this was a simple case. Most murder cases are. A young girl was abducted and killed. A suspect was arrested. Kiszko confessed to the murder while in police custody. Without that confession he would not have been convicted. After he had confessed, both orally and in writing, medical evidence proved that Stefan was suffering from hypo-gonadism, a defect in the reproductive system that results in the testes not functioning and not producing sperm. Sperm heads were found on the clothing of the murdered little girl. Stefan could not have been her murderer. Because this evidence conflicted with the detailed confession evidence, it was suppressed, resulting in the destruction and wrongful conviction of a totally innocent young man.

Amongst the very important individuals frequently mentioned in this case is Detective Superintendent Richard Holland, who effectively led the investigation into Lesley's murder. Linked with him is the forensic scientist Ronald Outteridge, a most important witness in the prosecution case against Stefan with regard to the forensic evidence. Third, is the trial judge Mr Justice Hugh Park, who clearly believed that Stefan Kiszko killed Lesley Molseed and that belief coloured his view of the evidence and the conduct of the trial. Next is Stefan's solicitor, Albert Wright, who, I consider, let Stefan down, arguably quite badly, at the outset of the police inquiry. Then there is David Waddington QC, the leading defence counsel at Stefan's trial. He was appointed as Home Secretary in Prime Minister, Margaret Thatcher's last Government. He had been a barrister for some 24 years. In my view he made tactical mistake after tactical mistake in the conduct of the defence case. First, he failed to apply for an adjournment to enable the defence to consider the contents of about 6,000 unused witness statements that were only handed to the defence on the first day of the trial (As far as is known, no explanation has ever been sought or given why these documents were not disclosed until the 59th minute of the 23rd hour). Second, he failed to challenge the admissibility of the confession evidence, so that the jury knew from the very outset of the case from the opening speech of counsel for the prosecution that Stefan had admitted killing Lesley. If there had been a challenge to its admissibility, the jury would not have known of its existence unless and until the trial judge had ruled in their absence whether or not the confession should be admitted and allowed in evidence. The law recognises that a confession can only be regarded as reliable if it is given freely and voluntarily and was not obtained by oppression or in circumstances likely to render it unreliable. The number of police interviews, six in all, their timing and content, and their effect, especially that following the conduct of Superintendent Holland on a vulnerable and frightened person, were factors the judge would take into account in deciding on the issue of admissibility. Third, he failed to question the admissibility of the police evidence obtained from Stefan who was not under arrest, not told he was free to leave the police station at any time, and further question whether Stefan's detention at that station was lawful or not. Fourth, he failed to challenge the admissibility of evidence of alleged misconduct by Stefan on other, previous occasions, namely that Stefan had been involved in incidents of indecent exposure only days before Lesley Molseed was murdered. Such evidence normally requires the leave of the trial judge before it can be admitted, mainly by considering whether it is more prejudicial than probative. The consequence was that Stefan was effectively put on trial for indecency offences with which he had never been charged. Fifth, even after allowing that evidence to be adduced by the prosecution, which evidence the defence were claiming was either mistaken or untrue, Mr Waddington allowed the prosecution to read the evidence of two young women, Catherine Burke, then aged 16, and Pamela Hind, then aged 18, rather than require their attendance at court to give live, oral evidence to the jury from the witness box. Years later those two witnesses admitted to a police investigation that their evidence was totally false. They had described, in the most offensive and graphic terms, an incident that had never taken place.

Notwithstanding all of this however, it is clear that Stefan had full and total confidence in his defence counsel, and that seems not to have been shaken even when two efforts on two separate occasions, once on the first day of the trial and second just prior to the judge's summing -up, were made by Mr Waddington QC to induce him to plead guilty to manslaughter. He would not do so.

Over and above that there were two even more serious mistakes which I consider Mr Waddington made in the course of the trial. First, the running of the special defence of diminished responsibility which in my view is no defence at all but a mitigating factor that can in certain limited circumstances reduce the charge of murder to that of manslaughter. Even then a sentence of life imprisonment was most likely to be imposed if that had been the verdict in this case. The second more serious further mistake was the failure to seek the discharge a woman juror, or even the entire jury, when it was disclosed that she was told in a public house on a Saturday evening during the trial that Stefan Kiszko had been advised by his lawyer to plead guilty. As will be seen later in the text she continued to sit on the jury that convicted Stefan. It is not known whether or indeed when she repeated to her fellow jurors what she had been told in the public house. No-one told her that she should not do so, and I suspect she probably did. Whether she did or not, when David Waddington QC asked the jury in his closing speech for the defence to acquit Stefan of murder, did she not ask herself, 'Why would I do that, when I know that you tried to persuade him to plead guilty?' It is my view that his decision not to seek at the very least the discharge of that juror, if not the entire jury, deprived his client of a fair trial. To make matters even worse, Waddington failed to tell his client about the juror incident and to ask him whether he wished an application be made to the trial judge for the removal of the juror or the discharge of the entire jury.

For reasons I cannot understand or explain the report of this part of the case in the Criminal Appeal Reports is at variance with the evidence I found in the file in the National Archives. Far from the juror innocently overhearing or 'eavesdropping' on a conversation in a public house during a luncheon adjournment at the trial as the report wrongly states, the juror actually met and talked to two men, one of whom passed on the incriminating information, in the bar on the previous Saturday evening. I find this variation both significant and sinister. As Professor Terence Walters had observed, this was not idle or speculative gossip. The man who provided that information worked for the prosecuting authorities and was thus very likely to know exactly what he was talking about.

Lord Justice Bridge's statement on page 63 of the report in Volume 68 of the Criminal Appeal Report is wrong on two counts. 'The discovery of the body naturally led to a massive police investigation. The applicant, a young man of 24, was seen twice in November when he denied all knowledge of the matter. But suspicion continued to centre on him, and he was arrested again on December 21, 1975'.

Stefan Kiszko had not been twice questioned about the murder; in fact as will be seen in the text that follows, not a single question was asked of him, if the police are to be believed, about the murder of the little girl, until he admitted that he was the killer. Second, there was no question of him being 'arrested again'. He was not arrested once, let alone twice, and this was an error of substantial importance in the eventual unsuccessful appeal.

The defence to what I regard as a simple case was to make it more complex by running two inconsistent defences. First an outright denial of the murder, claiming an alibi — that is, Stefan was elsewhere at the time the murder was committed. The second defence was diminished responsibility. If I had been serving on that jury I would, in the light of that defence, have regarded the putting forward of the alibi as an outright lie. The obstacle, which I consider was insurmountable, to running this second line of defence was that in law the legal burden of proof was placed firmly on the accused to prove on the balance of probabilities that first he was suffering from an abnormality of mind, and further that he was so afflicted at the time of the killing. Stefan Kiszko never did admit that he killed Lesley Molseed. When in 2013 the Criminal Division of the Court of Appeal was asked to decide whether the placing of the legal burden of proving diminished responsibility upon the defendant was incompatible with the presumption of innocence contained in Article 6(2) of the European Convention on Human Rights, the court said the issue of diminished responsibility depends on the inner workings of the defendant's mind, and further that it depends on the highly personal condition of the defendant himself, indeed 'on the internal functioning of his mental processes'. Did Stefan realise this, and if he did, why did he not give a full and informed consent to a medical examination by a doctor whose task it was to establish the inner workings of his mind?

I consider that from the very outset David Waddington QC did not want to fight the case, almost certainly on the basis that it was a hopeless one and that a conviction for murder was inevitable. He must have been greatly influenced by Stefan's two particular admissions of guilt to the police, as clearly the trial judge was. Mr Justice Park invited the jury in the course of his summing-up 'test the confession in relation to the description of the smears on the thigh of the girl' (Page 69 of the transcript). He went on:

'…at that interview with the accused on the morning of the 22nd December, after the accused had admitted killing the girl and after he had demonstrated to Holland the way in which he had done it' then there followed, first, in answer to a question put by Detective Superintendent Holland to Stefan: "Did you do anything before you left?" (meaning leaving the scene of the murder). He claims Stefan replied "I sort of remember wiping the knife on her or on her clothes". That was the first fatal admission. There then followed in the course of the written confession statement [see *Appendix 2* to this work] where Stefan said "I had a knife in my pocket and I took it out and stabbed her in the throat she was still crying I got a hazy feeling and I can't remember where or how I stabbed her. She slumped over away from me and I don't remember what happened after that. I left her where she was and I didn't bother to look. I got back into the car and drove back home. I didn't tell my mother what I had done I put the knife back in my pocket and I wiped it on her clothes of something. I can't remember what. I was a bit hazy then. I didn't cut myself.'

In the course of his evidence the pathologist Professor David Gee referred to a photograph, Exhibit No. 17, which is of the little girl's thigh with a smearing of blood across it. Professor Gee could not say what kind of surface had been smeared across the thigh. Obviously someone drew the conclusion the surface was the blade of a knife. This caused the trial judge to put the rhetorical question to the jury — 'How did Stefan know that something had been wiped on the girl unless he had wiped something across her himself?'

That question at the time was unanswerable — only the police, the photographer, the pathologist and the killer knew of those marks on the child. If Stefan knew about them, then it must follow that he was the killer. We now know that Superintendent Holland was the source of that evidence in Stefan's confession. Shamefully it emanated from him, so it is claimed, as he allegedly set about fitting-up an entirely innocent man. Of course David Waddington QC and his junior, Philip Clegg, did not, and could not have known at the time, that this was what appears to be perjured evidence from a senior police officer.

At the date of Lesley Molseed's death, the police were almost overwhelmed by increasing pressure from the public to end the seemingly endless cycle of violence against women and young girls, especially in the search for a man who murdered at least 13 women between October 1975 and November 1980. He was Peter William Sutcliffe, the so-called Yorkshire Ripper. As the body count of Sutcliffe's victims increased, so did the deep feelings of troublesome unease in the country about the ineffectiveness of police investigations into the crime of murder, increasing the vociferous demands on them to take dangerous killers off the street and into custody. In the Turf Hill area of Rochdale, families were afraid to allow their children out to play because of the fear that Lesley's killer might strike again, and no doubt with the same pitiless ferocity with which he had taken that young girl's life. Was it that pressure that caused the West Yorkshire Police to alight on an entirely innocent young man and convict him of a murder he had not committed?

Chapter Two

The Main Players

As described in *Chapter One*, one of the main players in the case of Stefan Kiszko was senior investigating police officer, Detective Superintendent Richard Holland of West Yorkshire Police. In his book *Wicked Beyond Belief* (HarperCollins, 2003) Michael Bilton described Holland as knowing what was expected of him as a police officer. It was 'results'. That is, clearing up a crime—the more serious and savage the offence, the greater need for a result. Bilton added, 'If Judges' Rules were broken, it was done in true utilitarian fashion and with honest intent' (See p.143 of that work). It is a mode of operating by police, especially from that era, which has been dubbed 'noble cause corruption'. The Judges' Rules were first formulated in 1912 and were rules of practice, not rules of law. They were instructions for police officers in their treatment of suspects relating to detention, arrest, search and interrogation, drafted to ensure that treatment is fair and any confession evidence, oral or written, is properly obtained. So it seems if Holland thought he was acting honestly and honourably then all that matters really was the resulting confession evidence. It is my view that, amongst many police officers including Superintend Holland, there existed a feeling that suspects in custody had too many rights, and the police were hidebound by too many rules.

Holland deceptively provided Stefan Kiszko with details of the murder that only the actual killer, the police officers and the pathologist would know. When Stefan first arrived at the police station there was virtually no evidence of any kind to connect him with the murder of the little girl. Superintendent Holland changed all that. He incorporated the highly incriminating details in the confession evidence, which he wrote out himself. Although Stefan Kiszko was a clerk with the Inland

Revenue and perfectly able to read and write, like so many others, he seemed to completely lose that capacity once he crossed the threshold of a police station. Holland then appears to have lied at the trial when he stated on oath that the confession had been freely volunteered and that all the details contained in it had been provided by Stefan himself. He and others misused their powers relating to the lawful detention of suspects and resorted to the most extraordinary interviewing techniques over two days and a night, until finally a full and detailed confession was forthcoming.

As also noted in *Chapter One*, the role of David Waddington QC was central. He had dedicated his life to politics rather than the law. After being Home Secretary he later became Lord Privy Seal and Leader of the House of Lords. He acted throughout the case in what he considered, in his professional judgment, in consultation with junior counsel in the case, and the defence solicitor, to be in the best interests of his client.

Waddington ran two defences, one of alibi, meaning the accused was elsewhere at the time the crime charged was committed, the other the special defence to murder of diminished responsibility. Stefan Kiszko never at any time admitted to his lawyers that he murdered Lesley Molseed. He adamantly denied it, claiming his confession to the police was untrue and induced by their improper pressure on him to admit to a crime he did not commit. Raising such an issue of diminished responsibility compels the jury to consider the accused's responsibility for this actions at the time of the killing. If the accused denies the killing, or it is not proved against him, it is arguable that the defence is not available to him. I consider the relevant wording of Section 2 of the Homicide Act 1957 makes this clear beyond doubt.

In the course of the trial, towards the very end of the prosecution case, when their evidence would be fresh in the minds of the jury, three young women gave very damaging evidence against Stefan which caused him to lose first his liberty, then his sanity and finally his life. Waddington's decision not to have the prosecution call two of those, Catherine Burke, then aged 16, and the other, Pamela Hind, then aged 18, to give live, oral evidence and cross-examine them before the jury was a major mistake. Instead he agreed to allow the prosecution to read their evidence so that it lay before the jury unchallenged, uncontradicted and untrue. The impression it left upon the jury can only be guessed at, but it would not have been favourable towards the accused man.

Although the murder victim was Lesley Molseed, her entire family, her parents, her two sisters and her brother were also victims, because when Stefan Kiszko was cleared of her murder in 1992 after spending 16 years in prison, they then realised that the man they thought was the killer was innocent and the actual murderer was still at large. They must have been distraught. It was not until November 2007, when Ronald Castree — the man who had in fact abducted and murdered Lesley — was sentenced to life in prison for that murder, that they were able to attempt to resume some normality in the rebuilding of their shattered lives.

A former police officer, now retired, who was involved in the original murder inquiry, told me that in a 30 year career with the police service he came across many incidents of great sadness and distress. He added 'It is true to say that the Kiszko case was by far the most unjust example of the criminal investigative system. I have never forgotten it.'

He remembered visits to the Kiszko family home, where he and his fellow CID officer were welcomed with generous hospitality by Stefan's parents. He described Ivan Kiszko, known locally as Big John, as a huge, confident, domineering man and Charlotte Kiszko as a tiny, gentle, highly intelligent, woman, who kept their little home in Crawford Street in Rochdale quite spotless. She doted on her only son and spent much of her free time with him. His personal health was not good, he suffered from anaemia and other medical complications. Amongst other things he felt compelled to record the registration number of motor cars, the drivers of which annoyed him or caused him some kind of trouble. That led him into some difficulty with the police and at his subsequent trial.

Most tellingly of all, the retired police officer recalls that:

'Stefan, who continued to grow into the huge size he became, would always sit in another room with his mother when my colleague and I visited their home. He was a quiet, reticent young man, somewhat clumsy and naïve. He seemed almost afraid of any form of authority, preferring to be with his mother rather than converse on a man to man basis...During the enquiry

I remember how shocked my CID partner and I were when Stefan was arrested. Even as experienced police officers we could not come to terms with what was happening, knowing Stefan as we did. On the night of the usual "end of enquiry" celebrations, Stefan having been charged with the offence of murder, we both could not take part, so we left the gathering.'

This retired officer and his colleague were troubled by clear and deep feelings of unease about the case. Their instincts, knowledge and experience indicated that something was radically wrong. What they could not have known and what made this case one of the most shocking miscarriages of justice ever was that, even before Stefan Kiszko stood trial, there existed plain and unequivocal evidence that he was totally innocent. That evidence was deliberately concealed with the result that an innocent man went to prison whilst a guilty man stayed free.

Chapter Three

Two Material Witnesses

When Lesley Molseed left her Rochdale home shortly before one o'clock in the afternoon of Sunday 5 October 1975 to go to a local shop, she was wearing a blue coat with a hood and carrying a blue linen shopping bag. Someone who did not know her may have seen her soon after that.

On 25 October 1975 the police discovered the existence of a very material witness named Christopher Coverdale. He was a building contractor, then aged 27 years. He made a witness statement to Detective Constable Perry on that day. He said he had driven along the A672 on Sunday afternoon, 5 October 1975, past the exact spot where Lesley's body was found. As he did so his attention was drawn to a man and a little girl climbing the hill that overlooks the carriageway on the Ripponden side, where there is a large 'pull-in' or lay-by for motor vehicles. He remembered thinking they were foolhardy for being out on the hill because of the adverse weather conditions that day. The man was facing the road, helping the little girl to climb up the hill. He described that man as being aged 30 to 35, light brown or fair hair, cut short, with a receding hairline, 5 feet six inches to five feet eight inches in height and of plump build. He was wearing a middle-brown jacket which was either plain or had a darker brown window-pane check pattern on it, a beige or mustard yellow cardigan and trousers that did not match his jacket, but contrasted with it.

I saw Ronald Castree in the dock at his trial in Bradford Crown Court in November 2007, and apart from the age and allowing for the passage of time, I regard this as a quite accurate description of him. If the police had ever put Stefan Kiszko in an identification parade to see whether Coverdale could identify him as the man with the child on 5 October

1975, I have not the slightest doubt that he would not have done so. But might he have identified Ronald Castree?

When the police took Coverdale back to the murder scene, he pointed out the position of the man and the child as being within a very short distance of where the mutilated body of Lesley Molseed had been discovered. It seems clear beyond any doubt that he had seen the killer very shortly before he killed. The only difficulty there might have been over his evidence, so far as the police were concerned, was that he put the time when he drove past the man and the child 'climbing the hill', as he described it, as being after 3.45 to 4 pm Lesley had gone missing some time after 12.30 pm that day, perhaps nearer 1 pm, but there was really nothing to show whether she was dead or alive by that later time, around 4 pm. I think it was simply assumed by the police (but of course not proved) that she was killed soon after she was abducted and taken the nine miles from Rochdale to the place where she was found—the place where she in fact met her violent death. Could it really have been the case that, first, Lesley and her killer climbed the hill on that Sunday afternoon and then, not long afterwards, another man with a little girl, both wearing strikingly similar outer clothing, climbed that same hill? Is it not significant that of all the road users on the A672 on 5 October only one came forward to say he had seen the two on the hill? As for the question of timing, the police had made three car runs from the spot where Lesley was last seen alive in Rochdale, to the place where she was found. One route was 9.6 miles and took 15 minutes travelling time, the second route was 16.6 miles and took 29 minutes, and the third was 9.8 miles, which took 20 minutes. Those journeys were direct, with no stops, and within the speed limit for the road in question.

Christopher Coverdale gave a truthful and convincing explanation for why he had not come forward until almost three weeks after the murder inquiry began. He was unaware of it until the previous week and the day on which he made the statement was the first opportunity he had to talk to the police. Apart from the time element, had the police not got compelling evidence of a positive and reliable sighting of the murderer? I would have expected at the very least that the police would have prepared a photofit from the detailed description of the man that Coverdale was able to provide. Whether that happened I cannot say. Nor is it possible to say when the defence were told about this piece of evidence, which I regard as vital. Was it among the material provided to the defence on the first day of the trial? If so, why did prosecuting counsel not bring this witness statement specifically to the attention of defence counsel, having regard to its clear importance and relevance, rather than leaving the defence to work their way through those statements as the trial progressed? In the event, Coverdale's evidence seems to have played no part in the trial of Stefan Kiszko when it clearly should have done so. His name appears on a schedule prepared by junior counsel for the prosecution at the trial, Matthew Caswell, but it is not known if, or when, that schedule was disclosed to the defence.

By far the greatest significance and relevance of the evidence of the potential witness Coverdale is his description of the little girl that he saw. He said she was wearing a blue gabardine-type hip-length coat and the hood was up and her legs were uncovered. That is what he told the police on 25 October 1975. Surely he could not have made that up? In addition to his witness statement there is a note made by a police officer that is numbered A 1485 to be found in the National Archives, setting out all of this detailed description of the man and the child. The police must have appreciated the importance of this evidence. Was it deliberately concealed from the defence at the trial and, if the answer is yes, by whom? For reasons never explained, Coverdale was not called as a witness by either the prosecution or the defence at the subsequent trial in 1976 of Stefan Kiszko, the man charged with the sadistic murder of Lesley Molseed. In fact, it is not clearly established that the defence even knew of Coverdale's existence, let alone his evidence, at the time of the trial.

On 20 October, the second material witness, Mrs Emma Tong, had made a statement to the police. The prosecution decided not to call her as a witness because they did not accept that her evidence advanced their case. They considered she was honest but mistaken in what she claimed to have seen. On Sunday 5 October 1975, Mrs Tong was at her home in Wellington Lane, Rochdale, which was not far from the Broad Lane area where Lesley was last known to be seen alive on that day. At about 1.30 that afternoon she saw a little girl sitting in the front seat of a car which was deep cream in colour with red markings, possibly one of the Ford range, and badly in need of a respray. The girl was wearing a dark navy-blue coat or raincoat with a hood. She did not appear to be distressed in any way but smiled at Mrs Tong. Because she was expecting her son to call she went to the front door. She could see the little girl leaning back in the car seat, holding something. As she watched she saw the child put one arm over it and pull the object, whatever it was, towards her. Mrs Tong could not see what it actually was, but she smiled at the little girl who smiled back and, as she did so, she pulled the object, which may have been some kind of parcel, upwards. When the little girl smiled, Mrs Tong noticed her front teeth; there was something unusual about them, so she thought — she saw there was a cleft (that is, a fissure or a gap) at the front. Contemporary photographs of Lesley Molseed show that there was such a gap in the central area of her front teeth. Emma Tong thought the child was about seven or eight years-of-age.

A man, whom Mrs Tong was able to describe, then emerged from the nearby toilets and got into the driver's seat. He was wearing 'a brown tweedy jacket'. When one compares the descriptions of the outer clothing of the man and the little girl whom Christopher Coverdale saw climbing the embankment above the carriageway of the A672 and the description provided by Mrs Tong, one is driven to the very strong inference that they had seen the same man.

Coverdale thought the man was of plump build and aged 30 to 35, Mrs Tong thought medium sized and aged late-20s or early-30s. Both noticed his hair; he thought that it was light brown or fair, cut short, with a receding hairline, whereas she said his hair was well brushed back (does that mean receding?) as if a lot of brilliantine had been used.

The next day, Mrs Tong learnt of Lesley's disappearance. The following Saturday, 11 October 1975, she went to the local market and saw a girl's photograph on a poster. That was Lesley Molseed's photograph. Emma Tong was convinced that it was the same little girl she had seen sitting in the car outside her house on the afternoon of Sunday 5 October.

On 20 October she made a statement to the police. If that was, in fact, Lesley Molseed in the car then she was alive about 1.30 on that Sunday afternoon in the company of a man who definitely was not Stefan Kiszko.

The approach of the prosecution to her evidence may have been that it could not have been Lesley because she had been abducted by the man who eventually went on to murder her. The little girl in the car was not distressed, in fact she was smiling and alone, so she could have left the car and sought the safety of Mrs Tong's house if she had wanted to do so. This overlooks one vital point. She was holding some kind of parcel or box. Had the killer lured the child into the car by giving her either a toy, perhaps a doll, in a box, or even more likely had he given her a small animal such as a kitten or a puppy which might have engrossed her attention and removed her anxieties about getting into a car with a man she did not know? Lesley and her two sisters and brother had owned a cat named Jinxy that had gone missing only a few days before that fateful Sunday. Indeed it was thought by some at the time Lesley first went missing that she might have wandered off looking for that cat.

If Mrs Tong was right in her sighting of Lesley Molseed, then was it not inevitable that she had seen that little girl with the man who murdered her? She had had more than a fleeting glimpse of that man, and it seemed very likely that she would identify him if she saw him again. That man was not Stefan, and she would have said so.

The defence were apparently given a copy of Mrs Tong's statement on the first day of the 1976 trial. It was thought to be of sufficient relevance and importance for them to call Mrs Tong as a defence witness at the trial. However, the prosecution, ably assisted by the trial judge, found it easy to throw doubts on the accuracy of her observations and recollections, while at the same time never suggesting that she was anything other than honest but mistaken about who and what she saw on that Sunday afternoon.

It is my view that if there had been full and proper advance disclosure by the prosecution of the vital evidence of these two eye-witnesses, the criminal justice system might have been spared yet another and most scandalous miscarriage of justice.

Chapter Four

Three Days' Events — 3 and 4 October and 5 November 1975

Events that led the police to Stefan Kiszko really began two days before Lesley's death. Some time in the middle of the evening of Friday 3 October 1975 there was an incident that was both upsetting and confusing for many of the young people at a youth club on the Turf Hill Estate near Kingsway School. It was soon known to the police what had in fact led to the incident, although their grasp of the detail was as uncertain as that of those who provided the facts about it. Did the events of that evening disclose the existence of another material witness whose evidence was withheld from the court and from the defence?

What had if fact happened was that a local milkman who had been collecting his weekly milk money in the Turf Hill Estate on that Friday evening had stopped in a clinic in the vicinity of the club in order to urinate. The clinic was closed at the time. He had left his silver Ford Escort car parked nearby. He had not the slightest intention of insulting or offending anyone; he simply could not resist the urge to relieve himself. While he was doing so, his presence was spotted by at least two young girls who were some distance away. They panicked and ran into the club. When the media reported this incident the milkman immediately contacted the police and made a written statement outlining what had occurred. He had nothing to hide.

Superintendent Holland included a copy of the witness statement made by that milkman when he wrote to the Director of Public Prosecutions on 14 May 1976. He told the director that he had not served a copy of that statement on the defence and said he awaited the director's further instructions on the matter. Whether the DPP ever replied to that note is not known. The defence did not see that statement and if they had might well have conducted their case differently when it was clear that the man involved in the incident near the youth club was not Stefan. Why the DPP did not disclose this statement defies comprehension because Superintendent Holland told the director that the Ford Escort car had been traced, its owner was the milkman and he had left it in the exact spot where one little girl described it as being parked under yellow/orange sodium street lighting. She described it as a yellow car. Tests carried out by the police indicated that a silver car parked under such a street lighting system would appear to be yellow in colour, and since the young girl described the milkman's clothing in accordance with what he admitted he was wearing, she was an excellent witness. It seems from this that the DPP and the police knew that the man who went into the clinic to urinate was identified, and he was definitely not Stefan Kiszko. The problem was that the judge, counsel and the jury were simply not told this as they should have been, and all seemed to have assumed that the man near the clinic was Stefan.

The two young girls who were frightened by the presence of the man were Ann Marie Storto and Sheila Woodhead. Both were ten years of age at the time. Neither child claimed they saw any indecent conduct. Ann gave evidence and Sheila's evidence was read to the jury. It is difficult to see how their evidence proved anything relevant to the charge of murder the jury had to decide. They were frightened but not offended by anything that happened on that Friday evening. Three other children, Colin Peers, Bevereley Mullins and Sarah Lord also made witness statements to the police. The statements of the first two were read to the jury; Sarah gave evidence from the witness box. None of them claimed to see any indecent conduct by anyone at or near the youth club. The purpose of their evidence being put before the murder trial judge and jury is not easy to understand.

Five other witnesses did make such a claim however. They were Debra Mills, Maxine Buckley, Debbie Brown, Catherine Burke and Pamela Hind.

It was canvassed by the prosecution at his trial, based on his confession to the police, that Stefan Kiszko was the man involved in this incident near the youth club. At no time however did the prosecution seek to prove in evidence that Stefan was the man involved, and it was never actually proved that he was.

At the time Stefan was 23-years-old. He was six feet two inches tall and he weighed in the region of 17 stone. Even in his late teens he was about 17½ stone and eventually that escalated up to 20 stone. He was a lumbering giant of a man, who could hardly be described accurately as being of slim build.

A further witness was a 12-year-old girl, Debra Mills. She made three witness statements to the police. The police seemed to have devoted a lot of resources into an allegation of indecent exposure. In the first state-ment dated Saturday 4 October 1975, Debra Mills describes events that occurred about a quarter to one mid day on that day. She was walking along Vavasour Street with her friend Maxine. Debra saw a man stop immediately in front of them. He opened his coat and exposed himself. He didn't say anything but stared straight at them. The girls ran away from him. Debra hadn't seen the man before but thought she would know him again if she saw him. He was about 20–30 years-of-age, good built, five feet ten inches in height. It was then that she added the words which some may regard as relevant and important, 'I haven't seen the man before but I would know him again if I saw him', for some may question why, if the police wanted to establish that man was Stefan Kiszko, they did not hold an identification parade to ascertain whether this witness would identify him at such a parade. There was of course no reason why the defence could not have asked for such a procedure to be arranged, if they were confident that the witness would not identify their client. They did not do so. The man alleged by the prosecution to have been Stefan Kiszko, committing that act of indecency on 4 October. Stefan lived at that time at number 31 Crawford Street (in which direction this witness said he walked after the indecency). and it was seriously suggested that he had behaved in the way described in broad daylight, in the middle of the day, within a fairly short distance of his home. He had also attend a nearby school the Newbold Junior School, which was in Vavasour Street, so the chances of being seen in the area by someone who knew him, if he was the person involved in this incident, must have been quite high.

In her second statement dated 9 October 1975, Debra Mills relates the events of the evening of Friday 3 October. She recited how she went to the youth club at about 8 pm on that evening with her two friends, Debbie Brown and Maxine Buckley. A girl aged about nine came into the club; she was crying. Her name was Ann Marie Storto, sometimes called Anna by her friends. Debra Mills made no allegation of indecency committed by anyone on that Friday evening. Debra Mills claimed she saw a man standing on the footpath, staring at the group. She said, 'I think he was a white man, 20 to 30-years-old, medium build, wearing a black beret and a dark three-quarter-length coat. We then went and stood by the clinic.' The man left the scene.

She made her third statement to the police on 2 January 1976. In this she describes both incidents. By this date Stefan Kiszko was in prison custody. Debra Mills repeated exactly the description of the man she had seen on the evening of 3 October. In any event, when she goes on to deal with the Saturday 4 October lunchtime incident she describes the man involved as follows:

'The man was about twenty-five years old, about 5' 10' tall, heavy build, light brown hair with a fringe.'

She then added the following, which may be regarded as having some significance:

'He walked funny, he sort of shuffled. He had staring eyes which were round. He was very clean shaven and had smooth skin as if he had no whiskers.'

It was a fact that Stefan Kiszko did have a rather unusual walk; he ambled from side-to-side, due perhaps to his excessive body weight, but also because in April 1974 he had fallen down the stairs at his home and broken his ankle. The complex break, a Potts fracture, was so serious it required surgery and four days' stay in Rochdale Infirmary. Two steel pins were inserted into the ankle bone. (His ankle remained encased in plaster for the following five months.) Even then after the operation Stefan was not allowed home but had to spend five weeks convalescing at Springfield Hospital. It is also a fact that Stefan had staring eyes and, because of his medical condition, he had a very smooth complexion, devoid of facial hair. In fact, he did start to shave when he was 18 years-of-age, but even then he only shaved once a week. Many people might consider this evidence from this young girl to be very incriminating, but it would have carried much more weight if it had appeared in her two witness statements written before Stefan Kiszko's remand in custody and not in a statement written at least a week after it, when these physical characteristics were known to the police to match the appearance of the man in Armley Gaol.

In her third witness statement, Debra Mills described an incident of indecent exposure on Saturday 4 October 1975 while she was walking along Vavasour Street with her friend Maxine when a man exposed himself to the two young girls. His zip was unfastened and she could see his private which was sticking out. The girls ran away. Debra Mills described the man as being 'about 25-years-old, about 5'10' tall, heavy build with his hair in a fringe. He walked funny, he sort of shuffled. He had staring eyes which were round'.

The next witness relating to the allegation of indecency was Debbie Brown, a 13-year-old schoolgirl who lived on Turf Hill Road. She made a total of three witness statements. In the first, dated 8 October 1975 she described leaving in the youth club on Friday 3 October when, at about 8.35 pm, when Ann Marie Storto ran back into the premises. Debbie Brown said she saw a man nearby. She added,

'This man opened his coat and exposed himself to us. He dropped his trou-sers and I saw that he had a scar on his left leg from his hip down to his knee. We ran back and told Alf, the youth leader, and he came outside with us. When the man saw Alf still coming after him he ran down Delamere Road. Alf chased him but lost him.'

This version of events is not in accordance with the evidence of those witnesses she named and, more especially, Alfred Sutcliffe. He never claimed to have chased a man and then lost him in the course of doing so.

Debbie Brown's statement continues:

'I would describe this man as about 5' 9' tall, long thin face, his hair was receding and he had a dark beret over the right side of his head. He had a long black coat on and grey pants, black shoes and black socks. I would say he was about thirty to forty years old. When he exposed himself to us I was about ten feet away.'

This evidence is clear enough. The fact that it contradicts the versions of other witnesses is not sufficient reason for rejecting it. The weight to be attached to the evidence of a witness is not decided by counting heads. However, the police decided to take another statement from Debbie Brown and did so the next day, 9 October (For the sake of completing the record Debbie Brown made a third statement on 9 October 1975. This statement related to an alleged incident that she claimed happened at the end of July or beginning of August. A man in a van had called out to her 'come on darling, you can come for a ride'. She ran home to her mother. This statement, obviously for legal reasons of relevance, did not feature at the trial in July 1976). Debbie Brown, in her second statement, claimed that she was in the youth club at about 8.20 pm on 3 October when Ann Marie Storto back came into the club. She was crying.

'She told me that a man outside had been following her and trying to stop her as she walked home. Anna was crying and said the man had a knife and she asked me to take her home.'

It is a fact that at no time in the course of three statements did Ann Marie say that a man had been following her, that he had tried to stop her, or that he had a knife. According to her, the man who stared at her had been stationary in the clinic porchway. Her statement goes on:

'I asked her to wait a minute whilst I got my friends and one of the girls Maxine Buckley went to tell Alf the youth leader. Alf came to talk to Anna and asked her about the man. He told us to walk on home and he would follow.'

She described the man as follows: 'The man was in his forties, 5' 10', round face and slim build.' It should be noted here that at his subsequent trial the prosecution claimed that the man Debbie had seen indecently exposing himself to her and to others on the Friday evening was Stefan Kiszko. This, in spite of the claim this young girl made that the man was in his forties, whereas Stefan was only 23 and, as noted previously, he could hardly be described as being of slim build.

She added what may be regarded as a significant observation. She said, 'I can't recall seeing the man before but I would recognise him again.' Whether that was sufficient for the police to set up an identification parade is not known. Might she have identified the man involved if this had happened?

This young girl gave her evidence on oath at the subsequent murder trial of Stefan Kiszko. What impression she made on the jury it is not now possible to say. She may well have been a most convincing witness. In their book *Innocents* about this case (Fourth Estate, 1997), Jonathan Rose, Steve Panter and Trevor Wilkinson describe her, at page 285 as '... the third member of this unreliable triumvirate'. As Debbie Brown she had, at 13, lied along with her friends: 'As a young girl,' she said, 'I had a vivid imagination and frequently made up stories about things.' By the time she owned up and told the truth, Stefan Kiszko was dead and buried in Rochdale Cemetery.

The two untruthful witnesses, the other members of the 'unreliable triumvirate' were Catherine Burke, then aged 16 and Pamela Hind, then aged 18. In her witness statement dated 15 October 1975, almost two weeks after the incident, Catherine claimed that on the evening of Friday 3 October she and two friends, Pamela Hind and Gillian Cleave, decided to call in at the Kingsway Youth Club. She fixed the date of that incident by describing it as follows:

'...the Friday before Lesley Molseed went missing. When we were near to Kingsway clinic I saw a man standing in the clinic doorway. The clinic was shut. This would be about 8.50 p.m...I thought that the man standing in the clinic doorway looked a bit funny. I thought he might have been drunk...as me and Pamela reached the clinic door the man jumped out in front of us. At first the man was holding his coat closed, then he opened his coat and his trousers fell down to just above his ankles. I saw the man's penis was sticking out, and looked fairly large. The man said, "When I get you two bastards, I'll shove this right up you." We both screamed and ran round the man and ran to Kingsway gates where I stopped and looked round and the man had gone.'

Her description of the man was as follows:

'I would describe the man as being thirty-five to forty years of age, fairly tall and broadly built. He had dark collar length hair. He was wearing a dark mac which went just below his knees, dark trousers and a dark coloured flat cap.'

Catherine Burke went on to describe going into the youth club and telling Alf Sutcliffe what had happened. She added the description of the man she said had exposed himself to her and her friend Pamela. Her description, like that given by her friend, did not match Stefan Kiszko.

Her friend Pamela Hind made a statement supporting that version of the incident, although her recitation of the very insulting and offensive words used by the man differed. According to her he said, 'Come here, let me ram this up you.' She related how the incident began when she saw this man on the opposite side of the road to herself and Catherine. Their friend Gillian was nearby. The man crossed the road to the same side where she and Kitty (as she called Catherine in her statement) were.

'The man walked up to Kitty. I don't know if he said anything to her or not. Kitty turned round to me and Gillian and shouted, "Come on Pam" and when she turned back round I saw the man unzip his trousers and take his penis out. His penis was erect.'

She added,

'As we were running away I heard the man shout, "Come here, let me ram this up you." Kitty shouted something back to him, I don't remember what she said. I would describe the man as being thirty to forty years of age, about 5' 10' or 11' tall. He was well-built but not fat. I think he had dark collar length hair. He was wearing a dark coat, possibly a raincoat, which had a zip up the front. It was not fastened. He was also wearing dark trousers and I have not seen this man before. I don't think I would be able to recognize him again.'

There is no need to speculate on whether she was describing a quite separate incident from that alleged by the other girls, or whether the man was the milkman, because Catherine Burke and Pamela Hind did not give evidence at the trial of Stefan Kiszko. Instead, their evidence was read to the jury by prosecuting counsel under the provisions of Section 9 of the Criminal Justice Act 1967, with the express agreement of defence counsel. That meant that the jury received their versions of evidence without challenge, denial or any form of cross-examination from the defence. Why David Waddington QC agreed to this at the trial is incomprehensible. It was not until 1991, when the police were carrying out an investigation into the safety of Stefan Kiszko's conviction, that both young women admitted that they had not told the truth in their witness statements. That was a shocking admission.

It is now necessary to return to the narrative of events on Saturday 4 October 1975 when, as has been noted above, according to the evidence of Debra Mills, who had been in the company of Maxine Buckley, there had been another incident of indecent exposure.

In her first witness statement, made on 9 October 1975, Maxine Buckley, then aged 12 claimed that a man had indecently exposed himself while he was standing on the corner of Jackson Street as she and Debra Mills walked along Vavasour Street. That behaviour, not surprisingly, left Maxine in a very distressed state, almost to the point of hysteria. Debra Mills was upset and frightened by what she saw. Maxine ran home and told her mother, 'A man has exposed himself to me in Vavasour Street. I think it's the man who lives in Crawford Street, the house with the plants in the window.' The police were contacted. An officer attended and was told the man involved was '... a white male, aged approximately twenty-five years, very fat build, wearing a green "parka" type coat with the hood up.' The man was also described as being about 5' 10' tall and shuffled as he walked.

A thorough search of the area for a man answering that description proved fruitless. The officer was directed by the two young girls to 31 Crawford Street but there was no one there. The house did have plants in the window. The occupants of that house were Stefan Kiszko and his mother. They had lived there for more than 20 years but were now in the process of moving house to an address at number 25 Kings Road and in fact completed the move a month later, on 6 November 1975.

According to the police officer, 'The house appeared to be empty and there was no sign of anyone living in the house'. For reasons not readily apparent the police seemed to have made no further enquiries about the occupants (a check of the electoral roll would have been useful). Neither did they make any effort to follow up this inquiry into the allegations made by the two young girls by making a return visit to the house that had been identified to them. For the occupants of the house, life probably went on as usual, for they knew nothing at this stage of what was being said about Stefan Kiszko and the reckless and outrageous conduct being alleged against him.

On 5 November 1975, Guy Fawkes Night, at about 8.30 in the evening, Michael John Rigby, aged eleven, was walking along Vavasour Street with Maxine Buckley. They had been watching the fireworks at a bonfire in the grounds of St Peter's School. A man was staring at Maxine, pulling his face and grinding his teeth. She was terrified. Her mother was in a nearby community centre. They contacted the police who searched the area and found no-one. The two children accompanied by their mothers drove to 31 Crawford Stret, the Kiszko family home.

When they arrived there, Mrs Buckley saw that the front door was open and there was a very big man standing in the doorway, with a small grey-haired woman with him. It was possible to see them both easily as the light was on. There were plants in the front window. The curtains were still open. As the car stopped, the lady walked back into the house. Both women got out of the van together and, before they spoke, according to Mrs Buckley, the man shouted, 'What do you want me for, I've done nothing.'

Mrs Buckley tried to calm the situation by saying they had got the wrong house, even though by this time the two children had got out of the back of the van. Maxine was crying, saying, 'That's him, Mum', while Michael agreed, saying, 'It is him.' Whether the eleven-year-old was influenced in any way by the purported identification of the man by Maxine is not known. Certainly, he claimed that he immediately recognised him the moment the van pulled up outside the house, but he added that, 'I do not know this man by name, but I have seen him before standing at the door of his house.' Michael Rigby gave evidence for the prosecution before the jury at Stefan Kiszko's trial for murder.

How his evidence helped that jury to decide whether the prosecution had proved that he was the murderer of Lesley Molseed I find difficult to understand. To what issue in the case was it relevant? All that he could give evidence about was the reaction of Maxine Buckley when they saw the man in the street, contorting his face and grinding his teeth, and the fact that he, Michael Rigby, was as frightened as she was.

Mrs Sheila Buckley also gave evidence for the prosecution. She dealt with the incident of the 4 October 1975 as well as that on 5 November. The relevance of her evidence is questionable.

Two police officers went to 31 Crawford Street, arriving at about 10.20 pm on the same evening of 5 November. Stefan Kiszko was at home when the police arrived. So was his mother. One officer told Stefan, 'I have received a complaint from two girls that a man fitting your description indecently exposed himself to them on Saturday 4 October 1975 at about 12.45 pm in Jackson Street, Rochdale.' Whether the officer was being fair and accurate in telling Stefan that he matched the description of the man involved given to the police by the girls, is questionable.

When told of the accusation of indecent exposure by the officer it was Stefan's mother who rather indignantly replied, instead of Stefan, 'You have no right to accuse my son of such things, he is a sick boy, he has only been out of hospital a couple of days, after being in for six weeks.' To this the officer replied: 'We are not accusing your son, we are only making enquiries.'

Charlotte Kiszko said, 'My son wouldn't do a thing like that and I don't like what you're saying about him.' Clearly this wasn't taking the matter very much further forward so the officer suggested to Stefan that they go into the front room of the house, asking his mother, rather strangely some may think, 'Can we interview him on his own?' to which she replied, 'Why, don't you want me there?' This is not just the conduct of an overprotective parent, but the sign of a deep-seated anxiety that a rather vulnerable individual needed her presence to ensure fair and proper treatment from the two police officers. Stefan Kiszko was a man of unblemished character. He had no criminal convictions; he had never been in a court for any reason whatever and had never been accused of criminal conduct of any sort.

Police Constable Shaw told Mrs Kiszko that her son might be embarrassed to talk about it in front of her and if he wished to tell her about the incident he could do so later. With that, the three proceeded to the front room, leaving Charlotte Kiszko outside. There were further questions and answers about the incidents but Stefan admitted nothing.

The police concluded the interview by asking Stefan, 'Do you deny exposing yourself on the 4th October 1975 in Jackson Street near to Vavasour Street?' To which he replied, 'Yes, I do.' When she told him that the police would be making further enquiries, Stefan told them, 'Don't come tomorrow, we are moving.' The interviewing officer later notified the officers investigating the murder of Lesley Molseed of her interview with Stefan Kiszko.

When Superintendent Wilkinson prepared his report for the Chief Constable he noted, at paragraph 172,

> 'In the statement Kiszko made retracting his admissions, he does agree there was an incident in Vavasour Street at lunch time on the Saturday. According to him he had been disposing of an old carpet in that area. In his first statement he describes unzipping his trousers and his shirt flap coming out. There was an old lady and a man in the street at that time. He insists that he did not deliberately expose himself. In the statement he does not say why he unzipped his trousers'.

The superintendent continued at paragraph 173 'In the second statement he appears to be saying that he unzipped his trousers because his shirt flap had come out, whilst lifting the carpet. Quite clearly something occurred in Vavasour Street that lunch-time'. He could not take it any further than that.

Chapter Five

Police Interrogation

Stefan Kiszko was born in Birch Hill Hospital in Rochdale on 24 March 1952 and had lived for his entire life at 31 Crawford Street. His father Ivan was a Ukrainian who came to Britain in 1949. His mother Charlotte was born in Yugoslavia. Both parents treasured their only child and were very protective towards him, especially since his physical health was not good. He was found to be asthmatic at the age of four and was unable to start St Peter's Infants School, until he reached the age of seven. Before that time he lived in Austria with his maternal grandmother, in the hope that the bracing fresh air there would alleviate some of the difficulties he had with his weak chest. He later attended Kingsway High School and then Rochdale Technical College, where he obtained a certificate in office studies. He was a lonely student leading a solitary life, not mixing with others, and he formed no friendships during his academic career. At the age of 17 he passed the Civil Service Examination and took up employment as a clerk in the Inland Revenue, in the centre of Rochdale. It was a matter of great pride for his parents that he had attained such a prestigious position, the first member of his family to do so. Stefan was however almost as lonely there as he had been at school, devoid of any close friendships with persons of either sex, though he was courteous and helpful to everyone who met him.

He drove to work in his bronze-coloured Hillman Avenger, returning home for lunch each day. His mother bought that car for him and he repaid her by collecting her from work at the local mill at the end of every evening shift. It had been his father's dying wish that his son should have a car. On occasions, Stefan would take his mother and her sister Alfreda, on trips to the seaside at Blackpool and Southport.

Stefan and his mother were regular churchgoers, attending Mass every Sunday morning, and very frequently going on Sunday afternoons to the cemetery in Rochdale to lay flowers on his father's grave. Charlotte Kiszko said of her only son that he was 'a devoted home-loving boy'.

The only time Stefan socialised with work colleagues was at the annual Christmas party. He was, however, working within the limits of his intellectual ability and did extremely conscientiously and well all that was required of him by his employers.

His physical health did not improve. Early in 1974, he required medical supervision because he was suffering from internal bleeding. Then, in April 1974, he broke his left ankle. This was not the end of his troubles. In August 1975 he was admitted to Birch Hill Hospital (the same hospital in which he had been born) for treatment for acute anaemia, for which he received blood transfusions. Medical tests showed that he was suffering from a condition known as hypogonadism, that is, underactivity of the testes. Its cause may be a disorder of the pituitary gland that results in deficient production of gonadotrophin hormone. The condition can be treated by androgen drugs that stimulate the development of sexual characteristics, such as growth of facial and pubic hair, enlargement of the genitals and deepening of the voice. This treatment improves libido and potency but does not increase the production of sperm. Further examination and treatment at the Manchester Royal Infirmary, where Stefan was an in-patient between 18 August and 15 September, resulted in a decision to administer Primotesterone.

It would not be unfair to Stefan to describe him as 'a loner' with poor health, limited social skills and virtually no friends, someone whose human contact was confined largely to the family home with his mother and her sister, Mrs Alfreda Tosic. Throughout his life he could not escape the snide comments, the pointed jokes at his expense and the realisation that his overall condition would only deteriorate rather than improve. His physical and mental wellbeing could not have been helped by the sudden death of his father on 26 September 1970. Ivan Kiszko collapsed and died from a heart attack in the street as he and Stefan walked together. He was only 56-years-old. That tragedy would have had a devastating effect on any 18-year-old who was devoted to his parents; in Stefan's case it served especially to drive him closer to his mother than ever before. Some would regard Stefan Kiszko as a 'man-child', an extremely vulnerable individual who, if he came into contact and conflict with the law, would require highly competent, robust and courageous lawyers to defend him. The legal profession in England and Wales is full of such individuals. Whether he got the legal representation his case required and his legal interests deserved is open to question.

Stefan read the newspapers and listened to the news, especially with regard to items that concerned his own town of Rochdale. He knew that on Friday 7 November 1975 Lesley Molseed was buried in Rochdale Cemetery. There was a substantial media presence, for the death of this little girl had aroused profound sympathy throughout the nation. Did the funeral that day accelerate the pressure on the police to arrest someone for this horrific murder of a defenceless child?

At 4.45 pm that same day, two plain clothes police officers, Detective Sergeant John William Mawson of No. 1 Operational Area Drug Squad based at Bradford and Detective Constable Colin Ernest Sutcliffe of the Greater Manchester Police, arrived at 25 Kings Road in Rochdale.

Stefan was clearly not pleased to see them and made his displeasure apparent to them. Detective Sergeant Mawson realised from the presence of household items and articles of furniture that the family was in the process of moving into their new home, and asked Stefan, 'Have we called at an inconvenient moment?' Stefan replied, 'It's not just that, your lot have been here the other day accusing me of things I haven't done and upsetting my mother.'

There is a problem about Mawson's next question, which was either naïve in the extreme or it contained a hidden agenda. According to Constable Sutcliffe's typewritten statement, he asked, 'Do you know what you *are* [emphasis added] being accused of?'; for much would depend on who was making the accusation. Was he referring to the previous police visit, about which he appeared to know little or nothing, or was he giving the game away by indicating that the real purpose of the police visit was to accuse Stefan of the murder of Lesley Molseed? The difficulty arises because, according to Mawson's own typed witness statement, the question was, 'Do you know what you *were* [emphasis added] being accused of?' — which would appear to indicate that he was referring to the previous police visit on 5 November.

Stefan told him, 'I was supposed to have been doing something to a young girl in Vavasour Street but it wasn't me.'

Sergeant Mawson asked him, 'Do you know when that was?' and Stefan replied, 'They said on a Saturday afternoon the 4th of last month.' The sergeant then asked, 'Were you in the vicinity of Vavasour Street on that day?' and instead of replying 'Yes' or 'No' Stefan replied, if the evidence of both officers is correct, 'I have been giving it a lot of thought, and as far as I can recollect I was in hospital on that day. I had an operation on my foot.'

The conversation continued. 'So you were still in hospital on that date?' the sergeant asked him, to which Stefan replied, 'Yes, I was.' The sergeant then told him, 'I am making enquiries into the murder of Lesley Molseed which occurred on the 5th October. Were you still in hospital then?' Stefan told him that he had a discharge letter from the hospital somewhere and offered to find it. He could not. He went and searched upstairs rooms and when he returned downstairs his mother was with him. He had not found the letter because the house was in such disorder, but he offered to telephone a friend 'Who may know where I was on 5th October'.

The three men went into the hallway, where Stefan made a telephone call. The officers could hear clearly what Stefan was saying: 'The police are here again. I know my mother is very upset. Do you remember what day I came out of hospital?' The person on the other end of the phone line said something and Stefan remarked, 'Oh, it's just that I'm supposed to have killed a little girl now.' Unless the police have not recorded something that was said by them, they had not suggested to Stefan that he had killed a little girl. They had merely said they were making enquiries into Lesley Molseed's murder (Of course, Stefan did not have to ask who she was, since her funeral was covered by television and radio and details about her brutal death had been all over previous editions local and national newspapers). The telephone conversation concluded with Stefan saying, 'She can't remember.'

The next question is unusual in the context of what had gone before and it was followed by a most bizarre comment. Detective Sergeant Mawson asked, 'Would you care to say what type of vehicle you drive?' to which the answer was, 'A Hillman Avenger, it's on the road outside.' 'Do you have access to any other vehicles?' asked the sergeant. 'No, just the Hillman, I've told the other police,' Stefan replied. The officer then commented, 'I see, I just wondered if you'd any second thoughts.' What this actually means I cannot comprehend. Just what did the officer have in mind that Stefan should have second thoughts about?

The police officers then set the trap, asking Stefan if he was willing to make a statement concerning his whereabouts on Sunday 5 October, and in my view they should have cautioned him — telling him he had the right to stay silent and not say anything, because whatever he did say might be used in evidence — but their real intention was to get him to make a statement from which he could not retreat. If it was false, so much the better for the murder inquiry team. At least they would have a suspect who seemed to be telling lies. Detective Sergeant Mawson then produced a blank witness statement, the endorsement at the top of which complied with the requirements of Section 9 of the Criminal Justice Act 1967. That endorsement is as follows:

'This statement, consisting of 1 page signed by me is true to the best of my knowledge and belief and I make it knowing that if it is tendered in evidence I shall be liable to prosecution if I have stated in it anything which I know to be false or do not believe to be true.'

That was signed by Stefan and the officer to whom he dictated the following:

'I am the owner of a spice coloured Hillman Avenger VDK 157K which I have had since 1971. I do not have access to any other vehicle. As far as I can remember on Sunday 5ᵗʰ October this year I was an in-patient at Ward M.4.M at Manchester Royal Infirmary where I was receiving treatment for an old ankle injury by Dr English and [another doctor]. At that time I was living with my mother at 31 Crawford Street, Rochdale. I cannot remember the date of my discharge but it was early in October. If I had been discharged from hospital on 5th October I would certainly have spent all that day at home, as I was unable to walk at that time.'

He read and then signed that statement. Again, it is not possible to ascertain why he told one set of police officers on 5 November that he was discharged from the hospital on 15 September and another set of officers, this time in writing, two days afterwards, that he could not remember when he was discharged. According to the witness statement of Detective Constable Sutcliffe, 'the interview was concluded at this stage and we left the house'. No time is recorded for this in either police statement (Sergeant Mawson doesn't describe it as an interview at all in his statement), so it is not possible to find out from those statements how long the two officers were actually in the house and how long this interview lasted.

They did not, of course, let the matter rest there. They contacted Manchester Royal Infirmary and were obviously told the day of Stefan's discharge from hospital. It was 15 September. They also spoke to Police Constables Shaw and Oliver. On Monday 10 November 1975, Sergeant Mawson and Constable Sutcliffe went back to 25 Kings Road, and it is suggested that the police began misleading Stefan Kiszko from the very outset of the interview they now conducted with him in his home. He had told the police on 5 November that on 4 October he had been with his mother until after lunch and that he later went out with his friend in his car to take some 'stuff' to Kings Road. It was his mother who unintentionally caused difficulties for Stefan by claiming at that time that he had been in hospital for the last six weeks, and he put that right in answer to the direct question, 'So you were out of hospital on the 4th October 1975?' when he replied, 'Yes, that is right.'

Detective Sergeant Mawson and Detective Constable Sutcliffe tried to turn what he had said to them on 5 November to their advantage by ignoring this information. They did not caution him. Did they not have some information that they could put before a court as the beginnings of a case? This was the third time the police had called at his home to question him in the space of six days. Some of the questions covered the same ground again-and-again. They did not say on this occasion whether they were making enquiries into an offence of indecent exposure (as the officers on 5 November clearly did) or into the murder of Lesley Molseed. Why did they not do so?

They arrived at the house at 1.30 in the afternoon of that Monday. Stefan answered the door and invited them into the living room, where his mother was sitting. She was not asked to leave while questions were being put and answers given. It was a most unusual setting where an adult aged 23 years was accompanied by his elderly mother during the course of a police interview, unless that adult suffered from some mental or physical disability. Detective Sergeant Mawson said,

> 'Since I last saw you I've spoken with the officers who came to see you earlier about the incident in Vavasour Street. Can you explain why you told them that you were moving furniture from your old house with your mother on Saturday the 4th October and yet you told me you were in hospital on that day?'

Would it not have been more reasonable to acknowledge that Stefan had actually accepted on 5 November that he was not in hospital on 4 October and to ask why he had changed his account on 7 November to say that he was? Was it not misleading him to claim that Stefan had told the officers on 5 November that he was moving furniture from his old home with his mother, when in fact he had said that he had gone out with his friend in his car to take some stuff to Kings Road? That friend had picked him up at about 3 pm. There was no mention of furniture, according to the witness statement of both Constables Shaw and Oliver, and 'the stuff' Stefan did mention could have been anything from shoes to bed linen to books. It seems that Stefan was never asked to identify that friend, who might or might not have supported his version of events on 4 October, especially since it was alleged that Stefan had committed the indecency offence only about two and a quarter hours before the moving of the stuff took place.

Stefan's answer, to what I regard as a misleading question, was likely to cause him further trouble. 'As far as I could remember I was in hospital then but if I wasn't I would certainly have been helping my mother to move furnishings from the old house.' I fail to see how that follows at all, but Sergeant Mawson moved on and said, 'I have checked at the hospital and they confirm that you have been in hospital; however, their records show that you were discharged from hospital on 15 September 1975, which is almost three weeks prior to the incident in Vavasour Street. Can anyone other than your mother confirm your whereabouts on the weekend of the 4th and 5th of October?'

Had Sergeant Mawson overlooked the claim that a friend had helped Stefan on the Saturday afternoon? Why did he not follow this up? My suspicion is that by this time Stefan Kiszko was in an utterly confused state. He fell into further error. His answer to the question was: 'Not that I can think of, I have been talking it over with my mother since you came last Friday. We remembered visiting my father's grave on Sunday 12th October and that was the first time I went out anywhere.' So the existence of the friend is now not claimed, and Stefan now denies something he had previously admitted, that he went from Crawford Street to Kings Road with a friend in his car. 'I am sure I would have stayed in all day on the 5th October. I know I was having difficulty walking and I am still off work.'

The sergeant asked Charlotte Kiszko, 'Is what your son said correct?' and she replied, 'Yes, he has been with me most of the time at weekends but it is a long time ago. I cannot remember fully.' This has all the appearance of an honest and open answer. Some people may find it surprising that the police were prepared to allow one person to put forward an explanation in the presence of another, thereby giving them the opportunity to tailor any evidence that they might subsequently give in accordance not with what they knew, but with what they had heard.

The next question from Detective Sergeant Mawson is also troublesome. 'My information is that you have access to a white saloon car, probably a Vauxhall Viva?' He quite naturally did not disclose the source of that information but was he hinting that the police knew more than they were prepared to say at that moment in time? But could this be a reference to the colour of the car that Mrs Tong had seen outside her house with the little girl she thought was Lesley Molseed inside? Did they have information that Lesley Molseed had been abducted by a man in a white Vauxhall car? In the event, Stefan was never asked again, and never told again, anything about a vehicle of this make and colour. Stefan's reply was clear. 'No, I've told you only my own car. A white Viva used to park outside the newsagents next to the old house in Crawford Street but I think it was a customer's car. It was there regularly.' Sergeant Mawson then asked him, 'Are you willing to make a further statement to the one you made on Friday covering what you are now telling me?'

Stefan readily agreed. Again, a witness statement form was produced, setting out the declaration at the top. Stefan dictated a statement that Sergeant Mawson wrote down. Stefan read it and then signed it.

The statement reads:

'Further to my statement of the 7th of this month I have now found my final discharge papers and I realize that I was mistaken when I said I had been in Manchester Royal Infirmary on Sunday 5th October this year. I was in fact discharged from hospital on the 15th September 1975. I have been off work since that time. I could hardly walk after I returned home for a few weeks. My mother will confirm that I stayed in the house most of the time. The first time I drove my vehicle was on Sunday 12th October when I took my mother to the cemetery at Bury Road. We went there about lunch time and returned home about 1 pm The Sunday before that on the 5th October I stayed at home all day. I have only ever driven my own Hillman Avenger. I have never driven a white Viva, however a white car used to park outside the paper shop next door to my old house at 31 Crawford Street. I have never seen Lesley Molseed at any time.'

I consider that the purpose of this police interview was to establish that Stefan Kiszko was lying about his whereabouts on the day Lesley was murdered. Up to this point, after three interviews, there seemed to be no question of charging him with an offence of indecent exposure allegedly committed on Saturday 4 October 1975. I further consider that the police had sufficient evidence to charge him, based on the claims of Maxine Buckley and Debra Mills, who both said a man had exposed himself to them on that day. There was one reason why they might have hesitated to bring a charge. There would have been no point in arranging an identification parade for Maxine to attend, because she would without doubt have identified the man from the house in Crawford Street with the plants in the window. But there would have had to be an identification parade for Debra Mills to attend, even under the rules of procedure at that time, and if she had failed to identify Stefan Kiszko this would have damaged the prospects of conviction immensely. Moreover, anyone reading her statements, and those of Maxine Buckley, would immediately realise that there were two incidents of indecency mentioned, and yet up to this point, in the course of three interviews involving four police officers, Stefan Kiszko had not been asked a single question about the events of Friday 3 October 1975 or to account for his movements and whereabouts for around 8 pm to 9 pm on that Friday. So, at this stage in the police inquiry into his whereabouts and behaviour on 4 and 5 October 1975, it could be said, from one viewpoint, that Stefan Kiszko had given confused and contradictory explanations to the interviewing officers. From another viewpoint it could be said that he was lying to them. If the latter, and if he was a suspect for the murder of Lesley Molseed, one is bound to ask why the police did not immediately subject his motor vehicle to the most detailed forensic examination to see whether there was anything at all, and especially a fingerprint, that linked that little girl to the car.

That evidence apart, the investigation into this most terrible murder seemed to be going nowhere until someone decided that Stefan Kiszko should be brought to a police station and interviewed. That decision must have been reached some time between 10 November and 21 December, for it was on that day, a Sunday, that there was the next contact between the police and Stefan Kiszko. Why it took so long is not known.

Chapter Six

More Questions

On Thursday 18 December 1975, three police officers, Detective Sergeant John Michael Akeroyd (a member of the Molseed murder inquiry team since 8 October 1975), and Detective Constables McFadzean and Whittle went to the Turf Hill area of Rochdale to make enquiries about a number of incidents of indecency. They were surely going over old ground. In any event, according to them they were acting 'on information received' when they presented themselves at the door of 25 Kings Road in Rochdale in order to see Stefan Kiszko at 10.30 on the following Sunday morning. Why Sunday was chosen must now be a matter of speculation. Some defence lawyers would have raised it at the trial. Were many lawyers available in Rochdale, or nearby, to accompany someone to a police station for interview on that Sunday morning?

Does it really require the presence of three police officers to call at a house to see a suspect where, on two previous occasions, two sets of police officers (one of whom was a woman) had been to the same house and never had cause to complain of any use, or the threat of use, of violence against them? And this time the police were at the house for a different purpose. It was their intention to remove Stefan Kiszko from what he would regard as a place of safety, namely his home, with his beloved mother in the same room as himself or nearby, and install him in the extremely intimidating and coercive atmosphere of a police station. The question was, how most conveniently, to the police that is, to get him there?

There is a power of arrest for an offence of indecent exposure vested in a police constable if a person commits that offence within his view. That was not the case here. There was an offence at Common Law of outraging public decency by exposing the person or engaging in or simulating a sexual act. That was triable only on indictment in the Crown Court at one time, but now it is an offence triable either summarily in the magistrates' court or on indictment in the Crown Court. Whether there was in 1975 a power of arrest for the Common Law offence is unclear.

What the police did here was to invite Stefan Kiszko to attend the police station voluntarily, without arresting him. As a volunteer, he had fewer rights than a detained person held there under arrest. Under Rule VII of the Judges' Rules a person in custody should be allowed to speak on the telephone to his solicitor or to his friends, provided that no hindrance was reasonably likely to be caused to the processes of investigation, or the administration of justice, by his doing so. Obviously, Rule VII did not apply to Stefan Kiszko since he was not in custody.

Apart from a few statutory exceptions (such as a requirement to give name and address to a police officer in road traffic cases) no-one is obliged as a matter of law to answer questions put to him or her as a suspect or a witness and furthermore any person being questioned at a police station is entitled to leave at any time if he or she so wishes. However, in 1975 the police were under no legal obligation to tell Stefan Kiszko of his right to leave or to advise him of any other rights he might have. It was essential then, as it is now, that a person having the physical attributes and unworldly nature of Stefan Kiszko should be treated humanely, that his basic rights should be observed and that any statement he made should be reliable.

Whether it is admitted or not, a person being interrogated at a police station is in a very vulnerable position. As the American Supreme Court noted in 1966,

'[A]n individual swept from familiar surroundings into police custody, surrounded by antagonistic forces, and subjected to the persuasions described in various interrogation manuals cannot be otherwise than under compulsion to speak...As a practical matter the compulsion to speak in the isolated setting of a police station may well be greater than in courts or other official investigations, where there are often impartial observers to guard against intimidation or trickery... unless adequate protective devices

are employed to dispel the compulsion in custodial surroundings, no statement obtained from the defendant can truly be the product of his free will.'

This approach recognises something that many police officers and some
members of the judiciary in England and Wales refuse to countenance,
namely that all custodial interrogation necessarily trades on the weak-
ness of the individual. I consider there to be no doubt in this case that
the police were determined to hold Stefan Kiszko until such time as he
confessed to a crime that they believed he had committed.

Sergeant Akeroyd recorded that, on arrival at Stefan's house,

> '...I there saw a man whom I now know to be Stefan Ivan Kiszko. I
> informed Kiszko of our identities and said, "We are making enquiries in
> this case regarding a number of incidents which have occurred where it
> is alleged that a man has been indecently exposing himself to young girls,
> and from the enquiries I have made so far I have reason to believe that you
> can assist me with my enquiries." I cautioned him and Kiszko said, "Yes,
> what do you want?" I said, "I would like you to accompany me to the police
> station at Rochdale so that we can discuss the matter."'

Stefan asked the next question, 'Well, why can't we talk here?' and
this seems a sensible approach to take, for if it was true that the police
inquiry was into incidents of indecency and he had been interviewed
three times in relation to such matters in his own home, why change
the venue now?

Sergeant Akeroyd's response to the question was to say, 'I would prefer
it if you would accompany me to the police headquarters at Rochdale.'
Stefan apparently readily agreed, saying, 'Yes, all right, I'll come along
with you. I'll just get ready.'

If the police had told Stefan Kiszko that they intended to interrogate
him about the murder of Lesley Molseed, would he have gone so willingly
to the police station, or would he have refused and therefore placed the
onus on the police to arrest him? The difficulty that faced the officers,
of course, was that if asked to point out the grounds of reasonable suspicion that he had committed that offence of murder, in order to exercise

the power of arrest, could they have done so? The answer is surely no because there was not a scintilla of evidence against Stefan that he was a child killer. Would Charlotte Kiszko have let her son go willingly to the police station if she had been told that he was to be questioned about the murder of a young girl? Would she have tried (as she eventually but belatedly did) to obtain legal advice and assistance for him, even on a Sunday morning? As it was, while Stefan was putting on his coat and shoes, she asked Detective Sergeant Akeroyd, 'What do you want from him now?' His reply was short and immediate. 'We're making some further enquiries in respect of certain motor vehicles.' That statement might have been partially true. I regard it as a lie. It should be noted however that Stefan said in his draft statement (see *Appendix 1* to this work) that the police officers made it clear to him that they wanted to talk to him about Lesley Molseed's murder. One wonders whether he was mistaken about that; in fact he could only recall two police officers, not three, who arrived at his house on that Sunday morning.

At that point in the conversation, according to the sergeant, Stefan left the room, without any objection from anyone. I find this extraordinary, because if he was guilty of some crime might he not take advantage of the opportunity either to flee or to dispose of some incriminating evidence? What he actually did was to go into his garage, because when Detective Sergeant Akeroyd went into the house the other two officers went into the garage and started to examine the outside of the Hillman car. It is virtually impossible to avoid commenting that it was a little late in the day, on 21 December 1975, to expect to find any relevant evidence linking Lesley Molseed to that motor vehicle. My suspicion is that they were trying to ascertain whether the vehicle had been resprayed, because at no time had any witness to the alleged indecency incidents described a car that matched Stefan's. Neither had any car been observed in the vicinity of the murder scene in October that matched the colour or the make of Stefan's car. If Stefan Kiszko had been arrested at his home, I believe the police would have been entitled to carry out a search for evidence at the place where he had been placed under arrest. Since he was not, I consider that the police had no legal right to enter the garage in order to search for evidence. They could have asked for his permission to search, or obtained a search warrant, but they did not.

According to the two officers, Stefan said, 'Do you mind coming out of my garage?' to which Detective Constable McFadzean replied, 'Why, have you something to hide?' Stefan said, 'No, it's a bit untidy that's all. Can I bring my car with me?' Such an offer might have caused some police officers to pause for thought, since a motor vehicle had certainly been used to abduct Lesley Molseed prior to her murder, and here was a suspect offering to bring his car to the police station without any reservation of any kind. Detective Constable McFadzean said, 'Yes, if you like, I'll come with you.'

No time is recorded in any of the three police officers' witness statements establishing when the quartet arrived at police headquarters in Rochdale. Nothing is noted either about where Stefan was between the time of arrival and the first interview. As he was a volunteer, as opposed to an arrested and detained person, I consider it would not have been proper to place him in a cell. The problem, of course, is that individuals cannot be allowed to wander unsupervised all over the interior of a police station and something has to be done with them. The question remains, where was he? It would also have helped if these three officers had complied with the Judges' Rules regarding the timing of interviews in their witness statements. All three, Akeroyd, McFadzean and Whittle, were present at the first. None of them noted in their witness statements when it began or when it ended, as required by Rule II. It may have commenced immediately after arrival at the police station (Stefan's recollection was that it did. He also said that there was a fourth officer there; his name was Steele. He was quite pleasant to Stefan and kept holding his right hand. (I found no witness statement regarding this or any other dealings that officer may have had with Stefan at any stage of the police investigation). There certainly was an officer in the station with that name. He is mentioned by, amongst others, Detective Superintendent Holland as being involved in the enquiry.

According to the summing-up at the subsequent trial the first interview started at 10. 30 am It went on until 1. 45 pm. The second interview started at 2. 35 pm and ended at 5. 25 pm. Three officers took part. The third interview started at 6. 45 pm and ended at 8. 30 pm. Three officers, Akeroyd, Whittle and McFadzean took part in the first two; Akeroyd and Holland were the officers who conducted the third. At 1. 45 am the early hours of the Monday morning there was a short interview conducted by Holland and Akeroyd.

I question again why three (or four) officers were required to be present during this interview. One answer may be, to intimidate by sheer weight of numbers. I also question whether a contemporaneous note was taken by anyone, and if not, why not? Why trust to memory when it was perfectly feasible for one of the three (or four) to note, even in summary form, the contents of the first interview?

The police say that Stefan was reminded that he was under caution. He apparently did not ask what that actually meant. 'As I have already told you we have been making enquiries into a number of alleged offences of an indecent nature in the Rochdale area where a man has been indecently exposing himself to little girls. As a result of the enquiries which we have made I wish to ask you some questions concerning your whereabouts on certain days since the beginning of October.'

This was intended to be clear and unequivocal. The questions to be put to Stefan related to indecent exposure allegations in Rochdale. Not unnaturally Stefan replied, 'I have already been seen by the police, in fact I told my boss about it and he rang the superintendent.' Sergeant Akeroyd said, 'Yes, I know the police have seen you but you have given different accounts on each occasion. We have information which is contrary to what you have already told the police.'

'I'm supposed to have done something indecent to young girls but I haven't done anything like that,' Stefan replied.

The next question from Sergeant Akeroyd I find puzzling:

'What did the policewoman say to you when she came to your house?' I am unable to formulate an answer to that question myself. Was the officer expecting a recital of each and every question that the police-woman put to Stefan, or was he asking for a summary, or even just one or more of the questions that she actually asked? Was he more interested in the questions than the answers? Would it not have been better for Sergeant Akeroyd to have produced a copy of Police Constable Shaw's witness statement and gone through it with Stefan, asking whether he agreed that it correctly represented what was said and by whom in that interview on 5 November 1975—that is, about 46 days prior to the day on which Stefan was now being questioned? Stefan replied, 'I don't know, I can't remember. I've been seen by the police on a few occasions.'

The next question was equally puzzling, and more especially because Sergeant Akeroyd ought to have known the answer. 'Well what did they see you about on the other occasions?' He replied, 'They came to see me about that girl Lesley Molseed and I told them that I never went out that day because I was weak and could hardly walk.'

'Why were you feeling weak, were you ill?' he was asked, and his reply was, 'I'd just been in hospital. I'd only just come out. I'd had a blood transfusion.'

Sergeant Akeroyd then asked Stefan a question to which I suspect he well knew the answer, that is, 'What day were you discharged from hospital?' To recap, Stefan had previously told the police on 5 November 1975, that he went into Birch Hill Hospital on 6 August 1975, was there for two weeks, following which he went to Manchester Royal Infirmary for four weeks. When he had indicated that, the police officer confirmed with him, 'So you were out of hospital on the 4th October 1975,' and Stefan replied, 'Yes, that is right.'

When he was seen by Detective Sergeant Mawson and Detective Constable Sutcliffe on 7 November, only two days later, he contradicted what he had said on 5 November and then claimed he was in hospital on 4 October. This was an area bound to lead to confusion, because the police were switching from the events of 4 October, the indecency incident, and 5 October, the day that Lesley Molseed was abducted and murdered. Consciously or otherwise they seemed to be linking the events of those two days together. Up to this stage, according to the officers, no mention whatever had been made of Lesley Molseed by any of the three of them. They claimed that Stefan Kiszko was the first to make a direct reference to her case when he said, 'Well actually it was the 15th September. I made a mistake and told the police that I was in hospital on the day the little girl went missing but I later realised that it was a mistake and I told them so.'

Sergeant Akeroyd then pressed for more detail, asking the following questions and receiving the following answers:

'Would you care to tell me what was the first day you went out after leaving hospital?'

'It was the Sunday following,' Stefan replied, 'I took my mother to the cemetery to take some flowers. We do that quite a lot.'

'Was that the Sunday after you were discharged from hospital?'

'No, the Sunday after the girl went missing.'

'Do you mean the 12th October 1975?'

'Yes.'

'Are you quite sure that that was the first day you went out after being discharged from hospital?'

'Yes I'm sure.'

'Are you saying that you never left your house at all until 12th October 1975?'

'Yes, I never went out, I was too weak.'

'I want you to think very carefully before you answer this question. Where were you at about 12.45 pm on Saturday the 4th October 1975?'

Stefan paused and then said, 'At home with my mother. I was very weak and depressed, what with the blood transfusions and the injections.'

'Where were you on bonfire night, did you go out at all?'

'No, I don't go out much at all.'

'Are you sure about that?'

'Yes, I'm certain.'

'I want you to think very carefully again because I don't think you're telling me the truth. Do you remember bonfire night?'

'Yes, of course I remember it.'

'Tell me how you can remember what you did on bonfire night so clearly as to know that you didn't go out?'

'Well it was the night before we moved to Kings Road.'

'I'm telling you that that's not true, you did go out on bonfire night, and you were seen by someone who later came to your house at Crawford Street. Do you remember a woman getting out of a vehicle outside your house on that night?'

'No.'

'I think you do. Your mother was standing at the door with you and you said to the woman, "What do you want, I've done nothing wrong?"' '

'No, I don't remember.'

'Are you telling me now that this woman never came to your house on bonfire night?'

'I can't remember.'

'Can you remember any other night when what I've described it took place?'

'No, not at all.'

'I also have to put it to you that you went out on bonfire night because you stopped near to a bonfire at St Peter's School, and the significance of that is that you were seen there and positively identified as the man who had exposed himself to a young girl called Maxine Buckley on the 4th October 1975 in Vavasour Street near Jackson Street.'

'I don't remember.'

'Can you think of any reason why a woman should come to your home on bonfire night?'

'No, I can't.'

Detective Sergeant Akeroyd said, 'Listen, Mr Kiszko,' when he was interrupted and Stefan said, 'You can call me Stefan.'

'You obviously went out, think very carefully, you were seen.'

'Can I be identified?'

'You were identified that night at the bonfire and at the door of your house. The girl recognised you at the bonfire and went to your house at Crawford Street with her mother and another woman, and they saw you standing at the door. Are you saying they are lying?'

'Well, they might want to get me into trouble.'

Detective Constable Whittle then spoke, apparently for the first time in the interview, saying, 'Why would any person try to get you into trouble by saying things like this if they're not true. They could get themselves into serious trouble, couldn't they?'

'They might have it in for me because I work for the Inspector of Taxes.'

Constable Whittle said, 'Do you really expect us to believe that people would make up a story like this to get you into trouble just because you work in the Tax Department?'

'Well, what other reason could there be?'

Sergeant Akeroyd asked the next question, tied up in the form of a comment mixed in with a statement of fact: 'Because you are telling lies. You did go out on bonfire night and you are the man that indecently exposed himself on the 4ᵗʰ October 1975. Is that not the case?'

Stefan's reply to that simply does not make sense. Was this an indication of the pressure he was under, being accused of lying and indecency?

'Well I suppose I could have gone up to the house at Kings Road with some things and she must have seen me but she's mistaken me for someone else.'

'So now you're telling us that you did go out on bonfire night then?'

'Well I may have done. I was taking things up to the house nearly every night.'

I'll ask you again. Did you go out on bonfire night?' 'Well yes, I suppose I must have done. I can't remember.'

Detective Constable McFadzean then asked a question preceded by a comment. 'Surely you can remember whether or not you went to the bonfire that night. It's not as though you go to a bonfire every night is it?'

'I can't remember. I've already told you that I could have done, but I didn't get out of my car.'

Constable McFadzean asked, 'Well did you stop your car or not?'

'Yes, I did stop, but I didn't do anything wrong.'

'Why did you stop then?' asked that officer.

'I was feeling tired with all the moving.'

'Is that the only reason you stopped?'

'Yes, why?'

Constable McFadzean asked a further question: 'Are you quite sure that you didn't get out of your car?'

'Well I may have done but I can't remember. It's all a bit hazy. It's these damned injections, they make me feel a bit funny for a few days after I have had them.'

Detective Sergeant Akeroyd resumed the questioning. 'What injections are those, Stefan?'

'They're the ones I have to help me with my complaint.'

'Would you care to tell us about them?'

'No, it doesn't matter.'

'In that case, I'll ask you again where you were at about 2.45 pm on Saturday 4ᵗʰ October 1975?'

Again the switch of times and dates from one to another without any pattern or logic in the approach seems almost calculated to confuse. Stefan replied, 'At home with my mother I suppose.'

'There's no suppose about it,' said Sergeant Akeroyd. 'I know where you were on that Saturday dinner time and so do you.'

'I don't know. It is obviously someone trying to get me into trouble.'

The sergeant said, 'We are going to leave you now whilst we make some more enquiries. I want you to think very carefully about what you have told me and I'll come back and see you shortly. Would you like some sandwiches?'

'No, but can I have a drink?'

That ended the interview.

Where Stefan Kiszko spent the time until the next interview is not known, and although he may have remained in the unlocked interview room on his own, the probability was that he was locked in a cell in the police station. Was he still regarded by the police as assisting them in their enquiries, as a volunteer, or was he now under compulsion to stay at the police station?

At 2.35 pm the second interview began. The time of commencement is properly noted by all three police officers who were there. It was the same trio as had previously interviewed Stefan. It follows from this that Stefan (and of course the officers) had only a break of 50 minutes between both interviews.

The police claim he was reminded he was under caution by Detective Sergeant Akeroyd, who said, 'I have been making some more enquiries into the matter we had discussed earlier and you have had a chance to think as well. Do you want to tell us where you were at 12.45 pm on Saturday 4ᵗʰ October 1975?'

Stefan replied, 'I don't know, I can't remember.'

Detective Constable Whittle said, 'I think you can remember, but you don't want to tell us the truth. I'm satisfied that you are the man that exposed himself to those two girls on that Saturday lunchtime, and that they recognised you on bonfire night as the man responsible.'

I cannot say whether this officer was allowed to get away with this very misleading statement when he gave evidence for the prosecution at Stefan's trial. Perhaps he was. Some barristers would have subjected him to a careful and forceful cross-examination on why he wrongly claimed that the two girls recognised Stefan Kiszko on bonfire night, because they had not done so. Only Maxine Buckley, accompanied by Michael Rigby, had seen him on 5 November. The other girl, Debra Mills, was not even there. No effort had been made to see whether she could identify Stefan Kiszko as the man she claimed had indecently exposed himself to her on 4 October 1975, and the police were content to hold Stefan at the police station entirely on the allegations made against him by 12-year-old Maxine Buckley. At least one police officer was deliberately representing that the case against Stefan was stronger than it actually was. He should have been called to account for doing so.

Stefan was told, 'I'm satisfied that you are the man that exposed himself to those two girls on that Saturday lunchtime'. That might have been so, but why then was Stefan not charged with an offence relating to Saturday 4 October 1975 if the police were satisfied there was proof he had committed a crime? Whatever the reason, Stefan was never charged at any stage with an offence relating to the incidents of 3 and 4 October 1975.

The interview continued with Stefan's response to the claim.

'I couldn't do anything like that, that's why I'm having these injections.'

Detective Constable Whittle asked, 'What are the injections for?'

'Well, I don't fancy girls,' was the reply. In my view, that was a turning point in the case. From that point onwards the police were convinced in their own minds that those injections had caused a harmless young man to become a dangerous monster who so lost his self-control that he savagely murdered a little girl.

The three officers then asked further questions of Stefan. Up to now the majority had been asked by the senior officer, Detective Sergeant

Akeroyd, in the interview room. Some may find it disquieting to be asked questions in this way, from different people from differing positions in the room. Were the four sitting around a table, with three in close proximity to the fourth person under interrogation? This was not a friendly social occasion. No transcript can give an indication of the speed and tone of voice in which these questions were asked.

Detective Constable Whittle said, 'What do you mean, you don't fancy girls?' to which the reply was, 'Well when I was in hospital I discussed my problem with a doctor and he gave me some injections to bring me on.'

Detective Sergeant Akeroyd asked, 'This is a very personal thing, but are you telling us that you are impotent?'

'Yes I am. That's why I couldn't have done these things they say I've been doing. My doctor will tell you so.'

Constable Whittle asked, 'Do I understand you correctly, you are telling us that you are receiving treatment to help you with this condition?'

'Yes, I am,' said Stefan. 'I've no interest in girls at all but the injections will help me.'

Then Detective Constable McFadzean said, 'Don't you have any girl-friends at work?'

'No, I've never bothered with them.'

At this stage a message was given to Detective Constable Whittle and he left the room, returning after a few seconds. He asked Stefan for his car keys, telling him he would like to examine his car. Stefan's response was, 'Yes, I suppose so, don't leave it untidy.'

Does that question indicate that Stefan still did not appreciate the significance of the danger he was in? Sometime during that Sunday, 21 December, the police removed a number of items from that car, including three pairs of gloves, a coat, a hyperdermic syringe and a seat cover. The car was then loaded onto a low loader, covered with a tarpaulin sheet, and transported to the Forensic Science Laboratory at Harrogate. The purpose of the exercise was obvious. The police and the forensic scientists were looking for fingerprints and for traces of blood from the body of that little girl? Lesley was stabbed in the heart by a person very close beside her. Would her killer have been heavily bloodstained as a consequence of what he had done to that little girl?

After that officer left the interview room. Sergeant Akeroyd asked Stefan, 'How long have you had your car?' and was told, 'Since 1971.' 'Was it a new one when you bought it?' 'Yes', Stefan replied.

Constable McFadzean asked, 'Do you have access to any other vehicles at all?' and received the answer, 'No'. No attempt was made to put to him again the fact that the police had, so they claimed, information connecting him to a white car, probably a Vauxhall Viva. That sank into oblivion, never to be revived. The importance of that information is that it is linked to the evidence of Mrs Emma Tong, who saw the man and the child she was convinced was Lesley in a cream-coloured car.

'Does anyone else use your car?' asked that same officer, to be told, 'No, only me.'

'Do you go out in your car much by yourself?' he asked Stefan, and was told, 'No, I only go to work and back and I sometimes take my mother to the cemetery in it.'

While these questions were being asked, Detective Constable Whittle and other police officers searched Stefan's car, and under the carpet he found what he described as 'several sex-type magazines'. Sergeant Akeroyd looked at them and described them as '…of the type which contain photographs of nude women'.

Detective Constable Whittle said, 'I have just had a look in your car and I have found these magazines hidden under the carpet in the boot. Are they yours?'

Stefan replied, 'Yes.' The same officer asked, 'But you have just told us you have no interest in girls whatsoever, so why do you have nude books in your car?'

According to all three officers Stefan began to tremble violently and started to bite his fingernails. He said, 'It's those damned injections. I never did anything like this before.'

Sergeant Akeroyd asked him, 'Anything like what?' and Stefan made no reply.

The sergeant pressed him, and tried to reassure him by saying, 'Look, there's nothing wrong with a man buying this type of book, it's quite common in fact. Would you like to tell us why you buy them?'

'I don't know really, I just started to fancy them.'

'When did you start to fancy them?' asked the sergeant, to which Stefan replied, 'When I came out of hospital in September this year.'

Sergeant Akeroyd then asked a telling question: 'What else started when you came out of hospital?'

Stefan did not reply.

Detective Constable McFadzean followed this up, however, and said, 'Is it fair to say that you have had some sexual urge since you left hospital?'

Stefan appeared reluctantly to agree, replying, 'I suppose so.'

Constable McFadzean went on, 'The matter we have been discussing with you occurred on the 4ᵗʰ October 1975 which is about two weeks after you came out of hospital, and I'm putting it to you that you are responsible for that offence.'

'I can't remember,' replied Stefan. 'Can I go home now?'

This is a highly significant question and one to which Stefan received no answer, for the police proceeded with the interview as if it had never been asked. In my view, Stefan should have been told that he was free to leave the police station if he wished, because he had gone there voluntarily and not under arrest.

Assuming he was not locked-up at lunchtime that day, he was still a volunteer and under no restraint or compulsion. As noted above, it was not entirely clear under statute law or the Common Law whether there was a power of arrest for offences of indecent exposure not witnessed by a police officer. It may have been a case of not wanting to arrest him in any event, because the real purpose of the interviews had not yet been established — in fact, the police were seeking a confession to the killing of Lesley Molseed and were at that time engaged in 'a softening-up process' before moving on to the central point of their investigation.

Constable McFadzean asked Stefan to empty his pockets out onto the table and he did so. (Stefan claims it was Superintendent Holland who asked him to do that). Among his possessions were two knives, one a penknife with a black handle and one a locking knife with an imitation bone handle. Some may find it surprising that a man should be allowed to keep in his possession in a police station after his arrival there any object that could have been used offensively to others or himself. Of course, if he had been arrested then he would then have been searched, and his property recorded and taken from him, but that was not the position here. It will be remembered that there was a stage, before he left his home that Sunday morning, when Stefan had the opportunity to rid himself of those objects if he so wished. Surely he would have done so if he had anything to hide in relation to them or their use?

Constable McFadzean asked Stefan if the black-handled knife was his and was told that both knives belonged to Stefan. That officer picked up the bone-handled knife and asked, 'What do you use this knife for?' and the response was not actually an answer to that question. 'Well, I always carry a knife.'

Sergeant Akeroyd said, 'Yes, I would agree some men carry a knife of some sort, but would you care to tell me why you carry two knives?'

He replied, 'Well, I use one for cleaning my battery and the other one I use for cutting string and other things at work.'

Sergeant Akeroyd asked, 'Which one do you use for your car battery?'

Stefan pointed to the knife with the black handle. The officer indicated the other knife, saying, 'So this is the knife which you use at work for cutting string.' In response to this piece of deduction, of which the fictional Inspector Clouseau would no doubt have be proud, Stefan unsurprisingly answered, 'Yes.'

The next question is difficult to understand in the sequence of questions, but it may be that the police were thinking of the suggestion, based on a piece of hearsay evidence, that the man involved in the incident outside the youth club on 3 October 1975 had a knife in his possession.

Sergeant Akeroyd asked, 'Can you tell me where you were on the night of Friday the 3rd October?' to which Stefan replied, 'I can't remember'. There are very few fair-minded people who would blame him for that, but the officer persisted, saying, 'Well try to remember where you were that night. Did you go out at all?'

'Well if I did,' said Stefan, 'it would only be to take some stuff to the other house.' This was highly damaging to him, because he had earlier claimed that he not been out after his release from hospital until Sunday 12 October 1975.

'Do I take it that you had the key to the other house at this time?' said the sergeant, and Stefan told him, 'Yes, the woman we bought it off let us have the key before the forms were signed.'

'Do you know where Kingsway School is?' Sergeant Akeroyd asked, and was told in reply, 'No, I don't.'

'Do you know where Turf Hill Road is?' asked the sergeant, and Stefan said, 'Yes.'

'Do you go down Turf Hill Road very often?' said that officer.

'I take my mother to the hairdressers,' was the reply.

Constable McFadzean then asked, 'How many times have you been down Turf Hill Road since you came out of hospital?'

'Only once, to pick my mother up from the hairdressers.'

'And you have never been down there for any other reason?' said Constable McFadzean, and he received the answer, 'No.'

Detective Constable Whittle then spoke: he had been silent for some time.

'Let me see if I understand you correctly. What you're saying is that you know nothing about the allegations made by the two girls about the 4th October and that you never went near Kingsway School on the 3rd October?'

When Stefan replied, 'Yes, that's right,' one is bound to ask which of the two questions, in what is clearly a rolled-up question (i.e. two disguised as one), he was actually answering. Was he saying, 'Yes, I know nothing about the allegations made by the two girls about the 4th October'? Or was he saying, 'Yes, I never went near Kingsway School on the 3rd October'? Constable Whittle ought to have been more than gently chided by counsel for the defence for this in the course of the subsequent trial, though I doubt he was, because at no stage had Stefan Kiszko said, even on the police officer's own version of the evidence, that he never went near Kingsway School on 3 October. He had been previously asked if he knew where Kingsway School was and he replied, 'No, I don't.' That is all.

Constable Whittle put the next question: 'A girl identified you at the bonfire where you had denied stopping but then you changed your story and admitted that you did stop. If you'd done nothing wrong why did you lie about the bonfire?'

Stefan began to dig himself further into the mire. He said, 'Well perhaps when I stopped I might have rubbed my trousers up and down.'

'What do you mean by that?' Constable Whittle asked him.

'It was one of those urges,' was the reply.

That officer asked, 'Do you mean a sexual urge?'

'Yes,' was the response, and he then asked Stefan, 'Did you have an erection?' to which Stefan replied, 'Yes, in fact I came.'

The officer said, 'Do you mean ejaculated?' and received the reply, 'Yes.'

'I thought you had just told us that you were impotent?' said Constable Whittle and Stefan's answer was, 'Yes, I was, but since these injections it is a lot better now.'

The officer followed this up. 'Would you like to tell us what happened at the bonfire?'

'Well I saw some little girls and I got it out and wanked myself off.'

'Did anyone see you?' asked the officer and Stefan said, 'Yes, I think a little girl saw me because she got frightened and ran off crying.'

Constable Whittle asked, 'How old was the little girl?'

'I don't know, she was about ten or 12', was the reply. The officer went on to tell Stefan that 'it may surprise you to know Stefan that you are telling us about something that we knew nothing about. Have you done anything like this before?'

'No, but I've done it twice since.'

'When was that?' the officer asked him.

'The next one I think was the 17th November up near the doctor's in Castlemere Street. I was sitting in my car. I saw a girl walking towards me I got the urge so I got it out and had a wank. The other time was up in Durham Street. I was sitting in my car again. I saw a girl and did the same again. It's those injections, they make me feel funny when I see girls, but I've never touched any of them. I wouldn't do that.'

Constable Whittle said: 'Why do you have the magazines in the car?'

'If there's nobody about I can park up and look at them and have a wank.'

Sergeant Akeroyd then said, 'As I understand it Stefan, you've admitted going to the bonfire on the 5th November at St Peter's School and in fact you elaborated and told us about three incidents that we didn't know had taken place. Am I to take it that the little girl was telling the truth when she said she saw you and identified you as being the man that exposed himself to her on the 4th October?'

Stefan's answer to that is somewhat ambiguous. 'Yes, I was at the bonfire, but I am a bit hazy, can I have some time to think?'

Was that a qualified admission of being present at the scene of the bonfire on 5 November, or had he admitted by use of the word 'yes' that he was accepting that he had indecently exposed himself to the girl on 4 October?

Detective Sergeant Akeroyd told him: 'Yes, we'll leave you for a while.'

No time is recorded in the witness statements for the conclusion of this interview, which had commenced at 2.35 pm. If there had been a record made by the police it might be possible to reconstruct the pace of the questions put and the answers given. Just why does it seem from reading the witness statements there was this wilful disregard for the rules relating to interrogation in a police station? As it transpired, by the time of the trial the officers were able to tell the judge and jury that the interview ended at 5. 25 pm on that Sunday afternoon. So the length of the second interview was some two hours and 50 minutes. Was this commented upon by the defence at the trial? Did they know of the timing prior to the evidence being given in court by the police officers concerned?

Again, it is not possible to say whether Stefan stayed in the inter-view room without any kind of supervision of his movements around the police station. Nor is it known whether he was given anything to eat or drink, or was able to use the toilet facilities. The Administrative Directions on Interrogation and the Taking of Statements attached to the Judges Rules requires that 'When a person is being questioned or elects to make a statement, a record should be kept of the time or times at which during the questioning or making of a statement there were intervals or refreshment taken. The nature of the refreshments should be noted. In no circumstances should alcoholic drink be given.' It is not possible now to say whether Stefan Kiszko was given proper refreshments throughout the time he was at Rochdale Police Station. He should have been, and the fact that, if he had, should have been properly noted.

At 6.45 pm that same day, Sunday 21 December 1975. Detective Sergeant Akeroyd returned to carry on the interview. This time a more senior officer was with him, Detective Superintendent Dick Holland. The two officers had with them a number of items that were to be exhibits at the subsequent trial. There were four knives, a bundle of sex magazines, three balloons and two bags of sweets. Also included were two pieces of paper. On the first were written several car registration numbers and on the second more car registration numbers, together with the name of a police officer based in Rochdale.

Their purpose in bringing these objects into the interview room, together with the presence of the most senior officer involved in the investigation of Lesley Molseed's murder, was abundantly clear. It was to ratchet-up the pressure on Stefan Kiszko.

This was how the interview went. Superintendent Holland identified himself to Stefan and cautioned him. He then said:

'I have come over here to see you because your name has been linked with a number of incidents of an indecent nature in the Turf Hill area. I want to talk to you about this.'

Stefan replied, 'I have told this gentleman all I know.'

Superintendent Holland said, 'First of all I want to consider an incident of an indecent nature when someone whom I think was you, exposed himself to two young girls in Vavasour Street'.

Stefan replied, 'I remember that now, but it's not like you think. I was moving a carpet and the carpet knocked my zip down and my shirt tail came out. There weren't many people about anyway and I zipped myself up as soon as I had put the carpet down.'

The superintendent said, 'Two girls attended a bonfire on plot [sic] night 5th November, and when they saw you near the bonfire one of the girls told her mother and as a result the mother and the girls came to your home in Crawford Street where you lived at the time. You came to the door and you were identified as being the person who had been involved in the incident at lunchtime on the 4th October 1975.' (Might it have been more helpful if the Superintendent had got the fact correct that those who went to Crawford Street on the night of Wednesday 5 November 1975 were two adults and two children; Mrs Sheila Buckley and her daughter Maxime, together with Mrs Carole Rigby and her son Michael?) Was Superintendent Holland trying to convey the impression that the two girls alleging the incident of indecency on 4 October had seen him again on the night of 5 November and were on that date identifying him as the person involved in that act of indecency? If he was, for what purpose did he do so?

One is bound to ask moreover what useful purpose could possibly be served by going over again the details of a single incident of indecency that had been the subject of questions by two police officers on 5 November, two further officers on 7 November when a written statement was taken, the same two on 10 November when another written statement was taken, and two interviews on 21 December 1975 involving three different officers, making a total of seven officers in all. Now here was another, the most senior officer, covering the same ground again, in the presence of a detective sergeant who had been involved in the two interviews earlier that day.

It will be noted that he made the same mistake as Detective Constable Whittle. It was wrong to tell Stefan Kiszko that is was two girls when it was a girl and a boy who attended the bonfire and when they saw him one of them told her mother, suggesting that Stefan had been identified by two girls when he had not. The one identifying witness, Maxine Buckley was only 12 years-of-age, and English law was still struggling with the concept of wrongful cases of visual identification where an honest witness was completely mistaken about someone they saw in difficult circumstances, such as a fleeting glimpse, on a dark evening in November. (It was not until July 1976 that the Criminal Division of the Court of Appeal ruled that wherever a case against an accused person depends wholly or substantially on the correctness of the identification of the accused, the trial judge should warn the jury of the special need for caution before convicting in reliance on the correctness of the identification. He should make some reference to the possibility that a mistaken witness could be a convincing one. The Irish Supreme Court had adopted that approach, using the formula 'a special need for caution', as long ago as 1963, some 13 years previously.)

Stefan replied, 'Yes, I remember someone coming to the door but I hadn't attacked any girls.'

'I'm not suggesting that you attacked the girls, what I am saying is that you indecently exposed yourself to them.'

'Well perhaps I did, I can't remember. Things keep going hazy.'

Superintendent Holland then moved on to the earlier incident. Detective Sergeant Akeroyd had not said a single word in the interview so far. 'Now let us consider an incident outside Kingsway Youth Club on Friday night, the 3rd October 1975. I have been told that you may have been the man who was acting suspiciously outside the club on that night.'

'No, that wasn't me.'

That was all. Why did the questions stop there? It will be noted that the allegation put was one of acting suspiciously, not indecently. There is a difference. It would be interesting to discover whether Superintendent Holland knew, or indeed had with him, at this point in time, the witness statement made by the milkman who courageously came forward to say he was in the vicinity of the clinic near the youth club. In one way or another that man learned about the girls' statements, realised that they were mistaken about what he was doing and went to Rochdale Police Station to make a statement indicating what had actually happened. He need not have done so. He could have remained silent but chose not to do so. My belief is that his statement was concealed both from prosecuting counsel and defence counsel at Stefan's subsequent trial by someone either in the prosecuting department or the police, in order to link the alleged 'flashing' incidents to Stefan when it must have been known that no such link existed. This was unforgiveable.

Does this explain why there was no follow-up question from Holland about the night of 3 October and the youth club incident?

'My colleagues have taken possession of your Hillman Avenger which is bronze colour. Does anyone else drive it?'

'No, only me. No-one else has ever driven that car.'

'Have you ever driven, or owned, or borrowed any other car?'

'Have you ever driven, or owned, or borrowed, any other car other than the bronze Hillman Avenger?'

'No, I don't think I could drive a strange car.'

'What is your job Stefan?'

'I am a civil servant. I work in the Tax Office as a clerical assistant.'

'I understand that you carry a large number of felt-tipped pens.'

'Yes that's right. Every time we do an amendment it's put down in a different colour from the last entry. I always have a lot of pens in my pocket, particularly coloured felt-tipped ones.'

'Have you lost any pens recently?'

'Not that I can think of.'

This was a highly significant set of questions, because when Holland attended the murder scene on the morning of 8 October 1975, a felt tip pen had been found on a rock some yards away from Lesley Molseed's body. There was nothing unusual about that pen, and nothing to connect it with those used by Stefan in the course of his employment except its manufacture, and in 1975 there were thousands of such pens in circulation. In the draft unsigned typewritten statement made after his release from prison (see the supplementary materials mentioned in *Appendix 4* to this work) Stefan thought that the pens he was provided with at work were used to write names on file covers, and his recollection was that those pens were marked to the effect that they were government property. Was this not something that could have been proved, and should have been proved at the trial by the defence, if his recollection is correct? Those familiar with Civil Service practice and procedures may well recognise the capacity of the service to endorse its ownership on everything, especially stationary, that it uses.

Superintendent Holland then moved on to the question of possession and ownership of the knives.

'If you are a clerk in the Civil Service why do you need so many knives? For instance, what is your reason for having this flick knife?' and he pointed to a red-handled flick knife which bore a gold motif of a bullfight.

A more astute person might have asked the police officer which of those two questions he should answer first, but Stefan did not. I find no record of the officer ever being asked about this rolled-up question by anyone at Stefan's trial. Which of the two questions was Stefan expected to answer first? Why did he need the knife or what was the reason for having it?

'My father brought that back from Austria. We used to go to Austria a lot and bring back things like knives as presents for people.'

'Well, what is this other knife?' asked the superintendent, referring to the bone-handled knife.

'That's the same, that's another present from Austria.'

Holland then indicated the black-handled penknife and Stefan said,

'That's just a penknife. I usually use that for cleaning the battery of my car. I have had a bit of electrical trouble.'

The questions then changed direction. 'What is the point in carrying balloons in your car, other than to attract children?'

I regard this as a prejudicial and loaded question, but Stefan's response was equal to it.

'It's Christmas and I had them for decorations.'

'What about the sweets?'

'I eat a lot of sweets. I always carry sweets with me everywhere I go.'

It seems he was absolutely correct on that, and the state of his teeth supported what he said to Superintendent Holland.

That concluded the interview at 8 pm.

Stefan was left in the interview room, but he was not left alone.

Detective Constable Whittle and Detective Constable McFadzean went into that room at some stage after the conclusion of the third interview. Neither of them mention this in their respective witness statements, so presumably not a relevant word was exchanged between the three men in that room. It must have been disconcerting for Stefan to be faced with two silent witnesses for any length of time in the environment of a police station.

Superintendent Holland and Sergeant Akeroyd returned to the interview room at 9 pm. It is not possible to say whether the two detective constables remained in the room or left. By this time, Stefan must have been physically and mentally exhausted. He had been questioned by the police for seven hours and ten minutes during that Sunday, and here he was about to be interviewed yet again.

According to Holland he began by reminding Stefan of the caution, that he need not say anything unless he wished to do so. So far, Stefan had answered every question put to him by a substantial number of police officers, and it was his contradictory answers that had placed him in a very dangerous position.

'We have just had a look round your car and there is some peaty soil around the back seat. How do you explain that?' asked Superintendent Holland.

'I just don't know.'

That was all. There were no follow-up questions. That soil had no evidential significance and was not relied upon in any way as connecting Stefan with abduction and murder. I find this evidence somewhat confusing because in Holland's witness statement dated 1 May 1976 he claimed the car had been transported to Harrogate on that Sunday. He did not give a time, but was it not before 9 pm that Sunday evening?

The officer moved on to the notes that had been found.

'How about these notes which contain car numbers, first of all one which indicates "bell rang" in red ink and three other car numbers?'

'I saw PC Bell and complained to him that some vehicles from the scrap yard had tried to run me down when we lived in Crawford Street. They were always doing things like that. He told me to write the numbers down and I did. It was in the early part of this year, I can't remember when, but it would be about Easter.'

'Are you saying that all these vehicles belong to people who are either connected with, or were going to the scrapyard at the top of Crawford Street?'

'Yes, that scrapyard near our house.'

'What about the second note with three car numbers in blue and one in red?'

'Those three in blue which says Pakis, there was a house near ours and people were going there at night receiving stuff and I thought it was suspicious. I was going to report it to PC Bell because he told me if I saw anything more that was suspicious to let him know.'

'Did you tell him?'

'No.'

'Now what about the other car number in red, ADK 539L?'

'I just don't know. I can't explain it at all.'

'Well is it your writing?'

'Yes.'

'And your paper?'

'Yes.'

'Well why do you write car numbers down?'

'Well I just can't remember anything when I've had my injections, I go all hazy.'

'Do you feel hazy now, or have your felt hazy since you came into the police station?'

'No, I'm alright now.'

That concluded that interview. Again, Detective Sergeant Akeroyd said nothing and failed to ask a single question. According to the judge's summing-up that fourth interview started 'at nine o'clock and went on to about 10 o'clock' (p. 15 of the summing-up).

Superintendent Holland's witness statement records, 'I then left him with DC McFadzean and DC Whittle.' Does that mean that these two officers were also present at this interview, and remained equally silent? For what purpose? Or did they just take over sitting with Stefan after Holland left the room?

Superintendent Holland, Sergeant Akeroyd, and Constables Merkin and Booth then went to Stefan's home and searched it. There is no evidence that they had obtained a search warrant to do so. Without one, such a search was unlawful. They found and took away a white-handled penknife, a pair of scissors found in a tin, and a box of ampoules of a drug containing testosterone of the type given for injections. The seizure of that property was also unlawful. Whether these points were made at the trial on the admissibility of illegally obtained evidence, I do not know. I suspect they were not.

In 1982, the Divisional Court of the Queen's Bench Division ruled that once a person has been arrested on private premises for a serious offence and the arrest was completed, a police officer has no right at Common Law subsequently to enter the premises without a warrant in order to search for or seize an instrument of the crime known to be on the premises. (This case, *McLorie v. Oxford*, is reported in the *All England Law Reports*, 1982, volume 3 at page 480). If the law extends this protection to a person under arrest, it surely would do so also in the case of a person who had not even been arrested. Although the case was decided some six years after the case under discussion, the judges in the Divisional Court were not making the law, they were stating what the law is and was. Why did the defence not argue this point at the trial in 1976?

There is something slightly odd about Holland's evidence on this point. In his witness statement, at page 7, he records '… I returned to Kiszko's house at King's Road and made a further search.' There is no evidence from him or any other officer that he had previously been to the house and made a search there at all. Accordingly, it is the use of the two words 'returned' and 'further' that I fail to understand. I cannot say whether he was asked to explain this when he gave evidence at the trial.

At 1.45 am, that is, in the early hours of Monday morning, having been at the police station since shortly after 10.30 am on the Sunday, Stefan was interviewed by Holland again. Detective Sergeant Akeroyd was there. Again, it is not possible to say with any degree of certainty whether the two constables who had stayed with Stefan previously, in the absence of the two senior officers, remained in the interview room on this occasion or not. The superintendent made a few comments of fact and asked all the questions.

'Are these the drugs with which you are being injected?'

'Yes, I have some from the doctor and some from the hospital. I also have to take tablets but I have given them all to Mr Akeroyd here.'

'I have found another white knife in a tin in your bedroom.'

'Yes, that's another present from Austria.'

'Let me talk to you for a few minutes about your injections.'

'Well, I've told this man [indicating Sergeant Akeroyd] about some incidents with girls after I've had my injections. You see they make me go all queer and hazy and I fancy girls when I've had my tablets and injections. I used to be alright before'.

'Is that why you got the books?'

'Yes I started fancying girls.'

'Will you try and remember again why you wrote this number in red on a bit of paper because I now know that car was at the scene of a murder at Ripponden at 2.30 pm on Sunday the 5th October 1975.'

This was a highly significant question, probably based on the supposition that Lesley Molseed was dead by 2.30 pm, whereas if Christopher Coverdale (see *Chapter Three*) saw her at about 3.45 pm climbing the embankment with the man in the brown jacket clearly she was not, and there was not a murder scene on that embankment, at 2.30 pm

'I just can't remember. I have been thinking all the time. I am hazy when I have had my injections and my tablets.'

That concluded the interview. No time is given. No mention of the time of its conclusion is noted either in the evidence of Superintendent Holland or at the end of the case, in the trial judge's summing-up; the judge simply noted it was a short interview. That may be so, but its contents are highly relevant to the issue of guilt in the case.

Both officers present noted that 'arrangements were made for Kiszko to be accommodated in the police station overnight'. I take that to mean he was locked in a cell. If there was any doubt about his status at the police station up to this time, there cannot be any doubt now. Stefan Kiszko was unlawfully under compulsion to stay there. He was detained because he was not free to leave the premises. He was unlawfully arrested because he had not been told of the fact and grounds of arrest. He was falsely imprisoned by the police.

Chapter Seven

A Confession to Murder

At 11.30 on the morning of Monday 22 December 1975, Superintendent Holland and Detective Sergeant Akeroyd interviewed Stefan again. He was asked about the car registration number AKD 539L. I consider that the superintendent's statement that the car, whose registration number Stefan had noted, claiming '… I now know that car was at the scene of a murder at Ripponden at 2.30 pm on Sunday the 5th October 1975', would only be accurate and fair if it was conclusively proved that Lesley Molseed was dead at that time. That was not proved by anybody. It was unfair to mislead Stefan in this way, by linking what he had written on a piece of paper with a piece of evidence that was probably based on a false premise. It will not be forgotten, of course, that Christopher Coverdale had driven past the scene at about 3.45 pm on that Sunday and had seen the man and a little girl on the embankment above the lay-by. That may have been Lesley and her murderer, but I think the interests of justice would have been better served at the time if Coverdale had been given the opportunity to say, in some form of identification procedure, whether Stefan was the man he believed he saw. Sadly for Stefan, Coverdale was never given that opportunity.

Superintendent Holland conducted the interview. For his part he did not say in his statement that there was another officer with him. Sergeant Akeroyd's statement claims he was there but said nothing and remained silent throughout. Holland reminded Stefan of the caution and then said,

'I am making further enquiries into you, particularly the note on the piece of paper with the car number in red ADK 539L. I know that that car passed the scene of the murder, how did you come to write that number down? Have you ever been involved in an accident with the vehicle or anything?'

Again, how useful it would have been if the officer had waited for an answer to the first question before he moved on to the second. I find it of interest that up to now he had not mentioned the name of the murder victim, Lesley Molseed, or asked a single question about her at any stage. He did not even indicate, for the second time, to which murder he was referring. Stefan's reply to the two rolled-up questions was, 'No I just can't remember. I can't tell you anything about that, my mind's a blank.'

'But the other numbers which have been written down on the two pieces of paper, three on the same page as the number ADK 539L, have been explained to us perfectly. Your job is being concerned with figures and your boss tells me you are most accurate and meticulous in your work.'

'Yes, I can remember most things but I just can't remember anything about that.'

At the trial the prosecution made great play of the relevance of this evidence, In fact, as it transpired, it was irrelevant and worthless.

This interview concluded with the words 'I will have to make further enquiries into this matter and I am going to leave you with Sergeant Akeroyd.' Superintendent Holland then left the interview room. He seems not to have subsequently explained satisfactorily why he did so.

Stefan broke the silence and spoke next. He asked the sergeant,

'What is going to happen now?'

'What do you mean?'

'Well, when can I go home?'

'Mr Holland has just told you that he is going to make further enquiries into the matter.'

That was not an answer to the question. Stefan must have felt he would never be allowed home. He finally broke down under the continuous pressure to which he had been deliberately subjected.

He then said 'Oh, this is terrible. It's those damn injections. All this would never have happened.'

'What has happened?'

'Well that thing at Kingsway Youth Club and that little girl that I picked-up.'

Stefan's explanation in court for this piece of evidence was that he had to say this 'to get Akeroyd off my back and that was the only thing I could find to say'.

The questions continued. 'Which little girl did you pick-up?'

'That little girl, Lesley. I don't know what happened. It's all a bit hazy. It's those damned injections.'

'Are you telling me that you picked Lesley Molseed up in your motor car?'

'Yes. You see I can't help myself when I've had my injection.'

'When did you pick Lesley up?'

'On that Sunday dinner time, the day that I killed her.'

Detective Sergeant Akeroyd then cautioned Stefan, reminding him he had the right to stay silent. That does not call for comment, save for the fact that it seems very unlikely that he wanted, or expected, Stefan Kiszko to remain silent.

'Are you telling me that you murdered Lesley Molseed?'

'Yes, I killed that little girl.'

Sergeant Akeroyd opened the door of the interview room, called out and almost immediately Superintendent Holland and Chief Inspector Steele arrived at the door to the room. The sergeant said, 'Now Stefan just tell these two officers again what you have said to me.'

The response was said to be immediate. The inference we are asked to draw is that there was no time to administer the caution to stay silent if he so wished.

'I killed that little girl, I stabbed Lesley.' It was then that Holland cautioned Stefan. That hardly calls for comment either. Did he really warn Stefan that he need not say anything, and would this not have created the impression that the officer was trying to stop him from saying anything further and more incriminating?

Akeroyd noted that Stefan was hesitant and obviously under some emotional strain when he said, 'I went out for a run on my own in the car and I went through Turf Hill towards Broad Lane. Lesley was on the side of the road near a pub.'

The superintendent asked, 'Is that where there is a little shop in a terrace of houses, the shop being open all day Sunday?'

'Yes, that's right, the shop's on the other side, same as the pub. I stopped and I can't remember what I said to get her into the car but I drove up there. I had been to Ripponden once before. Soon after I got the car I went up the motorway and came off there and I went down into Ripponden and I sort of got lost. I had to turn round near some bollards and I finished up going back home to Rochdale another way. I went through Littleborough to get back but I didn't take her so far, I just took her off the road.'

The superintendent said, 'What happened after you left the motorway with her?'

'I drove into a lay-by, a sort of pull-in of the spare ground at the side of the road, just off the motorway. I talked to her in the car and then something came over me. I go all hazy and queer when I've had my injections, like I keep telling you, and I had been on Friday teatime for it. I took her up the hillside onto the moor and she struggled a bit. I held her down and I played with myself onto her.'

'Which hand did you hold her down with?'

'My right.'

'How could you hold her down and play with yourself?'

'I always use my left hand for that.'

'Do you play with yourself a lot?'

'Not very much but only since I started with the injections. You will find a hanky near my bed.'

'What happened with the knife?'

'I got my knife out and stuck it in her neck.'

Clearly this is another most incriminating admission, for the number of those who knew that Lesley had been stabbed in the neck was extremely limited. The actual killer knew of this, of course, more than anyone else.

According to Akeroyd, Holland then '... sat in a chair to reduce his height to approximately that of the girl and invited Kiszko to stand up so that could be something like his normal height. With a pencil Superintendent Holland asked Kiszko to demonstrate how he stabbed Lesley Molseed and he put his arm around the superintendent over his right shoulder with his forearm under the superintendent's chin so that the pencil was to his throat.'

'Is that the position?'

'Yes, but we were lying down.'

'Well what happened after that?'

'Look I just went blank and hazy I just can't remember anything. I don't know what came over me. I don't even remember driving home or leaving up there.'

'Did you do anything before you left?'

'I sort of remember wiping the knife on her or her clothes.'

On any view of the evidence that was a most damning reply of all because the prosecution had produced a photograph, marked No. 17, which shows Lesley's thigh with smears of blood across it. The pathologist, Professor David Gee, found that smearing of blood but was unable to form an opinion as to what kind of surface had been smeared across the thigh. But only the murderer, and of course those involved in the investigation, would know that something, whatever it was (and here the police suggested it was a knife), had been wiped on the little girl and it therefore followed that Stefan must have been the murderer because he had said that he wiped that knife across her himself.

The superintendent placed the four knives on the table in front of the three police offices and Stefan. Stefan indicated the bone-handled locking knife and said, 'This one'.

Holland and two other senior police officers had just been provided with a confession to a brutal murder of a young child by a man against whom there was virtually no direct evidence of his involvement in that murder. What that senior officer did next was frankly ludicrous. He questioned the self-incriminating killer about an alleged offence of indecent exposure and asked him, 'What about the matter outside the youth club?'

'Look I'll tell you all about that as well. I have told Mr Akeroyd about that and I'll tell you everything. I just want to get it off my chest. I don't know what has come over me. It's the tablets and injections.'

'Do you mean by saying you want to tell us all about it that you want to make a statement?'

'Yes I want to get it all sorted out.'

It seems that Detective Sergeant Akeroyd's evidence ends there. He seemed not to be present when the forthcoming, quite expected and indeed most welcome written confession evidence was brought into existence. He was the person who had first heard the oral confession that Stefan made in the interview room, and it seems surprising if he failed to stay while that confession was put into writing. Instead, there appeared an officer who had not featured so far in any of the interviews. He now enters the scene. He was Detective Superintendent Derek Wheater. He was an officer of the Greater Manchester Police. His name is not mentioned anywhere in Stefan's statement. There seems to be no indication of the time this interview, which began at 11.30 am that day, ended, although as noted previously the Judges' Rules require this. Did the defence at the trial have any interest in finding this out. However, unless what is set out in full above took from 11.30 am until the commencement of the written statement, which began at 3.20 pm (just ten minutes short of four hours), then having agreed to make a written statement there was a gap in time before it was written down by Superintendent Holland. If that actually happened, an explanation should have been sought at the trial — why the delay?

Stefan Kiszko's overall recollection of the events from the time he left his home on the morning of 21 December 1975 is in marked contrast to the version given by the police. He remembered driving his own car to the police station, with Police Constable Whittle sitting in the front passenger seat. When he arrived at the police station he was taken to an interview room, where there were four police officers present. He named them as Whittle, Akeroyd, McFadzean and Steele. He remembered that Steele kept holding his right hand and was quite pleasant with him. They spoke to him for quite a while and, at a later stage, Holland came into the interview room. He told Stefan to empty his pockets, which he did. He was carrying the penknife he used at work for the parcelling of packages. He was interviewed on and off for the rest of the day and locked in a cell at the police station overnight. He remembered the interview on the following day, although he could not recall the time it started. He claimed that Holland was very aggressive and threatening in his manner. 'He kept poking me in the shoulder and saying, "I'll get the fucking truth out of you one way or the other."' Shortly after this, Holland left the interview room.

The result of this conduct directed towards Stefan by the superintendent (and always denied by Holland) was that Stefan felt very intimidated by what was said and done to him and he thought that he would get beaten-up unless he made the admissions that he thought the superintendent wanted from him. He did remember making some verbal admissions, not just to one officer (as the police claimed) but to three: Police Constables Whittle and McFadzean and Sergeant Akeroyd. The verbal admissions contained the statement that Stefan had something to do with the murder, but he could recollect that there was no detail contained in any admission. He did remember that Detective Constable McFadzean said to him, 'As soon as we get this wrapped-up we can all go home for Christmas'. The officer denied that.

Stefan also was under the impression that two other officers, Steele and Mawson, came into the interview room after the other officers left. Something was said between them and him but he cannot recollect what it was exactly; the officers were questioning him about the circumstances they thought were related to the murder.

Stefan only left the interview room to go to the toilet. He was sick on several occasions. Although he was offered food and a hot drink he refused both and drank only water. He later told the jury at his trial, 'I felt terrible, I wanted to go home to mother.' He added, 'During the interrogation when I was telling what was my story they wouldn't believe me so I started to tell them lies and that seemed to please them and the pressure was off so far as I was concerned. I thought the police would check out what I had said and find it was untrue and let me go.'

So far as the making of the voluntary statement was concerned, Stefan claimed that Superintendent Holland simply wrote it out without any discussion with him. When he had finished writing it he read it to Stefan (he did not read it himself) and Stefan signed it.

It will be remembered that the interview on Stefan's second day at the police station, where in my view he was now in unlawful detention, began at 11.30 on the morning of that Monday. I have been unable to find any evidence anywhere, or anything in the summing-up to ascertain the time that interview ended.

The confession statement began at 3.20 on the afternoon of Monday 22 December 1975. It finished two and a quarter hours later, at 5.35 pm From time-to-time Detective Superintendent Wheater asked Stefan some questions, the answers to which were incorporated in the statement. This procedure is permitted by the Judges' Rules. Where a police officer writes the statement he must take down the exact words spoken by the person making the statement, without putting any questions other than such as may be needed to make the statement coherent, intelligible and relevant to the material matters. He must not prompt the confessor. Although the case was one of brutal murder, I find it unusual to note that two such senior officers of the rank of superintendent were involved in taking this statement. It is set out below. It was handwritten by Holland.

When reading it, one should be bear in mind that there was medical evidence (given at the trial by the defence witness Dr Tarsh) that Stefan was 'socially and emotionally immature like an eleven or twelve-year-old rather than a man of twenty-four … he had the personality of a child'. I continue to wonder why this evidence was not put before the trial judge in the absence of the jury in an effort to persuade him to exclude the confession from the trial. In such a case, is it the chronological age of the accused person that counts, or is it his own personal characteristics? Had the judge excluded the confession, that would have been the end of the prosecution case against Stefan.

The statement is headed as follows:

Stefan Ivan Kiszko. 25 Kings Road, Lower Place, Rochdale.

3.20 pm Monday 22 December, 1975

I Stefan Ivan Kiszko wish to make a statement. I want someone to write down what I say. I have been told that I need not say anything unless I wish to do so and that whatever I say may be given in evidence.

(Signed S. I. Kiszko)

It continues:

From the 5th August 1975 I was in hospital in Manchester for treatment for haemoplastic anaemia. That was Manchester Royal Infirmary and I was under Doctor English. I came out of hospital on the 15th September, and I went back to live with my mother at Crawford Street. I had to go back to hospital every three weeks for treatment for my lack of sex life. I had tablets from the doctor and injections both at the hospital and from my own doctor.

When I had this treatment it made me go dizzy for three or four days after the injections and then I feel a lot better of myself and it helps me in my sex life. When I see a girl after I have had my treatment it makes me fancy her. A week or two after I came out of hospital, it was the beginning of October, a Friday or Saturday I was going from my home to my auntie's in Kingsway. [Here, Superintendent Wheater asked him to explain where he parked his vehicle and this was the reply.] I stopped my car on the left hand side of the road near a bus stop, facing towards Milnrow. I had come down Kings Road and turned left. It was fairly dark. There was a disco going on at the youth club and two girls came from down the road towards the disco. Something came over me and I got out of my car unzipped my trousers and got my penis out. I had a knife in my hand [here, at this point in the narrative, Stefan was asked by Superintendent Wheater why he had the knife in his hand and Stefan continued] but that was a mere triviality. It was a small one with a black handle. The two girls went off towards the youth club and I got back into my car and drove off towards my aunt's. I didn't stop very long at the house, as it isn't very safe parking near the bridge in the dark. The following day about dinner time I had put an old carpet into my car to take and dump on some spare ground near Vavasour Street. I stopped my car in one of the side streets off Vavasour Street. I got out, opened the boot up and took out the carpet, it was a pretty hefty one. It was all rotten and we were getting a new one for Kings Road. I unzipped myself and my shirt flap came out. I put that back in and pulled my zip back up. There was an old lady and a fellow in the street and I didn't deliberately expose myself that day. I drove back home. For the rest of the day I sorted things out with my mum [At this point, Superintendent Wheater asked Stefan to explain this and he replied that he had packed the crockery in the car and he replied, "you know what removal vans are like, one bump and it's gone". This was written down as] and packed crockery and took it up to the new house. I sometimes went up to the new house at Kings Road in my own car. The next day was Sunday and I got up about "tenish". I had a drink and I went out for a ride in my car on my own. [At this stage, Stefan mentioned picking up a girl in his car in Broad Lane and Superintendent Wheater asked him exactly where this had happened. This was how Stefan replied] I can't remember the time but after dinner time I was driving down Broad Lane from Charlotte Street towards Oldham Road. A girl was standing on the left near to a pub which is on the right hand side and which stands back from the road. I mean to say she was more or less opposite the pub. She was about nine years old. I stopped the car and wound my window down. I can't remember what I said to her but she got into the front of my car. I drove off down Oldham Road and into Queensway down to the roundabouts and onto the M62. She started shouting and I hit her with my hand. It was a flat hand. I drove up the motorway towards the moors towards the road that takes you down to Ripponden. When I had first got my car in 1972 I had been up there and I had got lost. I went right down into Ripponden and then went over the other road through Littleborough to Rochdale. That was the only time before this Sunday that I had on that road with the little girl in my car. I came off the motorway and took the same road towards Ripponden, but not very far off. I stopped on the left hand side of the road on a bit of a patch. [Superintendent Wheater asked Stefan whether the grass was level with the road, went uphill or sloped downhill and Stefan replied] It was up a sort of grass banking, it wasn't very high and then it went flat on a flat piece. [The officer then asked him what he could see from that spot and Stefan replied "I could see the road but I don't think anyone on the road could see me". That was recorded in the following form] I took her out of the car and up a sort of grass banking, it wasn't very high, and then it went flat onto a flat place. I could see the road but I don't think anyone on the road could see me. The first bit was the sex bit. She was standing up crying, I got my penis out. I started playing with myself I can't remember if she said anything. I laid down by her, side by side, and held her with one hand and used my left hand to wank with. She was laid facing me and I was laid on my right side. I shot between her legs over her knickers'. [At this point, Stefan was asked by Superintendent Wheater what he meant by "shot", to which Stefan answered] You know, ejaculated, when semen leaves your penis. [The officer then asked Stefan if he had interfered with the girl's knickers and he replied, "No, I did not touch her knickers". That was recorded as the following] I did not remove her knickers. I had a knife in my pocket and I took it out and stabbed her in the throat she was still crying I got a hazy feeling and I can't remember where or how I stabbed her. She slumped away from me and I don't remember what happened after that. I left her where she was and I didn't bother to look. I got back into the car and drove back home. I didn't tell my mother what I had done. I put the knife back in my pocket and I wiped it onto her clothes or something. I can't remember what. [At about this stage, Superintendent Wheater had asked Stefan how he stabbed the girl and according to that officer he had replied, "I don't have to go through all that again. I've told both these gentlemen." I find that surprising, because Detective Sergeant Akeroyd seemed not to be present at that time, and Stefan was recorded as saying something that he apparently did not wish to repeat about the stabbing, but what follows next is the sentence] I was a bit hazy then. I didn't cut myself. I think I got to our house about "fourish" that is about tea time. I always carry a lot of pens in my inside jacket pocket for work because at work every amendment has to be in a different colour. Some are issued at work and some are bought by me. I have only been wanking since I had the hospital treatment. Before the treatment I didn't ejaculate but after the treatment I have done so every time except once.

Signed S. I.Kiszko.

I have read the above statement, and I have been told that I can correct alter or add anything I wish. This statement is true. I have made it of my own free will. Signed S. I. Kiszko.

Witness D. Wheater

Concluded 5.35 pm 22/12/75

Signed Dick Holland Det. Supt.

The information in this statement could only have been provided by the person who killed Lesley Molseed or, alternatively, someone who knew the intimate and reconstructed details of how Lesley died, such as a police officer investigating her death who had access to the witness statements. It may be worthy of note, for example, that the police did not know the exact time either at which Lesley was abducted or when she was murdered, so Stefan's statement has no exact and specific times, save to say that he was out of bed at home about 10 am and after a drink he went out, not returning home until about 4 pm.

With the conclusion of the confession, the case against Stefan Kiszko appeared to be wrapped up. He had confessed in a very limited amount of detail to a murder and offences of indecency. It is now known that he was not Lesley's killer; that was Ronald Castree. However did he confess in some limited detail to a crime he had not committed?

After the making of the statement was concluded, Stefan was left alone with Superintendent Wheater. Suddenly, he asked the officer how soon he could go home. Then he added, 'What I said was lies'. Wheater then asked him if he realised what he had said and Stefan answered, 'Yes, I want to see my mum'. Anyone, apart from the defence lawyers in this case, would have realised that this was the plaintive cry of a distressed child, albeit in the body of a man.

Holland was informed of this conversation, which apparently took place at about 6 pm. It is not clear why, immediately following the confession statement, Holland left his colleague alone with Stefan Kiszko and did not charge Stefan with the offence of murder that the police say he had openly, freely and frankly admitted to.

As noted previously, according to the introductory paragraph to the Judges' Rules, '... when a police officer who is making enquiries of any person about an offence has enough evidence to prefer a charge against that person for an offence, he should *without delay* [emphasis added] cause that person to be charged or informed that he may be prosecuted for the offence.' Although he had evidence orally and in writing sufficient to support a charge of murder, Holland did not charge Stefan with any offence at that time. It may be suggested by some that Holland wanted to take legal advice from the prosecuting solicitors' department of the West Yorkshire Police. I do not believe that. At the time, the decision to prosecute was vested in the police, one which they jealously guarded, and only reluctantly surrendered with the conception and birth of the Crown Prosecution Service.

What Superintendent Holland did do however was allow Stefan access to legal advice, and a solicitor named Albert Wright attended the police station in order to provide him with advice and assistance. Up to now, if Stefan Kiszko had been wrongfully detained, as I think he had, even if that custody was unlawful he ought to have been allowed to speak on the telephone to his solicitor or to his friends, provided that no hindrance was reasonably likely to be caused to the process of the investigation or the administration of justice by allowing him to do so. People in custody should not only be informed of the rights and facilities available to them but, in addition, notices describing them should be displayed at convenient and conspicuous places at police stations and the attention of persons in custody should be drawn to these notices. That did not happen here. In fact it seldom happened anywhere, in any police station.

Stefan Kiszko claimed that he was never told of these rights, did not see the notices in the police station setting them out, and the notices were never drawn to his attention. One reason may be that even the police officers in the case would not claim he had access to these rights and information, simply because, in their eyes, he was not in police custody. He was helping with enquiries.

On the arrival of solicitor Albert Wright at the police station at around 6 pm on that Monday, the senior officer in overall charge of the case, Detective Chief Superintendent Jack Dibb, spoke to him in Stefan's presence. The officer asked Stefan if he had any complaints regarding his stay at the police station. Some may particularly like the use of the word 'stay' although it would be pointless to suggest that Dibb should more accurately have said 'while we unlawfully detained you at this police station'! Dibb said to Stefan, 'You know who I am, but I will remind you. I am Detective Chief Superintendent Dibb, the officer in charge of this enquiry. I want to ask you in the presence of your solicitor, Mr Wright, if you have any complaints to make in any way about your treatment since you have been here at police headquarters?'

Stefan replied, 'I have no complaints to make'.

The officer went on: 'It is my duty to ensure that you have not been ill-treated, under-fed, or been deprived of any of your normal functions whilst you have been here so as to induce you to make statements or admissions'.

Stefan replied: 'I have no complaint to make'.

He was then told that the senior officer intended to call the police surgeon to examine him as to his physical and mental state and to invite him to give certain samples which will be sent away for forensic examination.

Albert Wright replied on behalf of his client, 'I shall advise him accordingly and it is a matter for him to decide'.

Stefan was later to be heavily criticised both by the trial judge and leading counsel for the prosecution for failing to complain about his treatment at the station. Instead of adopting that rather sanctimonious view, both the judge and counsel ought to have addressed the question of whether what the police did to Stefan in holding him without legal justification and interviewing him six times until he confessed, might have affected this emotionally immature man with the personality of a child and caused him to confess where another more robust person would not have done so. Instead, they expected him to have complained, in their presence, in the very place and about the very people who had subjected him to unlawful detention for more than 24 hours when he could not eat or sleep in a cell—which have no star ratings for their accommodation and comfort; he had never been in a police station before and had no idea when, if ever, he was going to be released and allowed home.

The police surgeon, Dr Edward Tierney was sent for and he arrived at the police station to examine Stefan. As previously noted, Stefan's confession statement ended at 5.35 pm Within 30 minutes there was another development. Superintendent Holland was sent for by the solicitor and was told that Stefan wished to make another statement. Wright told the officer, 'I understand that he now wishes to make another statement retracting what he has said.' In my view Wright should simply have obtained Stefan's full instructions and written down his full statement, in Stefan's own words, retracting what he had admitted to the police very shortly before. Did Wright not appreciate the position Stefan was in? Stefan had no idea when he would be released from the police station and allowed to go home to his mother. The person who could decide and determine that, and of whom Stefan was probably terrified, was Holland. In my view it was wholly wrong to take Stefan back into the presence of the police officer who had intimidated him into confessing to a most terrible crime that he had not committed.

On receipt of the information from the solicitor, the superintendent then asked Stefan what some may regard as a very perceptive question.

'Are you suggesting that I promised you something if you made that first statement?'

Stefan replied, 'No, I just thought if I told you that you would let me out.'

That was a line to which Stefan adhered thereafter; he really believed that if he admitted what the police wanted him to admit, then he would be allowed home to his mother for Christmas. Stefan Kiszko is not the only person who has paid the highest price for believing that English law does not convict those who admit, but have not committed, offences with which they are subsequently charged.

The superintendent then asked, 'Do you want me to take down another statement then?'

Stefan replied, 'Yes'.

The officer obtained the necessary documents on which to write it, and retrieved the original confession statement which was at the time actually in the process of being typed-up. After discussing the methodology with Wright, something I question whether, as his defence solicitor, he should have become involved in, Holland went through the first confession statement line-by-line and he wrote out what he describes as '… a second statement correcting the first one in the manner in which he indicated.' Why Albert Wright agreed to this is strange I think. Why let the police officer dictate the course of events and formulate the approach when he could just as easily have asked for time to take instructions from his client, and have Stefan write down, in his own words and in his own way exactly what he wished to say? As it transpired, the way Holland re-drafted the statement meant some of the original confession statement stayed in and was admitted in evidence as representing the truth. That was very damaging to Stefan's case.

That second statement began at 6.30 pm on that Monday and ended at 7.25 pm This is the statement.

Stefan Ivan Kiszko

25 Kings Road, Lower Place, Rochdale

6.30 pm 22 December 1975

I STEFAN IVAN KISZKO wish to make a statement. I want someone to write down what I say I have been told that I need not say anything unless I wish to do so and whatever I say may be given in evidence.

S. I. KISZKO

I thought that if I made like the other one I would get home tonight. The first page and the top seven lines of page 2 are correct. From stopping my car in Kingsway what I said about the disco and the girls is not correct. I did not show my penis and although I have a penknife with a black handle I had no reason to have it in my hand. I drove off towards my aunt's. It's true that I didn't stop long there. What I have said about the carpet is correct. The business about the carpet and my shirt flap coming out as I got the carpet out of my car is true and I returned home after I had dumped the carpet. The account of the rest of the day is true. The following day my account of the time which I got up and of going out for a drive on my own is true but I didn't go to Broad Lane. I can't remember where I went on that particular day but I didn't go to Broad Lane. There was no little girl and no little girl got into the front of my car. I was nowhere near the M62 I didn't go on the M62 that day. I had no girl in my car to hit and I didn't go near to Ripponden. The part is true that I got lost and been over to Ripponden just after I got my car. That is the only time I have ever been down that road. All the piece about stopping the car and taking the girl up the banking is wrong. All the piece I have described about the girl and the sexual activity is wrong. It is not true that I stabbed a girl with a knife, sometimes I carry a black pen knife and sometimes a bone-handle folding knife which used to belong to my late father. What I said about stabbing the girl and getting to my car to go home is not correct. It is not true that I wiped my knife on the girl's clothes or body. What I said about carrying pens is correct. The last paragraph about the results of my hospital treatment is true, but I have only done it home. Signed S. I. Kiszko

I have read the above statement and I have been told that I can correct alter or add anything I wish. This statement is true. I have made it of my own free will. Signed S. I. Kiszko.

Concluded 7.25 pm

22.12.75

Witnesses Albert Wright Solicitor, Rochdale

Taken by Dick Holland Det. Supt.

This retracted confession document contains 467 words, with 1,789 characters, written in 55 minutes. It was therefore written at just over eight words per minute. Whatever hopes Stefan had entertained that his change of mind would effect his release from custody, he was entirely wrong. What some may find astonishing is the fact that his solicitor never seemed to have enquired into his status at the police station. Even a cursory examination of the facts and circumstances would have revealed that Stefan had entered the premises quite voluntarily and he had never been informed of the fact of and grounds for his arrest. Should not Albert Wright have picked-up on this? Maybe he mistakenly thought that Stefan had been properly arrested, but he could and should have asked for a sight of the Detained Person's Register, which has to be opened when a person is detained in custody at a police station. My belief is that there was no such record, simply because there had been no valid arrest. No-one ever proved otherwise, though there have been many false assumptions that there was a lawful arrest in this case. Otherwise, how could Stefan have been held at the police station for so long? In addition, ought not Wright to have asked when, if ever, it was proposed to charge Stefan, and with which criminal offences? He would have needed to make necessary arrangements to be available for a court appearance and for professional representation for Stefan after charge, if one was preferred. All this was going on two days before Christmas Day, and since the courts are closed on that and the following day, if Stefan was not charged before then, when was he to be charged?

Superintendent Holland was later to claim that he consulted lawyers before he charged Stefan with murder. That presumably would be the local lawyers who conducted police prosecutions in the area at that time. He says in his statement made on 22 December 1992 that at 9 am on Monday 23 December he had a conference with the then force prosecuting solicitor who appointed his deputy to deal with the case. My view is that the sole purpose of that conference was to arrange for the prosecution to be represented when Stefan was brought before the magistrates' court the following day.

Chapter Eight

The Medical Evidence and Dr Edward Tierney

Stefan remembered, as he recorded at page 7 of his draft statement, *Appendix 1* to this work, the doctor's physical examination and being asked to provide a sample of semen together with other samples. His recollection was that he was not given any explanation why the sample was required, but he did not question the necessity or relevance of it. Whatever the truth, this evidence was obtained from him while he was illegally detained at a police station. However, the experienced and expert police surgeon Dr Edward Tierney, does remember clearly explaining to Stefan why the semen sample was required since it could prove his innocence, and ultimately it proved to be the evidence that cleared his name.

Dr Tierney was called to examine Stefan at Rochdale Police Station on Monday 22 December 1975. He believes that the officer responsible for calling him there was Detective Chief Superintendent Jack Dibb. The purpose of the medical examination was to ascertain whether Stefan was fit to be detained in police custody and if necessary and appropriate to obtain certain samples from him, with Stefan's informed consent. One is bound to ask why Stefan was not examined for fitness to be detained when he arrived at the police station on the morning of the previous day. Would it not have been most embarrassing for everyone if at that time Dr Tierney had concluded that Stefan was not fit to be detained in the custody of the police at Rochdale Police Station?

On his arrival, Dr Tierney was told that Stefan had been arrested on suspicion of murder of a little girl, Lesley Molseed. He recollected that she been killed some two months previously. Part of that information conveyed to the doctor was not true. Stefan had not been validly arrested, or at all, for any offence. The doctor told the police (in a statement dated

9 April 1992) that the time he medically examined Stefan was approximately 8.30 in the evening of Monday 22 December. He was aware that Stefan had been interviewed by officers of the Greater Manchester Police about a series of indecent exposures that had occurred in the Rochdale area. He was not aware however of the results of any such interview or the progress that the police had made in the murder investigation. No one told him that Stefan had been interviewed by Superintendent Holland at 11. 30 that morning and that later between 3.20 pm and 5.35 pm on that Monday afternoon Stefan had confessed in a statement written by that senior officer to the offence of murder. Nor was he told that Stefan had made a further statement after he had been permitted by the police to consult the solicitor Albert Wright, and in that statement made between 6.30 pm and 7.25 pm he had withdrawn and fully retracted that earlier written confession to murder.

Some may find it quite bizarre that the doctor was not told of the existence of the murder confession evidence and its retraction. Dr Tierney made no mention of Albert Wright being at the police station. My guess is that after he advised Stefan about his rights of refusal, he then left the police station to deal with other matters and perhaps other cases. I think he should have been there at the time the doctor was being asked to decide whether Stefan was fit to be detained in police custody. It might have thrown the proverbial cat amongst the pigeons if Tierney had decided Stefan was not fit to be detained. If he was not, then that might have led at the subsequent trial to the exclusion of any evidence obtained from Stefan by the police during his unlawful detention since the previous Sunday morning. This assumes that the defence team representing him at that time would have been prepared to argue a fairly contentious point of law, namely that unfairly obtained evidence should be ruled inadmissible by the trial judge and excluded from the consideration of the jury.

Stefan recounted to Dr Tierney his long medical history. He had suffered from asthma as a child, with an associated skin condition, eczema, for which he had received long term steroids. The doctor noted that Stefan was tall, approximately six feet two inches in height, with a heavy build. His voice was high pitched and had never broken, something, the police could not have missed during the interrogation sessions. His eyes were slightly popping. His flat-footedness caused him to walk with a distinct waddling movement. He had been treated for anaemia during the previous August in the Birch Hill Hospital. He displayed many of the signs and symptoms associated with hypogonadism. Stefan confirmed during the recitation of his medical history and in answer to questions that he had recently been diagnosed as suffering from that condition and had been given injections of Primotesterone, the last of which was two days prior to going to Rochdale Police Station. He was taking medically prescribed drugs namely Orovite, Grovite, Ferrogradumet and Distalgestic, none of which had been available to him whilst he was wrongly detained at the police station.

Dr Tierney advised that Stefan was to received that prescribed medication after the examination was concluded. He knew from his clinical experience that a male suffering from hypogonadism is sterile. He cannot produce sperm heads in semen. He also knew that seminal staining had been found on Lesley Molseed's clothing. He had been a police surgeon of many years experience. On one occasion during that time he had examined a man arrested on suspicion of rape. He had been vasectomised. Rape is a heinous offence but the allegation is easy to make and often difficult to refute. With the full and informed consent of that suspect Dr Tierney obtained from him a sample of semen, the forensic examination of which eliminated him as a suspect in the rape inquiry. Whether that was a case of mistaken identification or a totally false allegation against the suspect is not relevant here. The intervention of the doctor was crucial and in the public interest because it established the innocence of an accused man.

The information about the seminal staining on Lesley's clothing had been given to Dr Tierney by the two most senior police officers in the case, Detective Chief Superintendent Dibb and Detective Superintendent Holland. No-one, especially a highly trained and highly qualified medical practitioner like Dr Tierney, could have failed to realise that if those stains could be matched to a suspect that would provide extremely strong, perhaps even conclusive evidence, linking that suspect to the murder victim. It also followed however, as Dr Tierney well knew, that evidence could exonerate Stefan if he was not the killer of the little girl.

Dr Tierney therefore considered that he might once again take the most unusual step in relation to Stefan Kiszko in seeking a forensic sample from him that he was not obliged in law to give. He discussed the possibility of doing so with a number of police officers present. He cannot now, so many years later, identify who those officers were. No objections were raised by any of them.

He decided, for only the second time in his career, to become directly and purposely involved. He fully appreciated that his decision to do so would be subjected to the full glare of public scrutiny in a public forum, namely the court of trial where a judge and counsel might require him to explain and justify his actions in seeking to obtain what could be vital evidence in the case. He did not fear such questioning that might follow, because he acted, as he did at all times, in accordance with the ethics and parameters imposed by the medical profession, and also in accordance with his own conscience.

Dr Tierney also discussed with the police officer who was present at all times during Stefan's medical examination the possibility of obtaining the semen sample and he likewise raised no objection That officer was, according to Dr Tierney's recollection on 9 April 1992, when he made a witness statement to the Lancashire Police, either Chief Superintendent Dibb or Superintendent Holland. His note made at the time of the examination mentions only the first officer. Whoever that officer was, he realised how unusual this situation was. He must have understood exactly the aim, the object and the purpose of obtaining such a sample. Dr Tierney is aware however, for he says so in his statement to the Lancashire Police that Superintendent Holland was quoted as saying, with reference to Stefan's sterility, that it was 'as the police surgeon predicted', so he deduces from that that Holland was certainly aware of the reason why the sample was obtained and its relevance and significance. In fact, that officer told the journalist Steve Panter in 1992, after Stefan's release from prison, that he realised that the forensic sample contained no sperm heads, just as the doctor had predicted. Superintendent Holland could not remember how he found that out but he always thought that the semen tests matched. If he honestly and genuinely thought that (and

I don't believe he did) why did he not ensure that such evidence was placed before the jury at the trial in Leeds Crown Court in July 1976?

At the police station. Dr Tierney told Stefan what he proposed to do, namely to ask him to provide a sample of semen. He fully explained to Stefan, in the presence of the officer, that such a sample would either eliminate him from the murder enquiry into the little girl's murder or confirm him as the possible perpetrator. The entirely innocent man, totally convinced of his own innocence and perhaps confident that this evidence would prove it, provided the specimen without demur. There can be no doubt that Stefan gave his full informed consent to this procedure. He knew full well what he was doing and why he was doing it. The police did also. At the end of the medical examination the doctor completed his notes and made a list of samples, ten in number,that he had obtained from Stefan. Listed at No. 3 was the sample of seminal fluid. It was handed to a scenes of crime officer and arrangements were made to forward the sample to the forensic science laboratory. If that list had been disclosed, as it should have been, to defence counsel preparatory to the trial, then one wonders why David Waddington QC did not cross-examine Dr Tierney at the trial when he gave evidence as the last witness for the prosecution, to examine the reasons for the most unusual request for the provision of the sample.

'For what reason,' he could have asked, 'did you obtain this sample from the accused?' Waddington never asked and Dr Tierney, an experienced witness, was entirely familiar with the procedure of giving evidence: if counsel wants the jury to know about a piece of evidence, then he asks the relevant questions to introduce it. It is not a matter for the witness such as Dr Tierney to volunteer information about which he has not been asked.

The doctor gave his live oral evidence in accordance with his witness statement dated 23 December 1975. His appearance in the witness box at the trial was extremely brief. He was not asked either by the prosecution or the defence any questions about the semen sample, or its significance or even why it had, most unusually, been obtained. He did not know at that time in July 1976, and in fact only discovered it in April 1991, that the sample did not match the seminal stains on the murdered girl's clothing.

It was not his responsibility at the court of trial as a witness for the prosecution to decide on the relevance of an evidential issue and what matters he should reveal to the court. That is for counsel for decide. As far as the doctor was concerned all sides, the judge, the prosecution, and the defence all had copies of the witness statement he had made disclosing the evidence he was prepared to give. It was for counsel to decide what they considered to be relevant and material evidence and what they wanted to put before the court.

As for defence counsel however, the object of cross-examining a prosecution witness is, amongst other things, to obtain from him or her any evidence supporting the defence case, if it exists; further, it is to undermine or cast doubt upon the accuracy of the witness's evidence in chief and if appropriate to impeach the credibility of the witness and portray him or her as a person whose testimony is not to be believed. Over and above that, defence counsel must always be alive to how evidence is obtained and for what purpose. Why David Waddington QC failed to cross-examine Dr Tierney on his motive and reasoning for obtaining the sample of semen I find unusual. One simple question and answer in relation to it might well have changed the entire outcome of the trial.

The other samples that Dr Tierney took from Stefan included samples of urine, blood, saliva, head and pubic hair, skin shavings and a penile swab. It is now known that Chief Superintendent Dibb, Superintendent Holland and possibly forensic scientist Ronald Outteridge were at the police station while all this was being done in the medical room, elsewhere on the premises. Certainly the police officers would have known, and perhaps the scientist did also, that there was no lawful power at that time to demand the provision of a sample of semen and no penalty for failing to provide it in accordance with a request to do so.

Chapter Nine

Further Events

Returning now to the events of the night of 22 December 1975. Stefan's solicitor left the police station. His client had not been charged with any offence. If he had been charged, it would not have been permissible for the police to ask him any further questions about the offence with which he had been charged, save in exceptional circumstances that did not apply here (See Rule III(b) of the Judges' Rules 1964).

I would have expected Albert Wright to ask, before his departure, on what basis Stefan was now being held in police custody. I can find no record that he did so and if not the one person upon whom Stefan ought to have been able to rely for expert advice as to his legal rights and look to for support and reassurance seemingly just left him to his fate. Stefan had been at the police station since soon after 10.30 am on the morning of Sunday 21 December. It was now Monday evening. Did the solicitor not know the degree and extent of control that the police had over his client? Only they knew when he might be released from the police station. That was, as far as Stefan knew, to be decided by the police who questioned him again-and-again, and when little or no progress was being made, they returned him to a confined space until they decided to question him further. The police decided the length and timing of interviews, when Stefan should be allowed to eat, and what food would be provided (In fact, as described in earlier chapters, he ate little, because he started to vomit and could not eat. He drank only water). How had he spent the Sunday night? Did he sleep in his outer clothing? Where and when did he wash or shower or use the toilet facilities? Every aspect of his life must have seemed to him to be under the control of the police. A competent and confident solicitor, accustomed to practice and procedure in a police station where a client is being detained would have indicated to the police that if they intended for any reason to interview his or her client again, then the police must inform the solicitor and give them the opportunity of being present at that proposed interview. Of course the solicitor cannot compel the police to allow him to be present, but it would be a most cogent argument for the exclusion by the trial judge of any evidence obtained at such a time in such a way.

What followed next was extraordinary and should have been subjected to a legal challenge as to its admissibility at the trial. In the early hours of Tuesday, 23 December 1975, at 12.15 am according to Superintendent Holland, he decided to interview Stefan again. It seems that no other police officer was present at the time. Nothing is said about where exactly it took place—in an interview room, or more likely in a cell. I cannot say whether Stefan was roused from his sleep in order for this interview to take place, or whether he simply had not been allowed to sleep.

Holland said he cautioned Stefan and went on, 'I have been making enquiries about the number ADK 539L which you have written on the piece of paper.' It was shown to Stefan.

'Is this your handwriting?'

'Yes,' Stefan replied.

'Is it your paper?'

'Yes.'

'You have written the other numbers on there?'

'Yes.'

'I ask you again, how does that number come to be written on there?'

'I just don't know, I can't remember.'

'Well, I have ascertained that the owner of that vehicle lives in Manchester, works in Manchester Children's Hospital and so far as he knows he has never come in contact with you. He has only been over to Ripponden three times, once on the afternoon of the murder. How could you have got that number written down if you did not take it down on the journey when you had the girl Lesley Molseed with you?'

'I just don't know, my mind is a blank.'

'You remember income tax allowances and rates for the various excess taxable income don't you?'

'Yes, I can remember those figures, but I just don't remember that one in red.'

That concluded the interview. The time is not recorded. Some may regard these questions as derisory, although Stefan did not. Was it seriously being suggested that some time during a murderous episode, either during, before or after he carried out a brutal and sustained stabbing attack upon a little girl, Stefan Kiszko paused in order to write down the registration number of another motor vehicle passing by on the nearby carriageway? One is bound to ask: where was the evidence as to the time the number was written down? In fact there was none.

The authors of *Innocents* found that the vehicle involved was a red-coloured Renault. It had been owned by a man who lived in Rochdale. He sold it to a man in Manchester in February 1975. It was that person who had driven past the murder scene twice on 5 October 1975 but it does not follow that it was anywhere near the scene that Stefan wrote down the number or even that he wrote it down on 5 October. Why could he not have written it prior to February 1975 when the car's owner lived in Rochdale?

The mystery deepens with the disclosure of the information discovered by a private detective, Peter Jackson, one of the men to whom Stefan and his family owed much for his brilliant investigation work on their behalf. There is however one matter of contention. The *Sunday Times* journalist Margarette Driscoll records Peter Jackson as having traced the person who owned the Renault car at the time of the murder in October 1975 and 'found it had regularly parked at the Inland Revenue Building where Kiszko worked' (*Sunday Times*, 23 February 1992). I question whether there may be a mistake of some kind here, either in transmission of the information or its transcription in the newspaper. For this reason: at Stefan's trial the owner of the car on the relevant date, 5 October 1975, was Derek Hollos. The police had interviewed him and his wife.

His evidence was read to the jury (and was supported by his wife's witness statement), that he drove his car registration mark ADK 539L along the A672 on the afternoon of Sunday 5 October at about 2. 30 pm, passing the lay-by close to which Lesley's body was later discovered. In my view it is more likely that Peter Jackson found the previous owner of the car, and it was he who had parked it in the Inland Revenue car park in Rochdale, where Stefan worked. It is my view the mistake in the newspaper article was that of Margarette Driscoll, and it was not the only one. Earlier in the same article, she wrote that, 'Despite Kiszko's own denials, the [defence] team admitted the killing on his behalf but blamed his mental state and medication'.

That never happened. The defence team never admitted the killing in any way, shape or form but in the event asked the jury to acquit Stefan of murder. As set out above, this was the first defence, that Stefan did not kill Lesley—he was elsewhere at the time of her death. If however, the defence went on to argue, the jury were convinced he did kill Lesley Molseed, then and only then should they go on to consider the defence of diminished responsibility.

However that may be, it is self-evident that Superintendent Holland considered this to be an important incriminating piece of evidence. He questioned Stefan about the registration number of the car on no less than four separate occasions, i.e. at 9 pm on Sunday 21 December, then at 1.45 am on Monday 22 December, then at 11. 30 am, that is later in the morning of that same Monday, and finally at 12.15 am on Tuesday 23 December 1975. An astute juror would not have missed the fact that two of these interviews took place in the early hours of the morning at a time when Stefan must have been physically and mentally exhausted. It may be that Holland convinced himself that the written note of the car registration mark was conclusive proof that Stefan had been in the vicinity of the lay by on the A672 Halifax road on 5 October and had murdered Lesley on that date, at that time, on that day. Others shared that view.

However much speculation there may be there was no evidence to show that Stefan had written the car registration mark down either in the course of a journey in the area on 5 October 1975 or at the scene of the killing. That was pure speculation on the part of a partisan and manipulative police officer who was driven by the desire, as he was in other cases, to obtain a 'result'.

It was certainly repetitive and damaging evidence before the jury—they were told about it by Holland no less than four times, but was it right to leave them to draw the conclusion that Stefan did write that number either during the journey or at the murder scene on 5 October, rather than rely on that being proved, as I consider it should have been by the prosecution, beyond reasonable doubt, if the prosecution wished to rely on it as proof of murder?

For reasons not readily apparent, all the lawyers in the case, and the trial judge, seemed to regard the officer's reasoning as carrying some evidential weight. Some may question that. Should the defence have adopted a different approach to this evidence at the trial? The fact that Hollos and his wife drove along that carriageway on 5 October at a specified time was not of itself relevant to the issue the jury had to try, viz did Stefan Kiszko murder Lesley Molseed. It only became admissible evidence if it was proved that Stefan wrote down that car registration mark on that particular day at that specified time. That was not proved unless the jury accepted the truthfulness of the confession evidence. If they did not, I consider that Holland's approach was mere speculation, was ill-founded and the car registration mark was not admissible in evidence.

In fact the explanation for the existence of that number that Stefan undoubtedly recorded is short and simple. In the course of the subsequent police inquiry conducted by Detective Superintendent Trevor Wilkinson, two of his officers, Detective Sergeant John Mackerill and Detective Constable Alison Rose, simply sought the help of Derek Hollos — did he know the identity of the previous owner of the car? He did. It was Albert Oldham. Oldham told the two officers he used the same car park as Stefan. Is there an inference to be drawn there that more likely than not (which would not reach the requisite standard of proof in a criminal case) Stefan recorded the Renault's number for some reason while he parked there at the same time? If the defence solicitor had done his pre-trial work properly he should have realised the significance of the car registration mark. That mark established it was a Rochdale car, even though the current owner lived in Manchester. Because the vehicle was at least two-years-old (it could even have been three) why did Albert Wright, Stefan's solicitor, not try to discover who registered it as keeper and when?

I consider that the defence made a major mistake in allowing the evidence of Mr and Mrs Hellos to be read to the jury. David Waddington QC should have required their attendance to give evidence from the witness box. In my view evidence which is read does not make the same impact as live oral evidence where the jury see the witness and can remember their evidence more easily. He should have cross-examined those witnesses to reinforce their evidence clearly that their parents lived in Halifax; that they visited those two sets of parents from time to time, on Sundays. They did so on 5 October, 16 November and on 7 and 14 December. They always used the same route from their home to Halifax — taking the M62 up to Junction 22, then entering the A672 road to Halifax. That took them past the lay-by above which Lesley's body was found. The difficulty for Stefan regarding this was that he had told the police that he had been on that Ripponden road on Sunday 5 October and 'stopped on the left hand side on a bit of a patch. I took her out of the car and up a sort of grass banking…'. And because he could not explain to Holland when and where he recorded the registration mark of the Renault car, the jury were invited to conclude he must have recorded it on the day of the murder. We now know he did not; he could not have done — he was not in that lay-by on that day.

However, Mr and Mrs Hellos admitted in their statements a total of four visits to Rochdale in the Renault car at and about the relevant time. Should David Waddington QC have refused to allow the prosecution to read the evidence but required them to call Mr and Mrs Hollos to give live evidence? He could then have extracted in cross-examination the fact of the three admitted visits that Derek Hellos made to Rochdale in the Renault car, and ascertained how long he was there and what he did there. In her statement his wife admitted one visit to that town; she also drove the Renault car there. Counsel might even have elicited the information as to where they parked that car, if they did, on any of those four visits. Could it have been the same car park used by Stefan and by the previous owner, Albert Oldham?

Some defence counsel would have ridiculed the suggestion that Stefan wrote that car registration mark either before or after he stabbed a little girl no less than 12 times. If before, did he see the passing Renault car, which by simply driving along the carriageway could scarcely have caused him any problem, produce the pen and paper and write down the car number. Why would he do that? The longer he had the child with him in the vehicle or he stayed at the scene the greater the chance of being seen and apprehended. Where was the abducted little girl while he was doing so? In the alternative, did he after the ferocious killing pause and linger at the scene in the early afternoon of an October day, and with a bruised and bloodstained hand write down that number, for no apparent reason so to do, all in full view of any parked vehicle or passing traffic?

It is known that there were vehicles parked in that lay-by on that afternoon, including a white car. Was that the vehicle containing the little girl that Mrs Emma Tong had seen earlier that Sunday afternoon? It is also a matter of record that the combined police inquiry involved 300 officers from the West Yorkshire Police and the Greater Manchester Police who initially set out to trace a white vehicle seen in the lay-by adjacent to where the body of the little girl was found.

In addition, Holland reported on 14 May 1976 that enquiries had been made at 24 doctors' surgeries, clinics and casualty hospitals in the Rochdale area to find anyone with injuries to the hand that may have resulted from the infliction of the stab wounds to the deceased little girl, if say the hand of the killer rode up the knife when it struck a bone in the body of the deceased victim and stopped suddenly. No one ever saw an injury to Stefan's hand, nor is there any record of his receiving medical treatment for any such injury. If he had been away from home on that Sunday would his Mother have sought an explanation for his absence for quite a long time, and would she have missed seeing his clothing which, if he was the murderer, must have been bloodstained, and also missed any injury to his hand? How would he have got into the family home without being seen in a blood-splattered condition if he had in fact been the murderer?

Were the defence wrong in not challenging the evidence relating to this car and its registration mark ADK 539L? The prosecution wanted the jury to accept that because the owner lived in Manchester, then it followed the only real opportunity Stefan could have had to see and record the registration mark was on the day of the murder, Sunday 5

October. In reality, all their evidence proved was that Hollos and his wife drove their car along the carriageway of the A672 at about 2.30 pm on that day. That was not a matter in issue between the prosecution and the defence at the trial.

The great danger for Stefan was that the jury might have concluded that his confessions supported the Hollos' evidence, and worse still that their evidence supported his confession, making it more likely that it was true. In fact that was exactly how Mr Justice Park put it to the jury:

> '…and twenty minutes later, about 2.30 ADK 539L drove by, which car's number evidently had a fascination for this defendant. It is for you to decide whether that recording of that number on that piece of paper has assisted you in any way in deciding whether or not that confession is true'. (Pages 75–76 of the summing-up).

There is an opposite view to that. Unless the jury accepted the confession was true, then the handwritten note was not relevant and not admissible.

It should be remembered that, apart from Stefan's confession, the prosecution had no evidence as to the day and the date upon which Lesley Molseed was murdered. It could have been any time between 5 and 8 October when her body was found. When Stefan was originally charged those were the dates set out on the charge sheet. That being so, was it was right without further independent supporting evidence for the prosecution to allow the jury to conclude that she was in fact dead at 2.30 pm in the afternoon of Sunday 5 October 1975 at the time Mr and Mrs Hellos drove past the murder scene in their Renault car? She may have been dead then, but the prosecution had no evidence from the pathologist or anyone else that she was. Clearly this evidence was of substantial importance and the jury might have taken that view at the trial. They were told by Mr Justice Park that 'the important part of their evidence' (page 74 of the summing-up) related to their use of their car to travel along the A672 carriageway. Was that fair? It is for the jury to decide which part of the evidence was important, not the trial judge. Just as important to the defence case was the number of times that Mr and Mr Hellos drove the Renault to Rochdale at the relevant time to explain what Stefan himself could not explain—when he had recorded the registration mark. Did the jury not see that?

And did they remember in their retiring room, while they were considering their verdict, Mr Hollos' statement that he used his car for work as a chief laboratory technician at Booth Hall Hospital, Manchester? (That was not the same hospital where Stefan had been an in-patient earlier in 1975). He said he used the vehicle mainly in and around Manchester. Did they remember the detailed evidence from these two witnesses whom they had neither seen nor heard that Derek Hollos admitted in his statement that he had driven his car, which he had purchased in February 1975, to Rochdale on one occasion in early-July 1975. He also drove it to Rochdale on a day at the end of September. He again drove to Rochdale on Friday 24 October 1975 when he collected his in-laws from the bus station there. His wife drove that car to Rochdale two days later, on Sunday 26 October, taking her parents back to the bus station. So there were no less than four separate occasions when it is possible to conclude that Stefan may have actually seen that Renault car in Rochdale where he lived and for reasons known only to him, noted the registration mark there and then on any one of those four separate days. The prosecution were allowed to choose one particular day that suited their purpose to incriminate Stefan, namely 5 October 1975, and just disregard those other four days that didn't incriminate him simply because of Stefan's confession. One more reason why its admissibility in evidence should have been challenged by the defence.

There is one further point. The letters in the Renault's registration mark are significant. On no less than four occasions Holland had questioned Stefan about why he had written them down. The letters ADK indicate it was registered in Rochdale. The letter L indicates it was registered in 1972 or perhaps 1973. I consider that the defence solicitor, Albert Wright ought perhaps to have made inquiries in order to brief counsel about whether the car had been previously owned by someone who lived in Rochdale. How long had he owned it, was he the first owner, when he had sold it and to whom? Was it driven or parked anywhere where Stefan could have noted it? Would Mr Wright have found Albert Oldham and discovered, many years before the two police officers did, that in fact he parked the Renault car, registration mark ADK 539L in the same car park as Stefan. Would that have helped to undermine the truthfulness of the confession evidence? Was it far more likely than Stefan saw the Renault in Rochdale, rather than at or near the murder scene which was least nine miles away from there.

Whatever the truth may be, the psychological pressure exerted by Holland in Rochdale Police Station on this shy, lonely and wrongfully detained man was being piled on more and more by the police. Another interview followed. Again, Superintendent Holland was alone in conducting it. This was the eighth time that Stefan had been questioned by the police since his arrival at the police station the previous Sunday morning. It followed the interview that had taken place in the early hours of Tuesday 23 December 1975. No time is given for this further interview, when it started or ended, so it is not possible to say how long the interview lasted. The Judges' Rules and Superintendent Holland seem never to have been introduced one to the other. Although he knew that Stefan had access to a solicitor, the superintendent must have intended not to contact him and let him know of his intention to interview his client in his absence. The reason is obvious. The solicitor might have insisted on being present while the interview took place and, for the superintendent, that would never do.

The interview took place 'in the cell area', a description that I find unhelpful. Presumably the door of the cell was unlocked and opened, Stefan stepped out and stood in the passageway and there, according to Holland, he was cautioned. In spite of being constantly reminded of his right to stay silent, Stefan never did.

'From your first statement you have described the effects of the drugs and if you were hazy and can't remember, how do you know that what you told me in the first statement is untrue?'

At the subsequent trial, should not David Waddington QC have heavily criticised this senior police officer for his shabby tactics. There is also the matter of the trick question that led to this highly incriminating response: 'I am all of a blue. I have told you the truth. I remember the girl by the shop in Broad Lane and taking her to the moors. I must have stabbed her. That's how I showed you the bone-handled knife.'

Such a response must have delighted Holland. He had got all he wanted. He told Stefan he would make further inquiries. By this time he knew that of all of the knives that had been linked to Stefan, the forensic scientists had established that only the bone-handled knife had traces of blood on the blade. That was the one that Stefan had previously identified as the murder weapon. Unfortunately for the police, however, the trace was so minute that the blood could not be grouped by the tests available at that time. In any event, the pathologist Professor Gee admitted in cross-examination at the trial that his calculations of the size of the blade used in the murder did not fit the knife that belonged to Stefan. As it turned out, the actual murder weapon was never found. Did the jury have the impression, if not the evidence, that it had been.

Amongst the murder file of papers, etc. I found a memorandum dated 14 May 1976 written by Holland, addressed to the Director of Public Prosecutions. It was written in response to the Advice on Evidence drafted by Mr Caswell of counsel and received by Holland four days previously. Under the heading 'Paragraph 5c Case against the Accused' the superintendent wrote,

'Professor Gee has now been shown the four other knives taken from the accused Kiszko and his conclusion is that none of the other knives could have caused the injuries inflicted on the deceased. One knife had a similar blade but did not have a pointed end and this blade could not have cause the boney injury from one of the stab wounds to the back. The Professor is preparing an additional statement and this will be submitted as soon as it is received and a further copy will be served upon the defence'.

I find this confusing. A total of five knives owned by Stefan were of interest to the police. Three were found in his home, the remaining two were in his possession when he drove to the police station on the morning of Sunday 21 December 1975. One of those, which became Exhibit 54 at the trial, had an imitation bone handle. It was that knife which Stefan identified as the murder weapon. I cannot say whether Professor David Gee's additional statement, if he made it, about this was ever served on the defence. Clearly it should have been. But what did it purport to prove? This is linked to more disquieting evidence.

When Gee first examined the body of the little girl he thought it possible that the blade of the knife that caused wounds 4 and 5 had been inserted to its full length because there was bruising at the mouth of those wounds. When he was given at a much later date, certainly after 21 December 1975, the imitation bone handle knife, Exhibit 54, he realised that knife if inserted to its full length would have caused different wounds — so it might not be the murder weapon. He therefore revised his opinion about the wounds, indicating that it could be, without necessarily saying that it was the weapon that was used to murder the child. What impression did the jury form about this evidence?

Again, there arises this question: was Stefan roused from his sleep for this interview containing this vital admission, or had he simply been kept awake since the conclusion of the interview that had commenced at 12.15 am? What was it about the content of those murder interviews that required them to be conducted in the middle of the night by one officer acting alone, without the supporting, corroborative evidence of at least one other officer? This was quite a change in procedure from the times when no fewer than at least three, if not four, police officers sat in on interviews with Stefan concerning allegations of indecent exposure.

Throughout that day Stefan was kept, quite unlawfully in my view, in detention at the police station. One wonders whether, throughout that long day, his solicitor made any enquiry of the police about what was happening to his client. He ought to have shown some interest in Stefan's welfare.

At 10.15 on the evening of that Tuesday, 23 December 1975, Stefan was taken from the police station to Halifax by car by way of the Queensway roundabout and the M62 motorway. Superintendent Holland and Detective Sergeant Akeroyd were in the vehicle with him. They chose to stop the superintendent's own car at the lay-by at Ripponden, just below the area where Lesley Molseed's body had been found. It must have been a pitiful and desolate scene in the darkness of that December evening, two days before a Christmas that a deeply loved little girl was destined never to see.

Stefan remembered that it was raining heavily that night and visibility from inside the car was very limited. It is difficult to determine what useful purpose was served by this visit to the crime scene in these circumstances. If it was for the purpose of evidence-gathering, should not his solicitor have been told? What were the police hoping for? Another confession statement? Or was it all just a charade?

According to both officers, Stefan began '... to shake and he held his hands in a praying position. He said, "I can hear noises, can't you?" He was obviously very upset.' Other innocent people, just as Stefan was innocent, might have been upset too if driven to the scene of the savage murder of a defenceless little girl, on a dark windswept night in the company of two police officers to whom a false confession to that murder had previously been made.

Stefan was then taken to the police station in Halifax and at 11.50 pm on that Tuesday, in the presence of his solicitor Albert Wright, Stefan Kiszko was charged with the murder of Lesley Molseed. He seemed unable to speak. The solicitor said, 'No reply' and that was noted by both officers. I cannot say whether the solicitor was told, as he ought to have been, that Stefan had again confessed to the murder while he was not present. I can find no record of Albert Wright being told of the visit by car to the murder scene. Should he not have sought an explanation why he was not asked about this taking place, and concerning whether he would have advised against it, before it happened? It does not look as if he did so.

Superintendent Holland records that the solicitor left the police station at 12.10 am It was Wednesday 24 December 1975. Christmas Eve. He certainly was not then available to advise, if not console, a mild, asthmatic, bewildered man of unblemished character who now faced a charge of murdering a little girl. Stefan was photographed and fingerprinted and then locked in a cell overnight.

Later on that Wednesday morning, Stefan was taken before Calder Magistrates' Court in Halifax. The hearing lasted for only two minutes. Stefan stood in the dock with a police officer on either side. He spoke only to confirm his name and address. The public gallery was empty and no-one but the police and court officials saw that Stefan was in a state of shock and bewilderment. There was no application for bail. He was taken from the dock and hurried from the court building through the back entrance, surrounded by no less than six police officers. He was taken by police van, in custody, to Armley Gaol in Leeds to await the committal proceedings that would send him to the Crown Court for trial. It is my view that this was the first time he was in lawful custody on an order from a court of competent jurisdiction. It is doubtful if Stefan realised that. He was far more concerned that this would be the first Christmas he had ever been separated from his mother. There was little of the Christmas spirit around Rochdale for either of them; both were vilified by those to whom the presumption of innocence meant nothing. While Stefan awaited trial there was a public clamour for the execution by hanging of those convicted of the murder of a child. That was the fate that would have awaited him if the law had not been changed some ten years previously.

For the first two weeks at Armley Gaol he was segregated from other prisoners. Then he was put in a ward in the prison hospital.

I consider that Stefan's cause was lost on the day he voluntarily drove from his home to the police station. When he was further remanded in prison custody on 31 December 1975, his solicitor Albert Wright made no criticism of the police officers who had unlawfully detained his client, unlawfully searched his house and caused him to confess to a murder of which he was innocent. Instead he thanked Detective Chief Superintendent Dibb and Detective Superintendent Holland in open court for 'their close cooperation and assistance'. He added '... they have given me full information about all the inquiries and the inquiries still to be made. They are keeping me fully informed of the results of those inquiries.'

How mystifying those words must have sounded to Stefan as he was escorted away from the dock to begin his descent into a life of hell. A nightmare for an innocent was now well advanced.

Chapter Ten

Stefan's 'Detention' at the Police Station

Some time after the conclusion of the confession to murder written state-ment at 5.35 on that Monday afternoon Albert Wright, a partner in a local firm of solicitors, was allowed to see Stefan and obtain his instructions. He was confronted with a man aged 23, very tall at six feet two inches, grossly overweight at more than seventeen-and-a-half stone, with a high pitch falsetto voice, bulging eyes, unsteady walk, and displaying few of the male characteristics one would usually find in a man of that age. This was because Stefan had, since childhood, suffered from a hypogonodal condition and endocrine deficiency for which he was receiving testos-terone hormone injections at Manchester Royal Infirmary.

In addition, Stefan had been at the police station since 10.30 am the previous morning, had not eaten a proper meal, but had drunk only water. He had been sick. He had not changed his clothes, in which it appears he had slept. Just to look at him one would have immediately concluded that here was vulnerable and confused individual, who would be lost in the presence of persons in positions of authority.

As already argued, Albert Wright should, I suggest, have obtained from the police, at the very outset, full and detailed information regarding Stefan's presence at the police station. Why he was there and for how long had he been there. On what legal grounds was he being held, and on what evidence, in outline, were the police exercising their powers? At the very least he should have asked for the production of the Detained Person's Register (otherwise and elsewhere described as 'the detention sheet'), and inspected it carefully to ensure that everything that should have been recorded actually was. The fact that no such record existed because no document had been opened indicated Stefan's status at the police station. Wright would have discovered at that moment that Stefan was not in lawful detention for he had not been arrested on the Sunday morning. The Detained Person's Register must record the full name of the person detained, their sex, their date of birth, occupation, nationality and the name of the officer detaining them. The time and date of detention must be recorded, time of arrival at the police station, and whether the person was placed in a cell or detention room. The officer authorising the person's detention must sign the register. The reasons for detention and for delayed or refused charge must be recorded, together with a list of the property found on the person, or elsewhere, and that list must be signed by the searching officer and the person, after the last entry on that list. Visits and interviews, of fundamental importance to the suspect, must also be recorded on the register. If that had been done, Albert Wright would have seen that Stefan had been interviewed for three-and-a-quarter hours after arrival at the police station on Sunday morning, then some 50 minutes later he was interviewed again, this time for two hours 50 minutes. Would he have asked himself, was this not oppressive and overpowering for any individual, let alone a vulnerable man like Stefan?

As noted previously, there were three further interviews, the last of which had taken place at 1.45 in the morning of Monday 22 December. Did the solicitor ever ask why? Did he wonder why Stefan confessed to Detective Sergeant Akeroyd soon after half past eleven that very morning, and the written confession to murder did not start until 3.20 pm that day? Why the delay?

As noted previously, I consider that Wright should not have allowed Superintendent Holland to write the statement withdrawing the confession. That retraction statement should have contained everything Stefan wished to be known about his treatment by the police, of whom he was clearly frightened, at Rochdale Police Station while he was unlawfully detained there. He had not the faintest idea when, if at all, he would be allowed to leave the police station. Holland should not have been present, let alone play a leading part, in the writing of that retracted confession evidence. Many solicitors would have taken their client's instructions alone and in private, away from the police officer, in a situation covered by legal professional privilege. Albert Wright apparently chose not to do that. It may be that Wright like others was overwhelmed by the forceful personality of Holland. After that incident was concluded, he should have asked when, if at all, was Stefan going to be charged and put before the court? If Stefan had been charged immediately or at least soon after confessing to murder, under Rule III (b) of the Judges' Rules it was only in exceptional cases that questions relating to the offence could be put to the accused after he had been charged or informed that he might be prosecuted. That rule would have prevented any questions being put to Stefan about the murder, as clearly happened in the cell area at 12.15 am, the eighth interview, on the Tuesday, and then even later again in the cell area when Stefan made the statement confessing he was 'all of a blue'. Why did Wright not tell Holland that in the event of the police wishing to interview his client again then according to the rules he must be told and given the opportunity to be present at any such interview?

Later, when preparing for trial, did it not occur to Wright to ascertain how many pens similar to the one found some 15 yards from Lesley Molseed's body had been manufactured and who were the main suppliers in the Rochdale area? How many were stocked by the Inland Revenue there, and were all identified as being government property? The police thought the pen was of some evidential significance, in the same way as they considered the finding of carpet strands discovered by the scientists on the clothing of the deceased little girl. When he was told about this why did Wright not discover the name of the manufacturer of the carpet strands and which the scientist said were 'similar' to strands from Stefan's car. That manufacturer could have established how many thousands of yards of that carpet were manufactured and where they were sold. The evidence was merely that the strands were similar, that is in manufacture, colouring and design, but it was not claimed, and could not be claimed, that the strands on the clothes came from the carpet in the car. One of the problems with this kind of evidence is its cumulative effect — a pen similar to ones used by Stefan plus a piece of material on the clothing similar to the carpet in Stefan's car on their own might mean very little in evidential terms. But add them together and they might amount to something of substance. Did the jury think the pen proved Stefan's presence at the murder scene, and did the strands of material prove that Lesley had been in Stefan's motor car? In the light of the eventual conviction of Ronald Castree it is apparent that this purported evidence proved nothing against Stefan at all.

Finally, should Wright not have sought forensic support for Stefan's claim that he had never lured the little girl into his car, and sought to establish whether a man who must have been heavily bloodstained after the frenzied attack on Lesley would have been able to remove completely all traces of blood from the inside of the vehicle? Stefan said he had placed the murder weapon, the knife, in his pocket after the ferocious repetitive stabbing. Would that not have heavily stained his clothes? Would it have stained the driver's car seat? Would the Harrogate scientists who examined the vehicle have been able to discover whether Stefan's car had been subjected to a deep clean, and would even that cleaning have eliminated every trace of blood inside the car, from the clothing and body of the killer?

It is a matter of record that Stefan's motor vehicle in which he was supposed to have driven the murdered little girl from near her home to the scene of her death was taken to be examined at the Forensic Science Laboratory in Harrogate. No evidence was ever given by the prosecution at the trial that proved in any shape or form let alone beyond a reasonable doubt that Lesley Molseed had ever been in that car. I have found no 'negative' statement from the scientists to say they found nothing inside the vehicle that linked her to it. Are these not all matters which an experienced solicitor with a knowledge of criminal practice and procedure such as Wright was would have investigated in order to brief defence counsel to prepare the most compelling defence possible for their client?

Chapter Eleven

The Court Hearings

The committal proceedings on 18 February 1976 were speedy and uncontested. It was intended that Stefan should be sent to a higher court, the Crown Court, to be tried there. There was no consideration of the evidence; the defence told the court and the prosecution that they accepted that there was a case to answer on the basis of the papers containing the evidence served on them in accordance with the law. Since the defence indicated they proposed to rely on an alibi defence it was a requirement under section 11 of the Criminal Justice Act 1967 that an alibi notice be served on the prosecution either at the committal proceedings or within seven days thereafter. Failure to comply with the terms of this section meant that leave of the trial judge had to be obtained for evidence of an alibi or evidence in support of an alibi to be given at any subsequent court hearing.

In fact the defence did not comply with the requirements of section 11 at the committal proceedings on 18 February 1976 (*Chapter Eleven*). It is ordinarily imperative to obtain full instructions as soon as it emerges that alibi will be a defence and to serve the statutory notice in the required form with the committal papers. I cannot understand and have never seen any explanation as to why Albert Wright only served such notice, if that is what it correctly amounted to, by letter on 13 May 1976 (i.e. seemingly almost as an afterthought) stating:

'The defence propose to adduce evidence to establish an alibi. The accused will say that he was not at or near the scene of the crime on or between the days of 5th to 8th October 1975 inclusive, but he cannot recollect his precise whereabouts at any material time'.

Wright named Charlotte Kiszko as an alibi witness and added that she would say that Stefan was never away from home on the material dates for any period long enough for her son to have committed the crime with which he was charged.

I do not consider that this was a proper and appropriate approach to alibi evidence. Evidence, whether from the accused himself or from any other person, which goes no further than that the accused was not present at the place where the offence was committed is not evidence in support of an alibi within section 11(8) of the 1967 Act. That sub-section reads:

> '..."evidence in support of an alibi" means evidence tending to show that by reason of the presence of the defendant at a particular place or in a particular area at a particular time he was not, or was unlikely to have been, at the place where the offence is alleged to have been committed at the time of its alleged commission'.

By the clear words of that sub-section evidence in support of an alibi has to be evidence that the accused was at some particular place, or in some particular area, at the time of the commission of the offence. Stefan was not here claiming that he was 'elsewhere' — he was simply claiming he was not at the crime scene on the day of the murder. That being so, there was no requirement to serve that notice of alibi in that form in respect of his evidence.

With regard to his mother, all that Section 11 required the defence to do in relation to an alibi witness was to tell the court and the prosecution the name and address of that witness. There was no need to disclose the evidence, as opposed to the identity, of that witness called in support of an alibi. All this was rather inappropriate and confusing.

On 30 June 1976 a second notice of alibi, clearly prepared by defence counsel, this time in proper form, was served upon the prosecution. This was only a week before the beginning of the trial. Why was it left so late?

After Stefan was committed for trial he first appeared at Leeds Crown Court on 5 April 1976. He entered a plea of not guilty and was remanded in custody to await his trial which was fixed for 7 July 1976 at Leeds Crown Court. Following the usual practice, the leader of the North-Eastern Circuit, Peter Taylor QC, was nominated by the Attorney-General to prosecute the case. His junior counsel was Matthew Caswell. David Waddington QC was briefed as leading defence counsel, with Philip Clegg acting as his junior. At a later stage Stefan had a two hour meeting with both counsel and he felt great confidence in both men. At all times throughout that meeting he maintained his innocence. It was not suggested to him then that he should plead to murder or manslaughter.

Stefan later recollected receiving copies of the witness statements from his solicitor, Albert Wright. He was also told about the existence of over 6,000 other statements but Stefan did not see them. He was at that particular time appearing at Halifax's Calder Magistrates' Court for weekly remands in custody so this must have been before 18 February, 1976. He had told Wright that Superintendent Holland had frightened him. That he had kept poking him. Stefan thought that Holland was going to beat him up. There was no response from his solicitor on this point. Was Stefan however making it clear to Albert Wright that the original written confession made by him and written by Superintendent Holland was induced by the use and threats of force, was untrue, and not freely made? At a much later stage, Stefan explained the reasons why he confessed to the police.

> 'I started to tell lies and that seemed to please them and the pressure was off so far as I was concerned. I thought if I admitted what I did to the police they would check out what I had said, find it untrue and would then let me go'.

Chapter Twelve

Preparations for Trial

When the police submitted their first file to the office of the Director of Public Prosecutions for advice in the case against Stefan Kiszko, they included the witness statements in relation to the allegations of indecent exposure in October 1975, on Friday 3 and Saturday 4. Superintendent Holland said that this evidence was included in the file on the advice of the force prosecuting solicitor, Mr M Shaffner. He seemed to have considered that such allegations were relevant to the issues involved in the murder trial.

On 5 February 1976, a conference was held at the Department of the Director of Public Prosecutions in London. That was arranged at the request of Detective Superintendent Holland on 27 January 1976. At that conference the case papers show that the Assistant Director (East) decided to exclude the indecency allegations from the evidence. That would not be welcome news for the police officer, but that was the view of the assistant director and accordingly had to be followed. Advice on evidence was given orally to Holland that he was to prepare the committal papers without including the statements relating to the alleged incidents of indecency. That officer was also advised that the department should be supplied with two copies of each of the 6,100 non-material witness statements. Holland asked that a letter be sent to the Chief Constable about this matter.

When informed of this, junior counsel for the Crown, Matthew Caswell, later advised in writing that the evidence of the indecency allegations should be included in the disclosed papers served on the defence, because in his view that evidence was admissible. He gave reasons for his advice, overturning and completely reversing the decision made by the Assistant Director of Public Prosecutions on 5 February 1976. I do not agree with those reasons. I wrote to Mr Caswell, now living in retirement, making contact through his former chambers. I wished to discuss the point that the assistant director had considered the evidence was inadmissible, and seek to discover why had he reached a contrary conclusion. I was also interested in Caswell's failure to cite the then very recent House of Lords decision in *DPP v Boardman*[2] on the admissibility of similar fact evidence, that is evidence of misconduct by an accused person on other occasions, to support his advice, if it did. I received no reply from Mr Caswell.

It was the practice at the time that following the Attorney-General's nomination of prosecuting counsel in a case of murder, the decision on the conduct of the prosecution case was left in the hands of that nominated counsel. There might well be a reason for changing a decision on admissible evidence, for example if other incriminating evidence was uncovered by the police after the DPP's decision had been conveyed to the police. I found nothing to establish that happened in this case.

Matthew Caswell advised at the time that various witness statements relating to those incidents of alleged indecency should be served upon the defence and, in addition, the prosecution should serve statements of those witnesses they did not propose calling. The latter course was unusual.

The established practice at that time, in 1976, was that where the prosecution had possession of a statement from a witness whom they knew could give material evidence but decided not to call him or her as a witness, they were under a duty to make that person available as a witness for the defence, but they were not under the further duty of supplying the defence with a copy of the statement the police had taken. So in doing what he did, counsel went further than the law and practice then prevailing strictly required. There were, however, a number of other statements which may not have been disclosed by the police even to the prosecution team, as well as some which the prosecution did have, but did not disclose. There was, on any view, a very substantial number of documents. Among them were some 6,000 statements taken from

---

2.   (1975) 60 Cr. App. R. 165.

witnesses. There is a note on the case papers that after the committal proceedings on 18 February one of the DPP's professional officers, John Walker, asked for two copies of each of the some 6,000 non-material statements still in the possession of the police; he wished to send those to counsel for the prosecution.

There is a further note signed by Graham Grant Whyte, another professional officer, dated 4 May, 1976 stating ,'I have copies of the 6,200 non-material statements in my room. Contact me about collecting them'. No action seems to have been taken by anyone in respect of that request. The responsibility for the late service of those statements (now termed unused material) accordingly lies with someone in the Department of the DPP and not the police.

In the event, it was only on the first day of the trial that the prosecution handed over a large volume of documents to the defence. I take the view that this constituted an ambush for them and that they should in the interests of justice have been granted an adjournment in order to have time to digest the contents. The trial judge however, was not going to grant an adjournment, no matter how strong the argument in favour of doing so. The case was going to proceed to trial on the day fixed for it to start.

It is my belief that these bundles of documents did not include in them the statement of the courageous milkman, and I consider that the tactics used by the defence would have changed if they had known fully the significance of what he said about his presence near the youth club on the evening of Friday 3 October 1975.

Moreover, I would have hoped, rather than expected, that the police would tell the defence team about the witness statement of the milkman relating to the incident near the youth club on 3 October and, perhaps even more importantly, Christopher Coverdale. His witness statement was included and identified both in a schedule of sightings near the murder scene, and the actual witness statement itself, amongst the documents handed over on the morning of 7 July 1976 at Leeds Crown Court. Was that not too late in the day for such important evidence that would have been so helpful to the defence?

However, the officer given that responsibility was Detective Superintendent Holland. He was the last person I would look to to help any defendant in any criminal trial. His judgment as an investigating officer was just as catastrophic in this case as it later turned out to be in the notorious case of the Yorkshire Ripper, Peter Sutcliffe.

I think in the final analysis that Holland regarded his initial responsibility as a police officer to be to collect and collate the evidence for the prosecution, i.e. evidence that proved the guilt of the accused. It was not his task to provide information that undermined in any way that primary purpose. Even then, once the volume of material emerged on 7 July 1975, I still consider that the defence ought to have been given more time to examine carefully what that material contained. The overall end result however was that the jury was not allowed to decide the case on the whole of the evidence, but only on that which the prosecuting authorities decided they should be permitted to see. This was not an oversight, this was the suppression of the truth.

In preparation for trial, Philip Clegg, junior defence counsel, had previously gone to see Stefan in prison and had a conference with him there. They talked about his case in general, but Stefan did remember Philip Clegg mentioning the semen sample and the staining on the child's clothing, but he could not remember the context in which this discussion took place. He did, however, get the impression that Clegg placed a lot of importance on the sample.

After that there was a consultation between the two defence barristers, David Waddington QC, Philip Clegg and Stefan at the prison. There was a general discussion, but Stefan did remember telling both barristers about his alibi for 5 October, that at lunchtime on that day he was in a shop in Tweedale Street and that two witnesses, Mrs Baran and her daughter, could confirm this. He also recalled telling them that Mrs Baran was on holiday in Italy but he thought she would be back in time for his trial. He explained that the reason he had admitted the murder was because of what Holland had said to him and the fact that he had poked him on the shoulder. His recollection was that the defence barristers made no comment about this.

Counsel took him through the police statements but not that of the forensic scientist. Stefan told them that Holland had written the confession statement and he had just signed it. At all times during this consultation Stefan maintained that he was innocent, believing that only the guilty are convicted in the criminal courts.

Chapter Thirteen

Advice on Evidence

It is a long and well-established rule in the law of evidence that it is not generally permissible to attempt to prove that the accused committed the crime charged by evidence that he has a propensity or disposition to commit crimes of that type, whether by showing that he has committed such crimes in the past on other occasions or otherwise, for example by showing that he possesses articles associated with the commission of such crimes. The reason for the exclusion of such evidence is not that it has no relevance or probative value but because its probative value is outweighed by its prejudicial effect. However, the approach of allowing evidence to be given in certain instances of previous misconduct, which need not amount to a crime, is known to lawyers as the similar facts evidence rule, because the evidence of acts on other occasions deprives its cogency from the striking similarity of those acts to the present crime. Some might wish to ask what evidence at the scene of the murder of the little girl bore a strikingly similarity to the events of 'flashing' of 3 and 4 October 1975?

If in Stefan's case, David Waddington QC had invited Mr Justice Park to exclude the evidence of the alleged indecency on 3 and 4 October 1975 on the ground if it was not relevant then it was inadmissible, because the first ground of admissibility is relevance; further that the prejudice caused would outweigh the probative value of that evidence, the over-whelming probability was that it would have done so. For as the trial judge ultimately told the jury regarding the children's evidence '… it does not follow that he must have been the killer of a totally different girl on the 5th October'. In my view it was a massive mistake on the part of Waddingon not to argue this issue at the very outset of the trial.

On 28 April 1976 Matthew Caswell drafted his Advice on Evidence. He cited four cases which he considered supported his view that the evidence of indecent exposure on 4 and 5 October 1975 was admissible in evidence — contrary to the view of the Assistant Director of Public Prosecutions. His purpose seemed to be to establish that who ever was involved in that misconduct was also the murderer of a little girl on 5 October 1975. Apart from Stefan's confession it was never proved at the trial by the prosecution witnesses that he was the person involved in the Friday night incident, It is now known that in fact that was a confession to a crime that had never happened.

After citing the four names of the criminal cases Mr Caswell wrote:

'This evidence is of the utmost relevance in relation to several issues in this case:

(a) The stabbing to death of a child of 11 with a knife in the course of sexual assault consisting of no more than the assailant masturbating over her is quite unusual.

(b) the evidence that on each of the two days preceding the murder a man answering to the description of, and identified by one child witness as the accused masturbated in front of children with a knife in one hand is sufficiently proximate to the murder in time, place and method to make it relevant to the issue of identification'.

It is of course necessary to look at the information that Caswell had to hand when he drafted the advice in April 1976. It is now known from Superintendent Wilkinson's report that there was no witness prepared to say that there was any act of indecent exposure on Friday 3 October 1975 or that any person was in possession of a knife. However, Stefan's confession of 22 December 1975 contains the admission that he was in possession of a knife during the alleged incident near the youth club on 3 October. It was there that he added the mysterious comment to that confession '... but it was a mere triviality'. That must have done enormous damage to his case in the eyes of the jury.

Under (a) above Caswell considers that the events he describes are 'quite unusual'. He may be right about that.

However, when he claims in (b) that '... a man answering to the description of, and identified by one witness as, the accused masturbated in front of the children with a knife in his hand' that simply is not right. I can find no evidence anywhere in the prosecution statements first that Stefan Kiszko answered the description of the man, and further than any witness said at any time that man involved in two incidents on successive days did any more than indecently expose himself—there was simply no question of that individual committing an act of gross indecency by masturbating in the presence of the children either on 3 or 4 October 1975.

Where was the actual evidence in the form of a witness statement that justified Matthew Caswell in drafting this part of his advice? Certainly no witness ever gave evidence at the trial claiming this had happened. Where then did junior prosecuting counsel get this so called evidence from? Were there other undisclosed statements which are not now amongst the file papers? If that evidence had ever been available to junior prosecuting counsel on 28 April 1976 when he drafted his advice, why was it not called as part of the prosecution case at the trial that commenced some eleven weeks later on 7 July 1976? I bear in mind that in the course of confessing Stefan had admitted to further indecency incidents about which the police said they knew nothing. That part of the confession evidence would not be admissible because it related to incidents with which Stefan had not been charged and was therefore irrelevant to any issue before the jury. Was it just the simple truth that Stefan was prepared to admit to anything to anyone just to get out of the police station?

Did someone, perhaps a police officer, tell Caswell that the unidentified man, supposedly Stefan, was committing not just one offence of indecent exposure but a further offence of gross indecency while in possession of a knife, an offensive weapon, in a public place on two successive days, the 3 and 4 October 1975? As I understand it, it was never the prosecution case at the trial that Stefan had masturbated in front of anyone near the youth club on 3 October or on Vavasour Street in front of Maxine Buckley the following day, 4 October 1975. If it was alleged that four offences were committed on those two successive days, why was Stefan not charged with those four offences?

It also begs the further question: if the defence wished to prove the falsity of the confession to the indecent exposure on the Friday evening in support of their tactical approach that Stefan had lied to the police about that offence and therefore he had lied to the police about the murder, why did the defence not ask at the very outset for a formal identification parade on which Stefan was a participant, to prove conclusively that he was not the man near the youth club on the night of Friday 3 October 1975? Would not that have established the falsity of his confession?

Caswell's Advice continued:

'(c) The above is strengthened by the fact that the accused had been given an injection of testerone (sic) on Friday 3rd October 1975, immediately before the happening of all the above events.

(d) The evidence in question is also of great relevance in evaluating the confession statement which the accused subsequently retracted in that in the confession statement the accused confessed to indecent exposure and to the murder on the 5th blaming them on the injections; and by his retraction he denied all these incidents.

(e) I was informed by defence counsel that a notice of alibi would be served on the prosecution. I do not yet know what this consists of though I would expect it to be to the effect that the accused could not have committed either the murder or the indecent exposure or any of them since he had not yet sufficiently recovered from his foot injury to drive a car until the 8th October at the earliest. He had been discharged from hospital on 15th September 1975

(f) What led to the accused in relation to the charge of murder were the complaints of indecent exposure and the identification of the accused in relation to the latter by the girl Maxine. (It should be noted there was no mention here of the masturbatory behaviour).

(g) The medical treatment for impotence which gave rise to a sexual urge and aggression, the masturbatory behaviour, the indecent exposure in the presence of children, the police investigation in relation to the exposure, the confession of the accused, the manner and the circumstances of the killing—all these matters are so interlinked that I would consider it proper that the whole body of this evidence be before the jury and not just a truncated part of it'.

I find nothing in Caswell's Advice on Evidence which would have persuaded any trial judge to admit evidence of the alleged misconduct on 3 and 4 October 1975 under the similar facts evidence rule. In any event Mr Justice Park made it clear (at page 19 of the summing-up) that if Stefan had been prosecuted for indecent exposure (there was no mention of the alleged act of gross indecency) based on the evidence of the children then, in the absence of his confession, Stefan would have been acquitted. Moreover, as noted above, the judge told the jury (at page 18 of the summing-up) that even if the evidence proved that it was Stefan who did expose himself to the little girls on 3 and 4 October 'it does not follow that he must have been the killer of a totally different girl on the 5th October'. The very essence of the admissibility of the evidence of previous misconduct under the similar facts evidence rule is that it goes to establish the issue of guilt—that the previous misconduct tends to establish that this was the work of the same man. If it fails to show that, then it is worthless.

Returning to paragraph 1(e) of counsel's advice, I have never known a case where the accused has served a notice of alibi in connection with an offence with which he had not been charged. Matthew Caswell seems to suggest that the notice of alibi would relate not merely to the murder but also to the indecent exposure. I do not consider that Stefan was obliged to give notice of an alibi unless or until he was charged with an offence relating to the alleged acts of indecency and his defence to those charges had they been laid against him was that he was elsewhere at the time of their alleged commission.

As for (f) above, it is right that the allegations of indecent conduct and the identification of Stefan by Maxine Buckley led to his arrest, but does that fact advance the case for the prosecution in proving anything in relation to the murder?

As for sub-paragraph (g) above regarding the medical treatment I consider Caswell ought to have concentrated more on what was admissible than what was proper. He certainly applied the correct test of relevance but I question whether his submission would have found favour with the trial judge and the evidence of the alleged incidents on 3 and 4 October would have been allowed in evidence. He also made a major mistake in confusing impotence with Stefan's condition of azoospermia—the inability to produce sperm. He was wrong in his statement, as if it was a proven fact that the medical treatment for impotence gave rise to a sexual urge and aggression. The police made exactly the same mistake. Stefan was being treated by Dr David Anderson for hypogonadism with the natural hormone testosterone. That is not a drug but a replacement male hormone which would stimulate sexual activity in the normal way. It would not, and did not, cause Stefan to become an aggressive monster and a vicious murderer. What should have placed junior prosecuting counsel and the police investigating officers on alert was the unlawful confinement in the police station of a man suffering from these conditions, who had been ill and malnourished, and who had received blood transfusions for severe folic acid deficiency anaemia in hospital only weeks before. Did it ever cross anyone's mind while advising on the evidence in the case that the oppressive way in which the confession evidence had been obtained might give rise to questions about it accuracy and truthfulness? Did junior prosecuting counsel have any reservation about the admissibility of the confession evidence? If he did, he did not say so.

On 26 May 1976 Matthew Caswell drafted another Advice. He wrote

'If Kiszko were to offer a plea of guilty to manslaughter on the ground of diminished responsibility this should be acceptable to the Crown. There is ample evidence already in our possession. Including the statements of several medical practitioners, indicating that Kiszko who was otherwise a weak and fastidious "mother's boy" was injected with testerone [sic] to give him a sexual urge and a male aggressive urge'.

I consider that lawyers and lay people alike will question whether that was clear evidence of a 'disease of the mind' requisite to establish the defence of diminished responsibility. It might persuade some people however to wonder whether confinement in a police station and hours of interrogation might induce a 'mother's boy' to confess to a murder he did not commit.

On 28 June 1976, that is nine days before the commencement of the murder trial, Caswell drafted a Further Advice on Evidence and sent it to the Director Public Prosecutions. In paragraph 3, under the heading 'Further Investigation' he made a statement that may be alarming. He wrote,

'Since the fibres from the car carpet is the cornerstone of the case for the Crown I shall be grateful if Mr Outteridge and the investigating police officers could be asked to consider how common is this type of carpet (in this respect their attention is drawn to Mrs Tosic's statement to the effect that this came from the remnants of one bought by her for the hallway in 1970)'.

I find this difficult to understand. Is Caswell assuming that the comparison between the fibres that made up the carpet in Stefan's car were identical in every way to the fibres found during the post mortem procedure attached to Lesley Molseed's clothing? No reference is made in any of the media reports of the case, no witness statement, no police report elevates those fibres to being the cornerstone of the prosecution case. Peter Taylor QC did not, as far as can be ascertained, tell the jury in his opening speech that he was relying on this evidence in the way Mr Caswell describes it. Most would regard the written confession as being the Crown's strongest point. The most that could be said about the fibres which were found on Lesley's clothing, was whether they were natural fibres like wool or synthetic like acrylic. Their colours might have appeared to be identical but ultimately the fibres from the clothing and the carpet were not proved to be identical but similar. Any juror who acted by bringing in a verdict of guilty based on this 'cornerstone' would realise after the conviction of Ronald Castree how fundamentally wrong he was. There never was any connection, not even the remotest, with the fibres and the carpet in Stefan's car.

Chapter Fourteen

The Trial

On Wednesday 7 July 1976, Stefan was taken from prison to Leeds Crown Court. He arrived there about 9 am His solicitor and both his defence counsel saw him in the cells. David Waddington QC now suggested, for the first time, that Stefan should enter a plea of guilty to manslaughter, Stefan would not do so. I very much doubt whether the trial judge, Mr Justice Park, would have allowed the prosecution to accept a plea to that lesser charge, and he would have insisted on a trial for murder going ahead.

Stefan did agree to David Waddington's suggestion that a dual defence should be run on his behalf. Stefan did not, in my view, fully understand what he was agreeing to. But he had full confidence in his defence team at that time. Media reports indicate that senior counsel representing Stefan at his successful appeal claimed that Stefan did not authorise the dual defence and were withdrawn in the appeal court on 18 February 1992, when Stephen Sedley QC (later a Lord Justice of Appeal) told the court that he was making no criticism of David Waddington's conduct of the trial. In an editorial dated 23 February 1992, the *Sunday Times* wrote,

'Nor did Stefan's defence do him any favours. Led by David Waddington QC, the former Tory Home Secretary and now leader of the House of Lords, he pleaded manslaughter through diminished responsibility. Stefan never authorised that defence, but his QC went ahead with it anyway. The effect was to undermine Stefan's denials that he was totally innocent and to destroy his alibis, which have since been established as true. Rarely has somebody been so comprehensively let down by the criminal justice system:

falsely accused by the police, vilified by the public, undermined by his own defence, unprotected by the judiciary'.

Those greatly mistaken assertions could not stand unchallenged, and they were not. The next day, on 24 February, David Waddington QC (by this date Lord Waddington QC) issued a press release which reads as follows:

'The Sunday Times yesterday reported as if it were a fact the allegation made at the hearing in the Court of Appeal in December that Mr Kiszko's defence team put forward an alternative plea of manslaughter at his trial without his authority.

As leader of the team at the time I must make it quite clear that there is no truth in that allegation which was not pursued at the resumed hearing before the Court of Appeal last week.

The last thing I would wish to do now is to say anything which might cloud the happiness which last week's Court of Appeal decision will have brought to Mr Kiszko and his family after their appalling ordeal and so I will say no more than that his defence at the trial was properly conducted in accordance with our advice and his instructions on the basis of information available to us at the time.

Had any of us then known of the forensic evidence which persuaded the Court of Appeal that Mr Kiszko could not have committed the crime, the matter would have taken a very different course.'

The last paragraph is a statement of the obvious. Of course if the forensic evidence had been properly examined, evaluated, and understood by the police and prosecuting authorities and then lawfully disclosed to the defence, Stefan would not have been put on trial at all, let alone convicted and imprisoned.

The dual defence put forward was this. The first limb was that Stefan denied the charge of murder completely and maintained that he did not kill Lesley Molseed. That involved putting the prosecution to proof of each and every material allegation relating to her death and that Stefan caused it. Tied in with that Stefan relied on the defence of alibi, namely that on 5 October 1975 he went with his mother and aunt to the local cemetery where flowers were placed on his father's grave, after which they made some small purchases in a shop. Stefan then took his aunt to her home in his car.

The second limb was that if he did kill Lesley Molseed, then at the time of the killing he was suffering from such abnormality of mind as substantially impaired his mental responsibility for his acts and omissions in doing or being a party to the killing. It mattered not whether the abnormality of mind arose from a condition of arrested or retarded development of mind or any inherent causes or was induced by disease or injury. The legal burden of proving diminished responsibility lay upon him. If it was proved by him, on the balance of probabilities, then Stefan would be convicted of manslaughter and not murder. In simple terms, the jury were being asked to consider that on the evidence they should either accept his denial that he killed Lesley and acquit him altogether, or in the alternative they should act upon the second limb of his defence that if they decided that he had killed Lesley they should find him not guilty of murder but guilty of manslaughter, because his mental responsibility was substantially impaired on the grounds set out above.

There are obvious difficulties about combining any other defence with alibi. In 1978 one criminal lawyer wrote, 'Where the defence is personal to the accused, as with diminished responsibility, it is almost impossible to combine it with alibi'. The report goes on to cite paragraph 19. 11 of the Butler Report on Abnormal Offenders (Command Paper, 6244) which says, because of the role of the jury in considering the medical evidence the diminished responsibility provision is not available to the man who has a mental disorder within the terms of the section but denies that he committed the act alleged against him. If his defence fails the sentence must be one of life imprisonment, notwithstanding that evidence of diminished responsibility could be given; he has ruled himself out of psychiatric disposal'. That is what however Stefan's defence team purported to do. Achieving the almost impossible is never easy.

Professor Glanville Williams QC, of the University of Cambridge, probably one of the most widely admired academics in the field of Criminal Law wrote in his *Textbook of Criminal Law* (Sweet & Maxwell, 1978) at page 630 under the heading 'Introducing the issue of 'Diminished' 'The prosecution are not allowed to charge manslaughter by reason of diminished responsibility. The issue only arises if the defendant introduces it or sets up a McNaughten defence' (That is, seeks a verdict of not guilty by reason of insanity). He goes on 'in practice the defence of diminished [responsibility] cannot be set up, for obvious reasons, if the defendant denies that he committed the Act'. From first to last Stefan always denied that he had any act, hand or part in the brutal killing of Lesley Molseed, so in the view of a most distinguished lawyer, he could not rely on the defence of diminished responsibility because he would not admit he was the killer.

There is a contrary view. 18 February 1991 the Lord Chief Justice, Lord Lane, said when allowing Stefan's appeal against conviction 'the case against this man on those facts was extremely strong. Of that there can be no doubt. No doubt the defence team realised that the evidence against their client was of that nature: overwhelming strong, they must have thought. As a consequence they decided to run an alternative defence; an unusual course to take, but in these circumstances no doubt they thought that an unusual course was more than justified. That alternative defence was this, that if the appellant was the killer, he was guilty only of manslaughter by reason of diminished responsibility'. Clearly Lord Lane did not share Professor Glanville William's view that it was not possible to run a defence of alibi with one of diminished responsibility.

Research carried out by Susanne Dell of the University of London Institute of Psychiatry shows that in ten cases in 1976 and 1977 the offence of murder was denied by the accused even though the doctors called by the prosecution accepted diminished responsibility. In a further case the accused denied the offence and the doctors called by the prosecution denied the evidence supported the plea of diminished responsibility. (See The Criminal Law Review 1982 at page 812). So the defence was being run in such cases without objection from some members of the judiciary. As Ms Dell records, in those two years no less than 194 accused raised the defence and in 155 of those the judge and the prosecution accepted the plea of guilt to manslaughter. 39 cases went to trial. Stefan Kiszko's case was one of them.

'Under Section 2 of the Homicide Act 1957 Persons suffering from diminished responsibility.

"(1) Where a person kills or is a party to the killing of another, he shall not be convicted or murder if he was suffering from such abnormality of mind (whether arising from a condition of arrested or retarded development of mind or any inherent causes or induced by disease or injury) as substantially impaired his mental responsibility for his acts and omissions in doing or being a party to the killing.

(2) On a charge of murder, it shall be for the defence to prove that the person charged is by virtue of this section not liable to be convicted of murder.""

That places the legal burden of proof firmly upon the accused. The standard of proof, on the balance of probabilities, is less than any burden placed on the prosecution, where the issue must be proved to the higher standard of 'beyond a reasonable doubt.

The clear and unambiguous wording of Section 2(1) in my view puts it beyond doubt that only in a case where murder is proved against, or admitted by, the accused is the defence of diminished responsibility open to him. The section deals only with the person who kills or is a party to the killing and the jury is asked to consider the accused's mental capacity *when he killed* (Emphasis added). If he did not kill, there is no point in examining whether he suffered from an abnormality of the mind. Apart from his confession to the police, now known to be false and fabricated, Stefan Kiszko always denied that he killed Lesley Molseed. In considering whether he was guilty of murder or manslaughter, the jury that tried Stefan had to consider his capacity to commit murder at the time of the killing. If the abnormality of his mind, resulting from one of the specified causes, substantially impaired his mental responsibility for his conduct, then the verdict would be not guilty of murder but guilty of manslaughter. But Stefan says he was not there in which case this becomes a complete nonsense!

Some legal writers deal with diminished responsibility as a defence to murder in the same way as insanity as a defence to murder (and almost all other criminal offences). I disagree with that. I consider that diminished responsibility is simply a mitigating factor limited in England and Wales, (unlike Scottish Law), to cases only of murder. If accepted by the jury it is not exculpatory but reduces the accused's liability from murder to manslaughter. The only reason for creating and then retaining the offence under Section 1 of the Homicide Act 1957 was the mandatory sentence, first the death penalty and later that of imprisonment for life. The Butler Committee on Mentally Abnormal Offenders which reported in October 1975 thought there was a strong case for giving the trial judge a discretion in passing sentence for murder, allowing him/her to impose a term of imprisonment for life or for a determined number of years, or make a probation or hospital order under the Mental Health legislation, or even impose an absolute discharge. If that happened, with the abolition of the mandatory sentence, then the issue of diminished responsibility would no longer be a relevant factor. Although judicial attitudes to punishment is mainly concerned with retributive and deterrent factors, there is possibly a tendency, as Professor T.B. Smith of Aberdeen University put it, 'to punish the bad and excuse the mad ... In modern times the treatment of the accused and protection of society have been given greater stress, and a sentence of life imprisonment may well be thought justified in some cases of culpable homicide after an original charge of murder has been reduced on grounds of diminished responsibility'. (See the Criminal Law Review 1957 at page 362).

I consider that the central plank of the case for the prosecution was the confession evidence.

In my view even if the jury that tried Stefan convicted him of manslaughter, he would still have been sent to prison for life. For this reason I think David Waddington QC did Stefan Kiszko a great disservice when he adopted this most astonishing and unusual defence tactic in a criminal trial for murder. What the jury made of it can only be imagined, especially if they were drawn from the substantial majority of people listening to the evidence in child murder cases, who so often want to convict immediately after they hear the opening speech for the prosecution.

This begs the question, why did David Waddington QC do it? Even though acting in the best interests of his client, could it have had anything to do with the difficult legal arguments that might arise in the case and did he want to avoid them and keep the central issue simple and clear? Let the jury decide: should they acquit Stefan completely or should they convict him of either murder or manslaughter?

Even if Stefan had accepted Mr Waddington's advice and pleaded guilty to manslaughter, thereby showing deep remorse and sparing the witnesses the ordeal of giving evidence for the prosecution, and that plea had been accepted by the judge and the prosecution and he had been sentenced on that basis, would public revulsion have been so intense concerning the brutal murder of a little girl that the only available and acceptable sentence would be one of (discretionary) life imprisonment. I doubt whether Stefan would ever have been released from prison, because it is difficult, bordering on the impossible, however extensive the campaign or prestigious the campaigners, to overturn successfully a conviction where the plea was one of guilty. That being so, if he had remained a convicted killer on the basis of his own (albeit false) admission, then Ronald Castree would almost certainly never have been caught and convicted of Lesley's murder, simply because someone else was serving time in prison for her killing. What a tragedy that would have been.

Whether a confession, oral or written, is admissible in a criminal trial is a question of law for the judge to decide; it becomes a question of fact for the jury to decide whether that confession is true.

David Waddington QC should, in my view, have sought to exclude the confession evidence at a *voir dire*, that is, at a trial within a trial, held in the absence of the jury, and obtained a ruling on the admissibility of that confession evidence from the trial judge. I believe that if the confession evidence had been excluded as a matter of law, that would have been the end of the case against Stefan. Confession evidence obtained by oppression or in circumstances likely to render it unreliable must be excluded

163

in English law. It was at that time the only instance of the mandatory exclusion of illegally-obtained evidence.

I mean no disrespect to Stefan's memory when I describe him as a mild-mannered, immature, timid and inoffensive 'mother's boy' whose resistance to pressure would be limited in the oppressive atmosphere of a police station. Medical evidence was available that, in August 1975, only four months previously, Stefan had received treatment for acute anaemia. He must have been exhausted in that police station. He was not a tough character; quite the opposite. He was refusing food, drinking only water and constantly being sick. The trial judge, Mr Justice Park, should have been asked by the defence (or arguably even the prosecution) to rule on the admissibility of that confession statement and he never was.

The following is the apparent reason why Waddington did not do so. He decided to ask the jury to accept that, when Stefan confessed to the police on 22 December 1975 to the offences of indecency of 3 October, he simply was not telling the truth. Is this another way of saying, 'Believe me now, I was lying then'? Of course, it was not known at that time that the prosecution would by relying on the evidence as part of their case of three witnesses who, in the course of time, would turn out to be self-confessed liars,and that Stefan had, in fact, confessed to an offence on 3 October 1975 that had not taken place. But it seems that Waddington hoped, and perhaps expected, that he would be able to show in some way, perhaps through cross-examination, that the girls were lying about the indecency incidents and therefore that a confession by Stefan to committing them must be untrue. If that was untrue, it would be argued, then he also lied when he admitted to Lesley's murder, not once but twice, to the police.

I find that approach incomprehensible, and I suspect the jury did too. I still cannot fathom whether the defence were claiming that the indecency incident never happened on 3 October 1975, or whether they did not challenge the fact it happened, but that Stefan Kiszko was not the man involved in it. It was someone else.

All of this must have been most confusing for Stefan, whom I suspect thought he was on trial for murder alone, and not for any other offence.

It took Peter Taylor QC (later appointed Lord Chief Justice of England and Wales) almost three days to open the prosecution case to the judge and jury of seven men and five women. It was a brilliant performance, factual and restrained. He told the jury the victim of the murder was an eleven-year-old schoolgirl Lesley Molseed who had left home at about mid-day to go shopping but never returned. Her body was found three days later on a stretch of moorland. Lesley died as a result of multiple stab wounds. Seminal staining was found on her skirt and underwear. The police began to take interest in Stefan Kiszko following allegations against him of indecent exposure. In the course of several interviews he admitted killing the little girl. He later retracted that confession.

Taylor told the jury that Stefan had been receiving injections for his medical condition and that these had given him a sex drive that had led him to exposing himself to girls and then onto murder. After that outline there followed more detail, beginning with the events of Friday 3 October near the youth club, moving onto the next day, the Saturday, and then up to the purported identification of Stefan on 5 November.

Counsel told the jury that two days after the youth club incident, on the following Sunday Stefan had seen Lesley on her way to the shops, picked her up in his car and driven her to the lay-by on the A672. Then he took her on the moor and stabbed her repeatedly (In fact, as the pathologist noted the child was stabbed with such ferocity that her body was heavily bruised by the impact either of the handle of the knife or the murderer's hand as he delivered blow after blow to here frail and defenceless body).

Taylor continued: the motive for the murder was clearly sexual but it was unusual not merely because of the age of the girl but because there was no sexual interference of her or displacement of her clothing. The little girl was, he claimed, used by the accused as a sex object whom he required to be there while he abused himself. That completed, he killed her and left the scene.

Counsel explained that on 5 November 1975 one of the girls who said she witnessed an incident of indecency was going home from a bonfire and identified Stefan Kiszko as the man who had exposed himself to her. That led to him being questioned by the police. When interviewed on 21 December the accused said in answer to questions that he had no interest in girls and the injections were there to help him. Later the accused admitted to the police, 'This is terrible. Its those damned injections. All this would never have happened'. It was then alleged that Stefan confessed to picking-up Lesley in his car admitting, 'I can't help myself when I have had these injections'.

Counsel then related to the jury that on 22 December Stefan Kiszko had made a written statement under caution in which he admitted killing Lesley but later he made a second written statement retracting that confession. When asked why he was retracting the original statement, Stefan replied that he had only made it so that the police would let him go home.

Prosecuting counsel then recited details of the evening when Stefan was taken to the lay-by on the A672 near where Lesley's body was found and described how Stefan started to shake, holding his hands in a praying position and saying, 'I can hear noises, can't you'. Counsel commented, 'He was obviously very upset'. (In my view it was yet another tactical mistake on the part of David Waddington QC not to seek to exclude this evidence on the ground of prejudice and irrelevance. What was it calculated to prove? How many other alleged killers are or have been taken to a place near the murder scene and had their reactions noted and interpreted? Standing alone that incident had no probative value and was irrelevant to the issue of whether Stezan murdered Lesley Molseed. But was its real purpose and design to link Stefan with the murder scene and invite the jury to draw the conclusion he was returning there and his physical reaction was that of the murderer. We now know it was the reaction of an innocent man).

At the conclusion of that opening speech, which must have made a substantial impression on the jury, Peter Taylor QC then began to call his witnesses to prove beyond reasonable doubt that Stefan killed Lesley.

Because there had been no objection from the defence to the admissibility of the evidence relating to the incident near the youth club on Friday 3 October, the prosecution were able to paint a vivid picture of the rapid descent downwards of the hapless individual receiving medical treatment relating to his sexual development, the indecent exposure to three young girls, Debra Mills, Debbie Brown and Maxine Buckley, finally indulging in filthy and disgusting language and behaviour directed towards Catherine Burke and Pamela Hind, as a prelude to the brutal murder of a child only two days later. The two important witnesses however, Catherine Burke, Pamela Hind, did not appear in court to give live, oral evidence to the jury. Their statements were read out, and were effectively to be treated by the jury in exactly the same way as if they had given evidence in person. The only problem facing the defence was that because they did not challenge this evidence, saying it was either mistaken or untrue, they seemed to admitting that the girls' evidence was accurate and true.

When the forensic scientist, Ronald Outteridge, gave evidence for the prosecution he told the jury of the finding of the semen traces on the victim's underwear. It was not possible to establish a blood grouping. He said that slides had been prepared from the semen staining, but nothing was said at that time about the sample taken from Stefan Kiszko by Dr Tierney. The doctor later gave evidence that he had taken this sample. The entire important issue of whether they matched was not canvassed by anyone. Either before, during or after the trial, the forensic slides that showed the existence of sperm heads were mislaid or lost (Certainly, they went missing after Stefan's conviction and were never recovered). The person who made up the slides was the forensic scientist Peter Guise. He knew of the existence of the sperm heads and it seems that if he made a statement to this effect its significance was not appreciated by anyone who read it. No one said that they realised that Stefan could not have been the person responsible for depositing that semen on the victim's clothing.

Outteridge did however convey to the jury some evidence which they may have regarded as being very relevant and incriminating. He told them that he had found a number of yellow or orange fibres on the inside and outside of Lesley's clothing. One pale yellow fibre was found on Lesley's jumper and vest. A bright yellow fibre was found on her skirt and on her sock there was found an orange rayon one. The police had removed a carpet from the floor of Stefan's car and handed it over to the forensic scientists for examination. It was a piece of stair carpet given to him by his aunt Mrs Tosic at a time subsequent to Lesley's murder. The scientists claimed that the fibres from the clothing were similar to the fibre strands of the carpet. Is there a difference between 'similar to' and actual conclusive proof that they were one and the same? In any event Outteridge concluded that such a finding was entirely consistent with Lesley Molseed having been a passenger in Stefan's car. How heavily that evidence weighed with the jury can now only be a matter of speculation.

The judge fairly put the matter in some perspective when he told the jury that in weighing the value of this evidence they should bear in mind that carpet fibres are not particularly unusual either in shade or variety and very considerable quantities of this carpeting must have been manufactured. As already queried in an earlier chapter, might the jury have been helped if evidence had been given by the manufacturers on behalf of the defence about the volume not merely manufactured but sold, particularly in the Rochdale area? Why did the defence solicitor Albert Wright not have that evidence available as part of the defence preparation for trial?

There seems to have been little serious and forceful challenge to most of the evidence of the witnesses for the prosecution although David Waddington QC put it in cross-examination to the police officers that it was they who had suggested what Stefan had allegedly done to Lesley. The officers claimed that Stefan had told his own story, in his own way. Many experienced detective officers are first class witnesses, practised and accomplished in their versions of the truth, and always well-dressed and of smart appearance. They are not generally easily discredited in cross-examination by the defence.

Detective Constable McFadzen denied the suggestion that he had said at one stage of the interview, 'Let's get this wrapped up and we can all go home for Christmas'. Detective Superintendent Richard Holland told the jury that there was no suggestion by the police that Stefan would be allowed home if he made a statement. He said that Kiszko had asked him to write his statement, claiming, 'He was obviously under stress, but he was not unfit to make a statement'. The statement which commenced at 3.20 pm on Monday 22 December 1975 was then read to the jury. Although the statement was witnessed by 'Superintendent D Wheater' I can find no evidence anywhere that he gave evidence at Stefan's trial. He, like Holland, is now deceased.

That confession statement took two hours 15 minutes to write. It was followed, as we have seen previously, no less than 55 minutes later, by the retraction statement. It was put in evidence by the prosecution as part of their case. Prosecuting counsel then began to adduce the evidence relating to the allegations of indecency on Friday 3 October 1975 at the youth club, moving to the events on the following day, and finally describing what happened on 5 November that led the police to Stefan. There was very little challenge and denial about that evidence. No witness ever said that Stefan was the man in the vicinity of the youth club.

The last prosecution witness to give evidence from the witness box was Dr Edward Tierney. He still did not know the result of the tests on the sample he had obtained from Stefan and how it compared to the seminal staining on the little girl victim's clothes. His evidence was short and to the point.

David Waddington QC then made an opening speech for the defence on Stefan's behalf. He told the jury that Lesley's killing was '… a crime of most unusual circumstances' and he explained why. He said that under the provisions of the Homicide Act 1957 a person who killed another in circumstances which would otherwise amount to murder was guilty of manslaughter if at the time they were suffering from such an abnormality of mind as to substantially impair their responsibility for the unlawful act. He continued:

> '[I]t may well be that at the end of the case that the real choice with which you will be confronted will not be guilty or not guilty of murder, but guilty or not guilty of manslaughter, depending on whether you are satisfied that this man was the killer'.

This I regard as a reflection of the difficulty that he had created by the deliberate conduct of the defence case where in reality the defence wanted to run a response to a charge of murder by admitting manslaughter but could not do so simply because Stefan would not admit that he had killed Lesley. He maintained he was not guilty of either murder or manslaughter. In any event, as I have already said, I consider that if the jury had convicted Stefan of manslaughter, as an act of mercy on their part, the circumstances of the killing were so horrific that the trial judge would have sent him to prison for life anyway

Whatever it was that Waddington was trying to convey to the jury in the words quoted above, some criminal lawyers would contend that before the jury in this or any other case could convict an accused of either murder or manslaughter, it must be proved beyond reasonable doubt by the prosecution that the accused had unlawfully killed the victim. Then, and only then, after such a finding, could the jury consider whether the unlawful killing constituted the offence of murder or the offence of manslaughter and any defence he accused might have to the charge against him.

David Waddington QC went on to tell the jury '[A]t this stage you cannot convict my client of any offence'. This was perfectly true; the jury can indicate at any stage of a trial after the close of the case for the prosecution that they do not wish to hear any further evidence and can find the accused not guilty, but they cannot convict the accused until after all the evidence in the case is before them. If Waddington used the expression 'at this stage' as the press reported, I would regard that as unfortunate, because the jury might have interpreted that as an invitation to convict him of something not then but at a later stage. I consider it would have been better if he had told the jury that the only verdict they could return at that point in time, before the defence evidence, was one of not guilty. If they chose not to do that, there would be other evidence, this time from the defence, closing speeches, and these would be followed by a direction on the law and a summary of the facts from the trial judge.

What is I think clear however is that Waddington was making it obvious to the jury that he was not necessarily seeking an acquittal, but if the jury was satisfied that Stefan Kiszko killed Lesley Molseed then their verdict should be one of guilty of manslaughter and not murder on the ground that the accused was suffering from a disease of the mind that impaired his responsibility for his conduct. It has long been my view that he was totally convinced from the very outset that his client was responsible for the killing of Lesley Molseed. That greatly influenced his conduct of the defence case, so much so indeed as to lead to the comment by the authors the book *Innocents* (at page 224/225) 'He attempted to limit the degree of Stefan's guilt, whereas Stefan denied any guilt. Waddington therefore did little or nothing to establish Kiszko's innocence'.

Defence counsel continued: 'Mr Kiszko's confession was the nub of the prosecution's case' and there was a wealth of evidence to prove it was untrue. He also pointed out that the fibres taken from Lesley's clothing were of a carpet that was sold widely across the country. It was a good point, and might have been even better if the defence had called evidence to prove it.

Stefan decided to give evidence on oath from the witness box in his own defence. He need not have done so He must have found it a most daunting experience at the outset to have the eyes of the trial judge, the 12 members of the jury, the prosecution and defence teams, the press and the public firmly focused upon him, listening to his every word.

There were difficulties at the beginning. Stefan spoke in such a low tone of voice that it was not possible to hear what he was saying and at one stage the trial judge had to tell him to speak up. After that he did so and his confidence, based no doubt on his knowledge of his own innocence of murder, began to grow.

After reciting some detail of his medical history and treatment, how he was ill in July 1975 and received a blood transfusion at Birch Hill Hospital in Rochdale in the August, Stefan told the jury of his transfer to the Manchester Royal Infirmary. He had been diagnosed as being anaemic and having a hormone deficiency for which he was given injections. He was discharged from hospital in September. Stefan told the jury that on the Sunday 5 October, the day that Lesley disappeared, he left home after dinner about 12.45 pm. He took his mother and auntie to Rochdale cemetery to tend his father's grave. Following that he went to a continental grocer's shop where he purchased a loaf of bread and a pot of mustard. Then they drove to a garden centre before returning home. Stefan claimed that during the police interviews he had constantly asked if he could use the telephone to ring his mother, but this was refused. Under the Administrative Directions attached to the Judges' Rules then in force a person detained at a police station had the right to use the telephone to inform a person of the fact and place of his detention. That was provided that no hindrance was likely to be caused to the process of the investigation or the administration of justice by doing so. Such a breach of those rules and directions could provide a ground for challenging the admissibility of any evidence obtained consequent upon that breach. No point was taken by the defence at the trial regarding this apparent breach of the directions as I consider it should have been. Stefan also wanted to telephone his employers at the local tax office on the morning of Monday 22 December, but was not allowed to do so. He described how he was in the same room in the police station from the time of his arrival at 10.30 on the Sunday morning until he went to sleep in a cell in that same building. He left the interview room only to go to the toilet. He was sick on several occasions. He refused the offer to food and hot drink and in fact only drank water. He summed-up his feelings by saying, 'I felt terrible, I wanted to go home to mother'.

Stefan said,

'[D]uring the interrogation when I was telling what was my story they wouldn't believe me so I started to tell them lies and that seemed to please them and the pressure was off so far as I was concerned. I thought the police would check out what I had said and find it was untrue and would then let me go. Akeroyd spoke much louder than he did in the witness box and on that occasion slapped his hand on the table. Sometimes I answered questions quickly, there were some pauses but never for very long but they asked the questions over and over again. McFadzean said "As soon as we get this wrapped up we can all go home for Christmas"'.

Stefan remembered the interview (which was in fact the third) that started at 6.45 pm on the Sunday. He recollected that Superintendent Holland sat in front of him and said, 'I am going to get the fucking truth out of you one way of the other'. As he said that he was poking Stefan on the shoulder with his hand. 'I was feeling very nervous and worried', he added.

Cross-examined by Peter Taylor QC who had an abundance of material upon which to conduct this, there can be no doubt that he gave Stefan a torrid time. His explanation for confessing to murder was short and simple. 'It was not true. I said it to get the police off my back'.

Both his mother and his aunt gave evidence relating to his movements on 5 October. Charlotte Kiszko had originally said she could not recall whether it was the 5 or 12 October that they all went to the cemetery, but after finding a bill relating to the purchase of a tape-recorder on 29 September she was able to recall it was the following Sunday, 3 October. Alfreda Tosic gave evidence to the same effect. Stefan came to her house after dinner on that Sunday, about a quarter past one, and they went to the cemetery where they put water in a vase with flowers. She remembered it was a misty day. She remember the visit to the shop and the purchase of the bread and the mustard. She agreed that she had told the police the previous December she could not then recall whether this happened on the 5 or 12 October. A young woman Miss Baran told the jury she remembered Stefan being in the shop, but was unable to say whether it was the first or second Sunday in October. Her mother made a statement to the same effect. Because she was overseas, that statement was read to the jury with the consent of the prosecution. These defence witnesses were cross-examined gently and courteously by Peter Taylor QC. He did ensure that the jury understood that Stefan's family and his witnesses were, in his view, honest but mistaken in what they recited in evidence to the court.

In his closing speech Taylor accused the defence of trying 'to ride two horses' saying 'I didn't do it but if I did it was because my responsibility was diminished'. He later commented to the jury that these were simply not horses to be ridden together. It is difficult to argue with that proposition which is also a fundamental thread of the arguments I am making in this book that Stefan was placed in an impossible situation. The jury could well have regarded that comment and allied it to the fact that by putting his mental state in issue Stefan's defence team were effectively undermining his defence of alibi.

I can find no evidence that the defence called any witness who could give evidence as to Stefan's good character. His former schoolteachers told the media but not the jury what a generous and gentle child he was, incapable of hurting anyone. His senior colleagues at the Inland Revenue offices in Rochdale were said to be shocked beyond belief that he had been charged with a vicious murder, and would no doubt have said many good things to his advantage if asked to do so.

One of his colleagues told the press he certainly was not a violent man; '[I]f a little bloke had threatened to thump him he would have run a mile'.

The defence did call however as an expert witness a consultant psychiatrist Dr Michael Austin Tarsh. He examined Stefan whilst he was on remand in Armley Gaol. That examination took place on a Sunday which I understand to be 11 July 1976, so some four days after the start of Stefan's trial. Does that mean that the defence were not in possession of any medical evidence which might support the issue of diminished responsibility until 11 July? That seems to be remarkedly late in the day to gather evidence that was so central to the defence case.

There was a second doctor called by the defence: Dr B Anthony Enoch, a consultant physician. He wrote on 12 July 1976 to Stefan's solicitor Albert Wright saying, 'As requested by Mr Philip Clegg I saw and examined Stefan Iwan (sic) Kiszko at Her Majesty's Prison, Armley, Leeds, on the 10th July 1976.' That day of course was a Saturday. So both medical examinations took place after the trial had started the previous Wednesday.

What was the reason Wright did not endeavour, much earlier than July 1976, to obtain medical evidence in a case in which he had been involved since the previous December, was it that it was not until the 59th minute of the 23rd hour that the defence decided to run the issue of diminished responsibility? Why wait so long before gathering that evidence which might not have supported the claim of diminished responsibility in any event? Was it the position that the defence simply did not know whether any medical evidence would support that plea until after the trial had started?

Whatever the answer to this, it raises some fundamental questions that go to the very heart of this case. First, was Stefan told by anyone the purpose of the medical examination by a psychiatrist? Second, did he know and accept that Dr Tarsh was appointed to ascertain whether at the time of the killing Stefan's responsibility for it was diminished by reason of: (1) abnormality of mind, arising from (a) arrested development or (b) inherent causes or (c) disease or injury; and (2) resulting in substantial impairment of mental responsibility for his acts and omissions in doing, or being a party, to the killing? Third, since Stefan would not admit the killing, how could Dr Tarsh obtain evidence of Stefan's state of mind at the time of a killing that he always denied? Fourth, was Stefan told that by running this defence, even if successful, he was likely to be sent to prison for life, and the fact that he had put on record his abnormality of mind would prejudice any future Parole Board in deciding when, if ever, he was likely to be released on licence, on grounds of public safety?

Dr Tarsh told the court that, in his professional opinion, Stefan did not have a normal personality, was unhappy, socially inept and mother-fixated. The witness spoke of Stefan's very close relationship with his father, his widowed mother and her sister, adding 'virtually all his contact that mattered to him had been within his immediate family and had been so all his life'. Dr Tarsh concluded that Stefan had a tragic sort of life, his motor car was like a private temple to him, which really meant an enormous amount to him, that he could drive around, sit in the car, presumably that he could read magazines in it, and take his mother and aunt out to garden centres, which was a very big thing in his life.

As far as he could discover Stefan had never had a friend of either sex, and apart from one of two Ukrainian parties and office parties he had never been anywhere or done anything. 'He had a remarkably restricted, isolated existence'. It was work, it was his immediate family and holidays in Austria until his father died and nothing else. Apart from one kiss exchanged with a girl at an office party he had no contact with young people at all. Physically Stefan was fat, was embarrassed by that, and it was a big thinking topic in his life. Asked if he could find any history of mental illness Dr Tarsh replied no except there might have been a paranoid episode some eight or nine months previously when he thought other cars in his neighbourhood were chasing him around and trying to interfere with and damage his car. For that reason he took a lot of car numbers because car drivers were against him in some way. Dr Tarsh thought that was unlikely to be true and was probably connected with his anaemia. He further thought Stefan's sexual interest seemed to have arisen when he was 17 or 18, these had become largely dormant by the time he was 19. So that for the previous five or six years Stefan had no sexual urges. Dr Tarsh recognised from the very outset the difficulty under which he laboured in his medical examination of Stefan when he said in answer to Waddington's question,

'You know Dr Tarsh that the defendant has denied killing this little girl?'

'I know that, yes'

Waddington went on, 'I think you recognise therefore that you are faced with a difficult problem when you are asked to express an opinion as to his mental state at the date when this girl died?'

Dr Tarsh said, 'Clearly, and I have said in my opinion from the beginning that I have to ask myself if he did this, why might he have done it, and of course the main burden of his conversation with me, it was a long interview — the best part of two hours, *was that he had not done it*' (Emphasis added).

When Dr Tarsh went on to speculate he did, in my view, the most terrible damage to Stefan's case, and it was a massive mistake for the defence to call him as a witness and to rely upon his evidence. Having said that, of course, once the defence had embarked on the course they elected to take, seeking the verdict of guilty of manslaughter and not murder, they were compelled to call some medical evidence to discharge the legal burden of proof that at the time of the killing Stefan's responsibility for that killing was diminished.

Waddington then began a series of questions relating first to the question of motive. He asked Dr Tarsh about the prosecution's suggestion that after picking up the little girl and then indulging in an act of gross indecency towards her Stefan would want to get rid of her as a witness. Waddington wanted to know from this witness whether Professor David Gee's evidence was compatible with that approach. Dr Tarsh thought that extremely unlikely because in his experience the more ferocious the more violent the killing the more aggressive and disproportionate the injury, the more in retrospect you can see the person concerned is either formally mad in the case where sometimes the injuries are bizarre, strange or so angry, so frenzied, so ferocious that they didn't know what they were doing so that where disproportionate violence is used, as it clearly was in this case (and the jury would not have been allowed to forget the horrendous injuries to Lesley Molseed's frail little body) one can say that usually the person concerned has been rejected or insulted something of that sort to the level where they become completely uncontrollable.

The judge asked Dr Tarsh, 'The fact that no attempt had been made to conceal the body, is a factor is it' Dr Tarsh did not think it was a factor, he said '… one would expect if he was merely trying to destroy the evidence, a vicious killing and an attempt to bury the body, and conversely if he had become uncontrollably violent, he would probably then be aghast at seeing what he had done and want to get away as soon as possible'.

Did the jury fully comprehend that Dr Tarsh was not actually describing what had happened, but what he speculated might have happened at the killing scene involving a person he had medically examined but who had denied in his sworn evidence prior to Dr Tarsh being called, as being present at that scene and killing the child.

The doctor was asked by Waddington, 'What was abnormal about his personality?' to which the answer was,

'I think of him as a fat, socially withdrawn, socially inept, mother-fixated, unhappy person. Dim socially, dim not knowing where to put himself, not able to form relationships'.

This was followed by the question: 'And apart from his sexual immaturity of which the Jury have already heard, what about his emotional state?'

Dr Tarsh replied: 'I see him as socially and emotionally immature, perhaps well like a pre-pubertal boy or eleven or 12-years-old rather than like as man of twenty plus'.

If the defence had been in possession of this information before the start of Stefan's trial, as I consider they should have been, would that answer have induced them to challenge the admissibility of Stefan's confession on the ground that the police were unlawfully detaining and continually interrogating for hours an individual with the social and emotional maturity of a boy aged eleven or 12 years?

Dr Tarsh explained to the jury that following the medical treatment Stefan had received for anaemia resulted in weight loss but in addition

Stefan's sex drive would be restored. He was not emotionally prepared for this. The injection of the male sex hormone (which Mr Waddington described as 'fairly large') subsequent to this restoration would have made a disproportionate physical endocrine impression upon Stefan.

David Waddington QC moved on: 'I think you say in your report that if his confession is taken as a guide as to why it might have occurred, it would seem likely his approaching a girl was only possible because he was in a state of sexual excitement?'

Dr Tarsh replied: 'Yes, I think in order to approach a ten-year-old girl he didn't know there must have been this rather unusual combination of personality and physical well-being, if it wasn't there before, and sexual stimulation, profound sexual stimulation, and I think his reduced weight might have had something to do with it'. Tarsh told the jury he did not think that Stefan's personal characteristics were such that he would have been able to control a profound sexual stimulant. For ordinary, young people, and it was being made abundantly clear that Stefan may have been young but he was not ordinary, if given an injection of testosterone it does not make them aggressive or unable to control themselves.

Waddington then asked Dr Tarsh: 'Can you express any opinion on this: assuming he killed do you consider that he would have been fully responsible for what he did?'

Dr Tarsh replied 'no'.

The jury by their verdict rejected this answer.

Things got rapidly worse for Stefan as Dr Tarsh continued his difficult task of speculating as to what happened next. He wondered whether Stefan would have been in a state of 'sexual exultation' otherwise he would not have approached Lesley at all. He said, 'I would speculate that some sort of rejection or fighting was going on, or careless words on behalf of the little girl have been the sort of trigger to promote this frenzied outburst which clearly there was'.

Here Dr Tarsh was combining speculation with established fact — the wounds to the little girl's body were proof positive of the frenzy of the killing. He went on, 'So, if you go back in the story the child has signed its own death warrant by something they said which has triggered … at which point David Waddington QC indulged in some speculation of his own, posing the question 'like, you are a dirty old man?' to which the doctor replied 'something of that sort or "you ought to be locked up" or something like that'.

The judge intervened at this point, asking, 'You say once that happens he would lose the ability to control the act of stabbing?'

Dr Tarsh replied, 'I would think so, yes. I would think he would become completely overcome, completely uncontrollably angry and any weapon that was to hand, well ...'

The judge asked the next question also, 'If I may follow this up, he had a weapon to hand' to which Dr Tarsh replied, 'I know'.

The judge said, 'Why was it there?'

Here again speculation was being married-up to established and proven facts. The trial judge was asking about Stefan, not the unidentified murderer. Did the jury appreciate when the speculation ended and the actual facts emerged, for we know that the police had found the four knives owned by Stefan?

The doctor replied, 'Well his story is that he needed it for making adjustments to his car. He wasn't very forthcoming about these knives when I saw him ... I think he likes knives. I think quite a lot of people do'. Did any of this advance the case for the defence as far as a complete acquittal of the accusation of murder was concerned? Obviously not, for Dr Tarsh was not called to give evidence for that purpose.

The examination-in-chief by Stefan's leading counsel ended with Dr Tarsh confirming that he agreed this was a case of Stefan suffering from an abnormality of mind because of retarded development of personality and retarded development of sexuality, and thus he fell within the special defence afforded by Section 2 of the Homicide Act 1957.

What Stefan made of all this evidence, given in his presence as he sat in the dock in Leeds Crown Court, can only be guessed at. Did he still think, as an innocent man, that he would avoid conviction for a most dreadful murder and walk free and return home to his devoted mother? Or did he appreciate he might be convicted of manslaughter on this evidence, meaning a return to the prison where he was in custody, perhaps for the remainder of his life?

Stefan's ordeal was not over by a very long way. Prosecuting counsel, Peter Taylor QC, closely questioned Dr Tarsh in a way which even the most detached observer would regard as a friendly, non-confrontational, brutally effective way. Taylor made it clear he was not challenging the views that Dr Tarsh had formed about Stefan's responsibility. He simply wanted to explore what he called 'a difficult field'. It was difficult because in other cases in which he was a witness giving evidence regarding diminished responsibility someone has killed and admits the killing, giving the doctor a description of what led up to the killing. Dr Tarsh did not accept, however, that in Stefan's case 'when I say it is a speculative exercise I do not want it to be understood that it is purely speculative and that is all. It is a speculation based on experience and based on trying to put the thing together in a way that makes sense'.

That answer must have pleased Taylor. He went on, 'Can I ask you first of all questions concerned with the likelihood of this man having done the killing, and let us consider after that whether it was diminished or it was not. But does the account that he gives in the (confession) statement, is that consistent with what you might well have expected from his medical background?'

'The account of picking up the child yes,' replied the doctor, '... the account of going hazy and sort of coming round to find he had done something a lot of people tend to suppress, or be amnesiac about, the actual details of the killing, but of course it is much easier where you have a person who tells you something about what precipitated the act, what was said or done to trigger them off into the explosion'.

I find it difficult to reconcile the content of the first part of the answer with the second part. The first part may well, in the view be of some help to explain why there is such little detail in the written confession statement about the act of murder. Was it the inference that Stefan had shut down his powers of recollection of the horror of what he had done?

Counsel pressed the doctor on this so as to reinforce this point. 'But your qualification was that in his case, as you were saying in effect, in many cases when a person gets to the point where he actually describes the killing something inside him in a way erases the memory so that they say well I can't remember that bit I went a bit hazy or I don't know what happened next'.

Dr Tarsh agreed. 'Yes' he replied. The jury of course knew that Lesley's murderer had savagely struck her 12 times. Stefan had said nothing about this so here Taylor sought to explain this lack of detail from Dr Tarsh, namely that Stefan was so overcome by the sheer horror of what he had done that his ability to remember the detail of it simply shut those details out of his memory.

Counsel moved remorselessly on. 'Then you have this problem, you have a young man who has got in some ways the personality of a child … Who is suddenly being physically restored to above par, perhaps?' To both these questions Dr Tarsh replied, 'Yes'.

'And so there is something bursting to get out and he has not really got the social capacity for making relationships with people of his own age?' Again the doctor agreed and said, 'Yes'.

'… in these circumstances' said Taylor, '… is it to be expected that he might go for masturbation rather than sexual intercourse?'

Dr Tarsh said, 'It is to be expected'. The doctor did not finish there. He added, 'It is also to be expected that he would approach children rather than adults'.

If I had been sitting in Stefan Kiszko's place in the dock in that court-room I would have asked myself: 'How is this witness helping my defence with this evidence and is it reinforcing or undermining my denial of a most foul murder?' Is this not an explanation why the murderer chose as his victim a young girl and not an adult female?

Counsel pressed the doctor even further. 'He would have the desire and the mental motivation but well, perhaps I can put it this way, he may have ideas of great sexual feats but not really be able to do that?' It is clear beyond any doubt that Taylor is now referring to Stefan in these questions. These were not hypothetical questions about an unidentified individual, this was an analysis of the behaviour of the man sitting in the dock.

Dr Tarsh said, 'That is right. He would not know how to approach a girl of 17. He wouldn't know how to go about intercourse. He would revert to the act of masturbation that was briefly present according to his evidence, years before.'

The jury was inhaling all this in the utter silence in that courtroom. Here was a defence witness giving an explanation of conduct which earlier, Stefan had failed or refused to give himself.

Peter Taylor QC then moved on to a another point and place in the evidence. It will be remembered that the evidence of Catherine Burke was read to the jury in the absence of any objection from the defence. They accepted that evidence, not knowing it later turned out to be completely untrue. Peter Taylor didn't know that either when he posed this question to Dr Tarsh.

'Can I just recall to you a piece of evidence which we had some days ago and say whether it is consistent. The girl says a man, a man who may have been the accused, was seen exposing himself and as the girl and her friends were running away he shouted something like "When I get you I will stick this right up you". Is that the sort of mental process he might be going through at that time?'

'Exposing certainly', replied Dr Tarsh. 'Aggression of that sort I don't know; possibly'. Pressed further with the question, 'Wasn't so much the verbal aggression but the mental idea of that is what he wanted to do, but couldn't do it?'

Here everything that could be turned to the prosecution's advantage was being done by prosecuting counsel. In reply to the question, Dr Tarsh replied, 'I think it would be consistent'.

Did this evidence help to convince the jury that Stefan's admission to an act of indecent exposure near the youth club on 3 October 1975 was a lie, as the defence contended, and that being so did the jury then go on to accept that he had not lied when he confessed to murder, but had told the police the entire unvarnished truth about how killed the little girl?

If the answer to that is yes, then there would only be one verdict; guilty of murder.

Some advocates would have left it there. But Peter Taylor QC moved in to administer the *coup de grace*. He asked Dr Tarsh about Stefan's very close relationship with his mother and wondered whether it was a quite understandable reaction for him, above everything else, to consider the impact it would have on her if he had done something like this — the terrible murder of a small child. Not surprisingly, Dr Tarsh agreed with that proposition.

'So', said counsel, 'the pressures on him would be even greater to keep that from her?' In other words because he could not admit the killing to his mother, he was maintaining a lie rather than face up to the truth when he entered a plea of not guilty to murder.

Dr Tarsh provided a lengthy answer. In my view it didn't help Stefan in any way.

> 'I would think that if the jury take the view that the actual offence is such that they are certain that he was responsible for this and that the only sensible motivation that he would have in maintaining the opposite would be this relationship with his mother and the shame which he himself would have in telling her that he had done this dreadful thing after all, and perhaps feeling that because she would have to leave Rochdale and so on'.

We know in the light of the conviction of Ronald Castree for the murder of Lesley Molseed that the reason Stefan did not admit that murder was because he was not her killer. It had nothing whatever to do with the close and loving relationship he had with his mother.

Before sitting down on concluding his cross examination Taylor asked Dr Tarsh to look at the last page of Stefan's written confession statement. He suggested that the words 'I got back into my car and drove home. I didn't tell my mother what I had done' supported the view he had just suggested to the doctor. 'One doesn't go home and tell one's mother I have just done this, but the fact he is saying it does that suggest to you that it was his mother and not telling her that was one of the most upper-most things on his mind?' Dr Tarsh agreed that it did.

After confirming in re-examination that nothing in the matters put to him by Taylor in any way altered his opinion that this was a case of diminished responsibility, Dr Trash concluded his evidence and left the witness box.

Dr B Anthony Enoch was the next witness for the defence. In his statement dated 12 July 1976 that formed the basis of that evidence he told the court that, from early childhood, Stefan has suffered from bronchial asthma. In June 1974 he fractured his left ankle. On 5 August 1975 another doctor, Dr Duffy arranged for his admission to Birch Hill Hospital, he had had difficulties breathing and walking. He suffered from severe megaloblastic anaemia. His haemoglobin level was only 20 per cent of what it should be. He was treated for these conditions and also for hypogonadism. This involved the administration of 125 milligrammes of testosterone, but lower than one would expect, so Dr Enoch said, for a man of his physical proportions. Stefan was transferred to the Manchester Royal Infirmary on 18 August, and remained there until his release from hospital on 15 September. According to Dr Enoch, Stefan at this time was extremely ill. This was only some three months before his unlawful detention and interrogation for many hours at the police station. On any view, Stefan must have been quite unwell to explain the stay in hospital from 5 August to 15 September. Yet another reason for challenging the admissibility of the confession evidence before the jury was allowed to know of its existence.

At no stage of his evidence did Dr Enoch state that Stefan was suffering from a disease of a mind and that accordingly his responsibility for murder was diminished for that reason.

Chapter Fifteen

The Trial Judge Sums Up

Mr Justice Park began his summing-up of the evidence to the jury on 20 July 1976. I do not consider that in doing so he was impartial, objective or fair. His view I believe, shared by others, was that Stefan was guilty of killing Lesley Molseed. He summed-up for a conviction. He left it to the jury to decide whether it was a case of murder or manslaughter. At the outset he said that the person responsible for Lesley's death probably owned a car, as Stefan Kiszko did, and secondly, that person had a sexual problem. The next six pages of the transcript of the summing-up are devoted to a description of the medical problems that had beset Stefan and the various treatments and medication he received in respect of them. Few would blame the jury if, on the totality of what the judge told them over those pages, they concluded that the person with a car and a sexual problem was Stefan Kiszko and it followed from that that he was Lesley's killer. The judge did emphasise that it was their decision on the facts of the case that counted, and not his.

The judge directed the jury that Stefan was a young man of perfectly good character who had never come to the notice of the police until November 1975. He had never been questioned by the police about anything up to that time. He failed, however, to direct them on how to approach the evidence in the light of that good character, and that the evidence of such a person carries more weight than that of someone who is not of good character (i.e. someone who has convictions for criminal offences). It also means that a person of good character is a reliable witness who can be believed on oath. He also failed to tell the jury that the accused, being a person of good character was not the type, i.e. has not the propensity, to have committed the offence with which he is

charged. In fact I believe he did the opposite. He reminded the jury of
the evidence of a defence witness, Dr Tarsh, who said that Stefan was
of good average intelligence, of grammar school level. However, his
personality was abnormal, he was fat, socially withdrawn, socially inept,
mother-fixated and an unhappy person not able to form relationships.
He was socially and emotionally immature, like an eleven-or 12-year-old
rather than a man of 24. He suffered from retarded development both of
his personality and his sexuality. He had the personality of a child, so he
did not have the capacity emotionally to cope with the sudden increase
both in his physical well-being and in his sex drive. After a rather detailed
description of the medical treatment Stefan received, the judge posed
the question to the jury:

> '...and it is a matter for you, that on the 5th October this accused was a
> person with a sexual problem. He is also a person with a car...'

By tying the two matters in together with the date of Lesley's abduction and murder, was Mr Justice Park pointing the jury in the direction
of a murderer who owned that car and had that problem? If he was not,
what point was he making?

The jury were told :

> '...the question for you to decide is whether the confession that he killed
> the girl is a true confession. There is no other evidence which establishes
> beyond all reasonable doubt that he was the killer... there is much evidence
> which goes to show that the confession is true, that is if you accept that
> evidence, but that evidence without the confession does no more than raise
> suspicions that he was the killer...You must feel sure of his guilt and that
> means that you must feel sure that the confession is true, and so if you feel
> that there is a doubt about the confession, that it cannot be relied on as a
> true confession, that what is written down may possibly be an invention by
> the defendant or put in his mind by the police officers, as he says, then you
> would acquit him.'

Nowhere in the 92 pages of the summing-up is there any reference by the judge at all about the legality of the detention or the lawfulness of the searches of Stefan's home. On the contrary, the judge invited the jury to consider whether Stefan was the type of person whose resistance would be sapped and who would speak when otherwise he might stay silent under interrogation. He said:

'So, members of the jury, when you are considering the evidence of the police officers about what happened in those interviews bear in mind what the accused has said happened and if you think that the accused's answers were unreliable for the reasons which he gave you then you must attach to those answers such weight, if any, as you think fit. But members of the jury you have seen him in the witness box; you saw him there for a long time, I think a whole day. How did he appear to you to be? Do you think he seemed to be able to look after himself? Do you think he appeared to you to be nervous or not? Do you think he appeared to you to be nervous or under strain although he was being cross-examined with great skill by Mr Taylor on this very serious charge? Do you think he kept his head, do you think he kept cool? Do you think he was able when necessary to parry Mr Taylor's questions? You are allowed to take into consideration when you are weighing his evidence about his state of mind at these interviews the impression he made upon you when he was in the witness box and being cross-examined.'

Was Stefan really in the same position — in unlawful custody, entirely on his own, unable to eat or drink anything except water, vomiting, in the same unchanged clothing day and night as when he gave evidence during the Crown Court trial? That was in open court, in the view of the public and the press and where the conduct of individuals is subject to unrestricted scrutiny; where the manners of the police may be better and their approaches more polite than in a police cell; where Stefan felt he had the support and assistance of his lawyers, David Waddington QC and Philip Clegg, in whom he had great confidence and to whom he was able to look for advice and reassurance, and most importantly of all, the presence in the courtroom of his mother and her sister. And, of course, above all, he had the assurance that he knew that he was innocent and the belief that the innocent go free.

The judge then moved on to the evidence relating to the incidents of alleged indecent exposure. He said,

> 'Now among the least important of these matters from the prosecution point of view is the evidence of all those little girls who say that a man indecently exposed himself to them near the Kingsway School on the evening of the 3rd October and also among those matters is the evidence of Maxine Buckley who says that the accused indecently exposed himself to her and Debra Mills on the 4th October and that she was able to identify him to her mother on bonfire night, the 5th November. *Let me make it clear to you that if this man did expose himself to the little girls on the 3rd October and again on the 4th October, it does not follow that he must have been the killer of a totally different little girl on the 5th October. That evidence of indecent exposure has no bearing on whether or not he is the killer'* (Emphasis supplied).

In that one sentence the trial judge highlighted the absolute folly of David Waddington's tactics of allowing the indecent exposure evidence to go before the jury without argument and without attempting to exclude it on the grounds that it was totally irrelevant. It is a fundamental rule of the law of evidence in criminal cases that in order to be admissible the evidence must be relevant to a fact in issue in the case. If it had no bearing on establishing Stefan as Lesley's killer then it failed the relevance test and should not have been admitted. As noted previously, evidence of misconduct on other occasions is admissible in certain cases, as similar facts evidence, especially if the prosecution can convince the jury 'this is the work of the same man'. But here I consider that if Mr Justice Park had been asked by the prosecution to admit in evidence the allegations of indecency on other occasions in order to prove that Stefan Kiszko murdered Lesley Molseed he would not have done so, simply because, in his own words, that evidence had no bearing on the question of whether or not Stefan was the killer.

The judge did go on, however, to canvas the prosecution approach to the indecency allegations. He put it in one important sentence, that when Stefan admitted, in interview and in writing, these allegations of indecency to be the truth, then 'the prosecution submit that the fact that he was telling the truth about these matters supports their case that he was telling the truth when he said that he killed Lesley and for that reason his confession to the killing can be relied upon as true'.

The judge told the jury if Stefan had been prosecuted for the indecent exposure incident of 3 October he would have been acquitted if the only evidence the prosecution relied upon was that given by the girls at or in the youth club. Stefan's confession to that offence changed everything, but the defence claimed that it was false and that the confession to the murder in the same document was equally false or '...at least very considerable doubt is thrown upon that confession'. Some may fail to see the logic of that approach. Does it follow that if a person confesses to two separate, distinct and unrelated offences in one confession either both are true or both are false? One may be, the other not. In dealing with the incident on the following day, Saturday 4 October 1975, the judge told the jury ,'The evidence of indecent exposure on Saturday the 4th October to Maxine Buckley and Debra Mills is much stronger'. That was quite wrong in my view, for while admissibility of evidence is a question of law for the judge to decide and rule upon, the question of weight of evidence is one of fact, entirely for the jury. The judge may have thought the evidence was much stronger, but that counts for nothing: the question was, did the jury think it was much stronger, and if yes, what then? To what use could they put that conclusion in the light of the direction about it having no bearing on the question of whether or not Stefan was the killer?

When dealing with the evidence of Catherine Burke, aged 16 and Pamela Hind, aged eighteen, he reminded the jury that in the written confession 'it would seem he was admitting indecent exposure to the two girls whose evidence was read to you'. The reason being that the defence did not want the evidence of these two girls to be given in person from the witness box because they accepted the contents of their witness statements and did not wish to challenge or deny that evidence and subject it to cross-examination. That was a major tactical mistake on the part of the David Waddington. As noted previously, both these witnesses later admitted to the police, after Stefan had served 16 years in prison, that their version of the events of the evening of Friday 3 October 1975 relating to the insulting words and behaviour was quite untrue. What they claimed had happened had not. They had made up most of it. Because their evidence was read to the court, the jury was left to consider whether they accepted it as representing the truth. How the defence reconciles their absence from the witness box with the declared tactic of showing that Stefan had lied with regard to their indecency allegations, and had not committed them, defies comprehension. Waddington needed to cross-examine them to test their truthfulness, challenge their account and put it to them in plain unvarnished terms that they were liars. If he had done so at the trial in 1975, would they both have lied on oath as they had lied in their written witness statements? My view is that David Waddington's approach to this evidence was ambivalent. Part of the problem, I think, was that he seemed unable to decide whether the two young women were telling the truth about the indecency incident and were insulted by the behaviour of one man, who was not Stefan Kiszko, or they were lying and the incident never happened at all. Because of the uncertainty of his approach one wonders why he did not cross-examine the police on their failure to hold identification parades to ascertain whether Ms Burke and Ms Hind could identify the man they claimed they saw and who spoke those insulting and threatening words to them before Stefan Kiszko confessed to a murder he did not commit.

This was in essence a simple case that could have been confined to one single issue: could the prosecution prove that Stefan Kiszko had voluntarily confessed to killing Lesley Molseed and was that confession proved by the prosecution to be true? As it was, the mistaken tactics adopted by the defence allowed the introduction of evidence of allegations of indecency that was so greatly prejudicial to Stefan's case, but proved nothing in relation to the murder. Far too much of the trial was taken up with the evidence of the children and young women, and this was reflected in the summing-up, where the judge devoted a great deal of his direction to that evidence. He even failed to notice how Superintendent Holland misled Stefan Kiszko when he told him that each of the girls had identified him on bonfire night (5 November) as being responsible for the indecent exposure on 4 October. In fact, it was only 12-year-old Maxine Buckley who had done so. I regard it as a very serious failing for a police officer to be allowed to go unchallenged in his evidence where it is clear that he misled the defendant, accidently or otherwise, and then for the trial judge to repeat that misleading evidence in directing the jury as if that evidence was the truth. Moreover, the judge apparently failed to even contemplate the possibility that this young girl might have been mistaken in her visual identification of a man she had seen, in difficult and distressing circumstances, a month before. It was on that occasion in October that she was with another girl, 12-yearold Debra Mills. On 5 November she was with a young boy, 11-year-old Michael Rigby. He never made any allegation of indecency against anyone on that day or any other time.

I think, however, that the most devastating point made in the summing-up that told against Stefan, and which in my view very probably turned the majority of the jury against him, was the rhetorical question posed by Mr Justice Park when he said, after describing how the forensic scientist Ronald Outteridge found seminal stains in the crutch region of the little girl's knickers and over parts in the back and the front of her skirt, 'Well how did the accused know that seminal stains would be found there unless he in fact had been responsible for the creation of those stains?' We now know that Stefan was not responsible for those seminal stains, and he could not have known about them unless he was told by someone else. Was that person Superintendent Holland? Or could it have been Detective Sergeant Akeroyd? The judge told the jury, 'All the officers deny that anything to that effect was said to him during those interviews'. I believe that one, Holland, should in the interests of justice have been investigated with a view to prosecution for providing information about the stains to an innocent man, and then lying on oath that he had not done so (Furthermore, we know that the police had evidence at the time of the trial that conclusively proved he was not responsible. That was successfully concealed for 16 years).

The judge started putting the defence case at page 76 of the transcript of the summing-up and most of the remaining 13 pages are devoted to the defence evidence, including that of Stefan himself. I regard it as particularly unfortunate that Mr Justice Park should have told the jury when he was dealing with the issue of diminished responsibility:

'This was a crime against an innocent defenceless child of the utmost brutality and in the course of his evidence in the witness box the defendant may have revealed himself to you as untruthful, dishonest, perhaps cunning, yet there is no question at all that up to the time of his treatment in hospital he, being a man in name only, stunted physically and in the development of his personality, he had never done anything wrong. He was a law-abiding, inoffensive member of the public holding down this job in the Tax Office, dutifully taking his mother and aunt out in the car, and that appears to have been his only recreation. He had never shown the slightest violence towards any living creature and then on the 5th October, two days after receiving this second injection, he abducts and kills this child in a frenzy.'

Is this not an astonishing descent by the trial judge into the area of fact? Was it not for the jury to decide whether Stefan Kiszko had abducted and killed the child in a frenzy? Of course, Mr Justice Park was only following the lead set by Stefan's own defence counsel, whose tactical approach was to run the defence of alibi and diminished responsibility at the same time. The question of whether Stefan's responsibility for the murder was impaired and diminished did not arise until it was proved or he admitted that he had killed Lesley Molseed.

The judge's summing-up of the law and the facts was almost complete at the end of that day, Tuesday 20 July 1976. The case was adjourned until the next day. On the Wednesday morning, the judge, anxious no doubt to help the jury with what he regarded as the core issue in the case, told them,

'I have to ask you to reach a unanimous verdict in this case and that really means this: first, you must decide whether the Crown have proved so that you feel sure that the accused killed the girl. If you reach a unanimous decision that that case has not been proved then of course you will acquit him, but if you unanimously reach the decision that he did kill the girl then you must consider the second matter, and you must decide whether on the balance of probabilities the accused at the time of the killing was suffering from diminished responsibility, and if you are unanimously of the opinion that he was suffering in that way your verdict will be not guilty of murder but guilty of manslaughter. However, if you are unanimous that he killed the girl but not unanimous that he was suffering from diminished responsibility at the time, then your verdict would be guilty of murder.'

He then went on to quite properly tell the jury that they must strive to reach a unanimous verdict and that it was only after some considerable time if they could not so agree that they would be brought back into court and be given a further direction about a majority verdict.

Leading counsel for the prosecution, Peter Taylor QC, had no quarrel with the first part, but he did disagree with the direction on diminished responsibility and in the presence of the jury he told Mr Justice Park so. He said,

'...I think your Lordship may have had a slip of the tongue. My Lord, there is one phrase, if I may with respect mention it; your Lordship said if the jury were unanimous that the accused had killed the girl but were not unanimous that he was suffering from diminished responsibility they should convict him of murder.'

The judge replied, 'Yes.' I think he was correct and Taylor was wrong. If Stefan had not persuaded all members of the jury that he was suffering from diminished responsibility, that is, he had not discharged the legal burden of proof placed upon him by the Homicide Act 1957 to the required standard, on a balance of probabilities, accordingly the verdict of the jury must be one of guilty of murder.

Peter Taylor said, 'My Lord, with respect I would have thought your Lordship meant were unanimous that he was not of diminished responsibility rather than they were not unanimous that he was.'

The judge said, 'Mr Waddington, do you prefer me to put it that way?' to which leading defence counsel replied, 'I was not going to say anything my Lord, but I suppose that is technically correct.' Even at the 59th minute of the 23rd hour Waddington chose not to enter into a discussion on the law, where it might have been preferable to turn up the wording of the legislation and help the jury fully understand his client's case.

The judge then said to the jury: 'Well, members of the jury; you have heard what Mr Taylor says, look at it in that way'. Some may regard that observation as completely unhelpful and devoid of any real meaning.

The jury retired to consider their verdict. Perhaps not surprisingly, they returned shortly after the mid-day adjournment and asked for further directions from Mr Justice Park on the law relating to diminished responsibility. They went as far as asking for a legal textbook on that subject. That was refused, but the judge did tell the jury once again his full direction on that issue.

On 21 July 1976, after a retirement of five hours and 35 minutes, the jury convicted Stefan of the murder of Lesley Molseed by a majority of ten to two. Did those who formed the majority ever wonder how they got it so wrong? What must have been their reaction when, many years later, Ronald Castree was identified and convicted of that little girl's murder? Did they blame themselves or others for their wrongful verdict?

Mr Justice Park sentenced Stefan to life imprisonment, the mandatory sentence for murder. The nightmare that began on 21 December 1975 was to last for 16 long years. Stefan had been betrayed by the criminal justice system, falsely accused by the police — who convinced themselves that he was a murderer — utterly let down by his own solicitor and leading defence counsel, and totally unprotected by the trial judge, who I believe ought to have insisted on ruling on the admissibility of the similar facts evidence before the prosecution were allowed to introduce it. He should also have questioned the legality of Stefan's detention at the police station, even if the defence team had failed or refused to do so.

Chapter Sixteen

The First Appeal Against Conviction

Stefan decided to appeal against his conviction and sentence. He received the first draft of the application for leave to appeal on 13 August 1976. He was at that time prisoner number 688837 detained in Armley Gaol, Leeds. He asked for an extension of time allowed to lodge the notice of the application and he gave the reason for doing so: 'extension requested as grounds of appeal only just received from counsel'.

Stefan then added two pages of script. 'Please note that information to hand is that one of the women jurors (of which there were five in this trial) had been in a public bar the night before the end of the defence case, and she had overheard a policeman state to another man, who had reported the matter, that Mr Kiszko's counsel had been 'trying to get him to plead guilty'. Was this the first time that Stefan was told about the juror incident, when he received the first draft of the grounds of appeal? Did he fully understand the importance to be attached to that incident? We now know from his later statement that if he, had been told of it at the time of the incident, he would have asked for a new trial. He never had the opportunity to do so.

The note continues:

'The consequences were the judge asked Counsel into his chambers where he made it quite plain that he was not anxious to stop the case and start again with a fresh jury, but subject to any objection, intended to carry on with the present jury, including the woman in question'.

This information could only have originated from someone who was there and there is quite a difference in the language used here and the version put before the appeal court. In this version, Mr Justice Park had indicated in strong terms that he wanted to go on with the case, even retaining the contaminated woman juror. He intended to carry on with the case and did so. There were no objections from anyone in that room to that course of action. I disagree with Lord Justice Bridge's view on this. There should have been objections in the strongest possible terms to the trial judge's approach to this problem.

The mystery deepens in Stefan's next paragraph.

'Both Mr Waddington and Mr Clegg for the Defence were taken by surprise, as they had previously been told the woman had been taken ill, and in any event they would have to proceed without this woman juror's attendance. That was not the case'.

This begs the question: How did Stefan know about the surprise caused to counsel? Will we ever know if they both were told that the woman juror had been taken ill, and who told them, causing them to be surprised? When if ever did they discover the truth, not that she was ill, but that her continuance on the jury had been compromised? Did someone initially lie to defence counsel in order to suppress the truth about the incident in the bar?

Stefan then wrote:

'Without the opportunity for consultation Mr Waddington had to take a snap decision and decided to proceed in the course proposed by the learned Judge'.

In fact Waddington did not have to take a snap decision. If he had asked the judge for time to consult his client, as I consider he should have done, that request could not have been refused. In my view Mr Justice Park should not have proposed any course of action at all regarding the continuance of the trial, but simply asked counsel on both sides for their submissions on the facts and the law as they knew them at that time.

In the next paragraph Stefan noted:

'I regret to say that I had no knowledge of this having taken place, until I actually received Counsel's notes on appeal yesterday the 13th August 76. In any event Counsel for the Defence note in their advice on appeal that the correct decision was taken in the circumstances of my behalf'.

It seems a matter of regret that there is no trace anywhere of a copy of that advice on appeal. That might help to resolve the meaning of this last sentence—surely defence counsel could not have decided in August 1976 that their decision was correct, and then proceeded to draft grounds of appeal in November 1976 claiming that in doing what they did, or more accurately not doing what they should have done, Stefan's trial had been prejudiced and in effect he had been deprived of a fair trial.

Stefan went on to write:

'From perusal through these comments I do not feel strongly about this having taken place (but evidently it may have also been one of the facts which swayed the jury's decision one way or the other) of course it does not please me, and I merely feel that it is a point that should be pointed out to the criminal division in making this appeal, and furthermore Mr Waddington QC and Mr Philip Clegg, Defence Barristers with their instructing solicitor Mr Albert Wright, trying their utmost best to lead a line of defence in the Law Courts of "British Justice"…I wish it to be known that I would like Mr David Waddington QC and Mr Philip Clegg with their instructing solicitor Mr Albert Wright to represent me for the purpose of this appeal'.

Stefan signed Form 20. It was lodged in the Criminal Appeals Office in London on 19 August 1976.

On 27 April 1977 the office of the Director of Public Prosecutions received a letter from the Criminal Appeal Office regarding Stefan's application for leave to appeal against conviction and accordingly briefed Matthew Caswell to advise on the appeal. Amongst the eight items they sent him was included at No. 8 'Papers re jury incident'. I take that to mean the notes prepared by the chief clerk at Leeds Crown Court relating to how he dealt with the incident without the intervention of the trial judge. In a handwritten note, Caswell advised 'I consider that as regards the 'Juror' point raised in the grounds of appeal it would be prudent to obtain the trial Judge's notes, if any, concerning this point. I do not consider that in relation to this point it would be either fruitful or proper for the purpose of the appeal to try to carry out an investigation as to what may or may not have been said or heard out of court and by whom'. I disagree. Why not find out what actually happened in the bar on that Saturday night and what was said by one to another. It would have been in the interests of justice and truth if there had been a full and transparent inquiry into the circumstances that led to the contamination of the juror but rather than do that I consider efforts were made, particularly in the report of the case in the Criminal Appeal Reports, during and after the hearing of the appeal, to suppress that truth.

Stefan's amended grounds of appeal were finally drafted in a document dated 19 November 1976 by junior defence counsel, Philip Clegg and served upon the court. That was in accordance with the usual practice. It would be done in consultation with leading counsel. On any view it is a most extraordinary document, not least because it disclosed material that was known only to a few people at Leeds Crown Court on Monday 19 July 1976, and later those gathered together in the trial judge's room, during the currency of Stefan's trial, on Tuesday 20 July, 1976.

Ground 1A stated that

'[D]uring the Appellant's trial all Counsel in the case were invited into the learned Judge's room and there informed that the previous evening a woman member of the jury had overheard a remark in a Leeds public house made by a policeman, who was not a witness in the case to a town hall official. The effect of the said remark was that the Appellant's Counsel had been trying to get him to plead Guilty. The said incident had been reported to the Court by the said official.'

Ground 1B goes on 'the learned Judge intimated that as the trial was now at an advanced stage, subject to the approval of Counsel, he did not intend to discharge the jury but to allow the trial to continue with all twelve jurors.'

Ground 1C notes 'Counsel approved the said course of action without taking the Appellant's instructions and consequently the Appellant was deprived of the opportunity of insisting that representations be made on his behalf that the jury should be discharged or that the trial should continue with only eleven jurors in accordance with the provisions of Section 16 of the Juries Act 1974.' Ground 1D claimed, 'In the premises it will be contented that the Appellant's trial may have been prejudiced'. The prelude to all four grounds made it clear what the defence were actually claiming. 'It will be contended that the matters ... Numbered 1A to D inclusive constituted a material irregularity within the meaning of Section 2(1)(c) of the Criminal Appeal Act 1968.

Under section 13 of the Juries Act 1974 a trial judge has a discretion to allow the jury to separate both for the luncheon and overnight adjournments. It follows from this that the jurors will have the opportunity, if they so wish, to speak about the case with others not connected to it. To do so would be highly improper. The then Lord Chief Justice, Lord Widgery, stated in 1973,

> 'It is important in all criminal cases that the judge should on the first occasion when the jury separate warn them not to talk about the case with those who are not one of their number. If he does that and brings that home to them, then it is to be assumed that they will follow the warning and only if it can be shown that they have misbehaved themselves does the opportunity of an application [for discharge arise].'

Lord Widgery's direction was that the trial judge was required to make it abundantly clear that no juror was to talk to anyone outside their number about the case, and they should not allow anyone to talk to them about the case either.

It is a matter of record that allegations of misconduct against a juror mostly involved them speaking to a prosecution witness of members of the public about the case.

Apart from a very limited number of people, no-one knew that on the night of Saturday 17 July 1976 one of the women on the jury spoke about the case to a member of the public—who just happened to be a member of the police prosecutions department involved in the case. And he spoke to her. Assuming the judge had properly warned the jury in accordance with Lord Widgery's caveat that they should not speak to anyone but their fellow jurors about the case, and there is no reason to believe he did not give that warning, that is exactly what she did.

If she had been told not to speak to anyone about the case, or let anyone speak to her, why did Mr Justice Park not call upon the woman juror to explain exactly why she had disregarded his instruction? Why did the defence themselves fail to ask that question of that juror in court even when the trial judge chose not to do so? Was the defence not interested in what influence this woman might have had, what arguments she might have used, in the jury's deliberations?

In the Grounds of Appeal were the defence admitting that effectively they had deprived their client of a fair trial? First, by not telling Stefan of the juror incident at all and taking his full instructions on what he wished to do, and further by allowing the woman juror with her prejudicial knowledge to continue to serve on the jury. She was not even told by anyone that she should not communicate that highly sensitive and prejudicial statement to her fellow jurors.

No-one seems to have asked the question at any stage: how, when and where did the police prosecuting solicitor know about the advice given by defence counsel to his client? Why was he not sent for by the trial judge and asked to explain this? If he had been, would not the full extent of the conversation in the bar have come to light? Was that something someone wished to avoid?

The record shows that the closing speeches by counsel were concluded on Friday 16 July 1976. The case was adjourned until the following Monday, 19 July for the judge to sum-up the case to the jury. In the event because of industrial action by prison officers, no prisoner in custody was taken to court. The court did not sit on that day.

What happened on the Monday morning is recorded in a note made by the chief clerk of Leeds Crown Court and further in a statement made by him at the request of the defence solicitors on 3 December 1976. Headed 'Note for the Judge' it gives the name of the case and the name of the woman juror involved in the incident. It goes on:

'My Lord. It has been brought to my attention by [name withheld], a Solicitor employed by Leeds County Council, that he was in a bar on Saturday last when he met the above named juror with whom he is acquainted. He was not aware, at that time, that she was serving on a jury. They were joined subsequently by a Police Officer acquaintance of [name withheld] and during later conversation the Police Officer mentioned to [name withheld] in the hearing of [name withheld] that Counsel for Kiszko had been trying to get Kiszko to plead Guilty. [Name withheld] then disclosed that she was serving on the Kiszko jury and [name withheld] properly decided that the matter should be mentioned to the Court.'

It is obvious from this that an unauthorised person had spoken about the case to the juror, and she in turn had spoken to him or her.

On the original note the words 'police officer' in lines 6 and 7 above appears as 'X' and later on the same page of the note the 'X' appears again, followed by the words 'police prosecuting solicitor'. The chief clerk explained this when writing to the registrar at the Criminal Appeal Office in London on 27 July 1977. He wrote 'reference your letter of 27 July, I enclose the original note for the Judge prepared by me on the 19th July 1976, upon which the Judge endorsed the outcome of a discussion in his room with Prosecuting and Defence Counsel. As will be seen the reference in the note to "Police Officer" should read "Police Prosecuting Solicitor", this amendment having been made prior to the discussion taking place. No other note was made of the discussion between the Judge and Counsel'.

What clearly happened was this. The chief clerk was told by the Leeds County Council solicitor at the Crown Court on the morning of Monday 19 July 1976 about the highly prejudicial conversation in the bar the previous Saturday evening. The clerk had rightly decided that the matter needed urgent attention. In the absence of the trial judge he dealt with it himself. That decision cannot be criticised, but if the judge had been sitting on that Monday, does anyone doubt that he would have, and should have, dealt with the matter himself? There was however, in my view, nothing to preclude the judge from exploring the matter fully, either in his room or in court sitting *in camera* in the absence of the media when the court reconvened on the Tuesday morning. Was he not interested in how the police prosecuting solicitor acquired the information about counsel's advice to his client, given in confidence and subject to professional legal privilege, as the solicitor must have known, and why was he indulging in idle gossip in a public place while the trial was still going on? Moreover it is clear that the suggestion that the woman member of the jury had overheard a remark in the Leeds public house, as set out in Ground 1A above may not be entirely accurate if it conveys the impression that she just chanced to hear accidently, while eavesdropping, something said by one person to another as she sat or stood nearby. In fact she was in conversation with a man friend in that bar, they were joined by a prosecuting solicitor who knew that man. Were they formally introduced to each other when the second man arrived? Did the solicitor just idly throw out the remark about defence counsel; that he had been trying to get Stefan to plead guilty, or were other words spoken about the case as well? If there were, what were they? Are we being asked to believe that no sooner did the second man join the couple in the bar than he waded into the conversation by mentioning counsel's advice to his client? Whatever the answer, the information was given directly to her, it was not something simply said in her presence as she stood or sat nearby. This was not a case of 'eavesdropping' by an isolated bystander as some would have us believe it was.

It also begs this question: Did anyone tell the woman juror that the solicitor worked in the police prosecutions department and was therefore unlikely to be inaccurate or untruthful in what he was telling his friend and the woman juror? It is also not right to claim that the incident took place 'the previous evening' — it had taken place on the previous Saturday. Was that a genuine error or was it a deception calculated to ensure that the story of the 'eavesdropping' isolated bystander was believed in the public arena?

What effect the provision of this information had upon the woman juror cannot now be established. That should have been looked into at the time. She should have been asked whether it would affect her view of the evidence she had heard and the verdict she was likely to deliver. It should also be remembered that on the previous Friday the woman juror had listened to David Waddington QC inviting her and the eleven other jury members with whom she sat to acquit Stefan Kiszko of the charge of murder. Yet here she was being told on the Saturday evening that the very same person had advised Stefan to plead guilty. Why should she acquit him in such circumstances? If Stefan was entirely innocent, why would he be advised by his counsel, who argued his innocence, tried to get him to plead guilty? How many members of the jury knew of that conversation in the bar? All of them, or just one? That one woman juror had not been directed by anyone not to disclose the information she had gathered there, and it might seem unlikely that she kept it to herself. However that may be when Waddington in the course of his closing speech to the jury asked them to acquit his client did at least one of them, the woman, if not the entire jury, to whom she may have told everything she knew in the jury retiring room when they were asked to consider their verdict, look at him and ask themselves amongst others the questions: (i) Does a barrister advise a client to plead guilty if he is innocent?; (ii) Would a barrister who advises his client to plead guilty do so because he disbelieves his own client's plea of not guilty?; (iii) Was the barrister in possession of some information not in evidence before the jury and about which they knew nothing, that persuades the barrister that his client ought to plead guilty?; (iv) Did the woman juror listen to the defence closing speech, hear the invitation to acquit Stefan, and then ask herself, 'Why would I do that when I know that you advised him to plead guilty?' Most telling of all, did that juror, and the jury, decide the case on evidence disclosed on a Saturday night, in the absence of the accused and his lawyers, not on oath and not subjected to challenge in cross-examination?

The note prepared by the chief clerk for the trial judge is endorsed in the judge's handwriting with this brief observation. 'This was shown both to Taylor QC (pros) and Waddington QC (def) and discussed with me in my private room. All agreed that no action was necessary'. He initialled his note and dated it, 20 July 76.

I find it incomprehensible that the matter should have been disposed of in this way. Does the notice of appeal drafted by Philip Clegg of counsel seem to support that view? Not telling Stefan about the juror incident did deprive him of the chance to make representations about discharging that woman juror. Why was he not told? It does appear that for perfectly understandable reasons the chief clerk tried to resolve the problem, in so far as he could, at the first available opportunity, and the probability was that no-one concerned in the trial was at court on Monday 19 July, and that almost certainly included all members of the jury. What would be the point of anyone attending the trial on the Monday when it was known that the industrial action meant that the prison officers would not bring Stefan to court on that day?

Be that as it may, was not the first and most important point for the defence to establish, once they learned of the conversation in the bar, was whether the juror had informed any or all of the remaining 12 jurors what she had been told by the police prosecuting solicitor the previous Saturday evening. Certainly no-one told her at any time that she should not do so. If she had done so, that was the end of the case against Stefan Kiszko. Seemingly, any possible chance he had of being found not guilty disappeared at that moment. I cannot see any jury acquitting a defendant charged with the brutal killing of a little girl when they realised that the defence barrister who urged them to acquit his client had previously tried to get him to admit the crime and plead guilty to it.

If the woman juror had not told the other jurors, and I consider it was the responsibility of the trial judge to establish whether she had, consideration could have been given to continuing the trial with eleven jurors. That still left unresolved the question whether Stefan Kiszko had the right to know the circumstances that might have led to that juror being discharged from continuing to serve on the jury. It would then have been for him to decide, after seeking advice from his counsel, whether to continue with the case with the remaining eleven jurors. Because this did not happen one if bound to ask: Is there any reason to believe, now, at the time of writing, that she did not tell her fellow jurors exactly what she had been told in the Leeds bar on that Saturday evening? Why should she not share that information with others? If the remaining eleven jurors knew of that advice on the Tuesday morning, 20 July, would that affect the weight they would give to David Waddington's closing speech to the jury seeking an acquittal when they retired to consider their verdict?

Finally, one is bound to ask: Had the woman juror resiled from her oath administered when she was empanelled on the jury on the first day of the trial, when she swore to try the case on the evidence she heard and return a true verdict in accordance with that evidence? According to page 10 of Stefan's draft statement he said, 'It was not until sometime after my conviction that I found out that a juror had come forward and suggested that she had heard that my defence counsel had been trying to get me to plead guilty, and despite this had been allowed to remain on the jury. Had I known about this at the time, I would have asked for a re-trial'. In fact he never had the chance to do so, and for that Waddington must bear full responsibility.

On 25 May 1978, Stefan's application for leave to appeal against his conviction for murder was heard in the Appeal Court. He was represented by the same two counsel who had appeared at the trial. Might it have been better if David Waddington had returned the brief for the hearing of the appeal since the grounds of appeal involved him doing what counsel should never do, that is giving evidence in the case in which he is concerned? He effectively had to give evidence why he had not told Stefan about the juror incident, and had not sought his instructions on what to do in relation to that. It is almost without precedent for a barrister to argue that his conduct of the case was not such that his client's case was unduly prejudiced. Lord Justice Bridge, dealt briskly with that. He said,

> 'At a late stage in the trial of this applicant, it was very properly brought to the notice of the learned judge that a lady member of the jury during one of the luncheon adjournments' had been in a public house, where she had overheard a gentleman who was employed in the Leeds Borough Council's Prosecuting Solicitors Department telling someone else, who happened to be a council official, that the applicant had been advised by his own counsel that he ought to plead guilty. That information being before the trial judge, he very properly called counsel on both sides into his room, and indicated his view there was no reason why the trial should not proceed, indeed there was no reason why the lady juror herself should be discharged, but he invited the views of counsel on both sides. No doubt his view was based

on the self-evident proposition that in these circumstances any intelligent juror would have realised that the advice that the applicant had been given was to plead guilty to manslaughter on the ground of diminished responsibility, for in truth the invitation to the jury to acquit him altogether was from the outset a perfectly hopeless prospect'.

Pausing there in the narrative, it is difficult to see why Lord Justice Bridge seemed not to know that the juror incident did not take place during a luncheon adjournment but on a Saturday evening. The chief clerk's note set out above was sent to the appeal court on 29 July 1977 with an accompanying letter stating that fact. Nor did the juror overhear the statement—it was addressed to her and to her male friend in the bar. Did Lord Justice Bridge deliberately misstate these facts in order to conceal the truth that this was not a brief, accidental bit of eavesdropping, but a social occasion when three people were engaged in conversation the details of which were never fully and properly investigated and accordingly might lead to the quashing of the conviction?

As for the proposition that any intelligent juror would have realised that Stefan had been advised to plead guilty to manslaughter, that was pure speculation on the part of Lord Justice Bridge, and is not based on a shred of evidence. As far as the jury knew, Stefan was charged with murder and nothing else. He never offered to the court or to the prosecution a plea of guilty to manslaughter as an alternative to murder for one obvious reason. He had not murdered eleven-year-old Lesley Molseed.

Surely the simple issue was that once the woman juror heard of the advice in connection with a guilty plea, which we know from Stefan Kiszko himself he was given by David Waddington not once, but twice, to plead guilty, she should have been discharged from serving any longer upon that jury. If she had passed on that information to the others, they also should have been discharged from serving as well and a new trial in front of another jury should have taken place. The ultimate decision whether the judge should be asked to discharge one juror or the entire jury on the ground of contaminated evidence was vested in Stefan Kiszko. He was not allowed to make it simply because he was not given the opportunity to do so, and no speculative meandering on the part of Lord Justice Bridge alters that fact. He continued:

'At all events what happened was that Mr Waddington and Mr Clegg, who appeared at the trial, as they have appeared for the applicant in this Court, considered the matter. No doubt they took the view, as Mr Waddington was candidly accepting here today, that the trial was going well for the applicant, that a verdict of manslaughter was confidently to be anticipated, and that it would be against his best interests to raise any objection to the trial continuing with the jury then impanelled, and so it continued'.

This means, and was intended to mean, that acting in the best interests of a man who protested his innocence his counsel decided that the case should continue because they anticipated it had gone so well that Stefan Kiszko would be convicted not of murder, but of manslaughter. It would be of interest to discover the evidence upon which that conclusion was based. Although it is accepted that Stefan was convicted by a majority of ten to two, the fact remains that the true killer of Lesley Molseed, Ronald Castree, was not in the dock at Leeds Crown Court on 21 July 1976, and even Stefan's conviction for manslaughter would have been an appalling miscarriage of justice. The fact that two juror disagreed with the other ten did not mean they were holding out for an acquittal. They might have wished to return a verdict of not guilty of murder but guilty of manslaughter.

The judgment continued:

'At all events counsel for the defence gave their consent; perhaps more accurately, raised no objection to the trial continuing before the jury then constituted and so it continued. The objection is now raised that that was a material irregularity in the conduct of the proceedings because, it is said, the applicant was not personally consulted as to his wishes, and it is suggested that the matter was not within the authority of counsel to deal with, in the way in which it was dealt with without specifically obtaining his client's instructions and consent to that course of action. That is a submission which we have no hesitation in rejecting. It seems to us perfectly clear that the decision whether or not the trial should proceed before the jury as then constituted, or whether to invite the judge to discharge the jury, or to discharge the single juror who heard about the advice which the defendant received, was a matter fairly and squarely within the authority of counsel to deal with as he thought best in his client's interests, without consulting his client about the matter. There is nothing in that first point'.

I disagree that this statement is acceptable as representing the duty of counsel in a criminal case when something or someone contaminates a member of the jury during a trial. The client must be consulted and allowed to decide, after receiving advice, whether he or she wishes any steps to be taken in the light of that contamination.

The next point that Lord Justice Bridge dealt with related to the defence ground of appeal drafted by Philip Clegg namely:

'The learned Judge, at the conclusion of the summing up, misdirected the Jury by instructing them that their verdict would be one of guilty of murder if they were:

1. Unanimous in their decision that the Appellant had killed the deceased girl, but,

2. Were not unanimous that the Appellant was suffering from diminished responsibility at the material time'.

Philip Clegg added in this ground of appeal:

'[A]lthough the said misdirection was pointed-out at once, and although he accepted the criticism, the learned Judge failed to restate the proposition before allowing the jury to retire, and consequently it will be contended that they may have thereby been confused between the concept of unanimity and the burden of proof'.

I do not pretend to understand the reference to the jury's possible confusion between unanimity and the burden of proof.

Lord Justice Bridge disposed of the point in this way. He sided with Peter Taylor QC saying,

'The correction of the judge's misdirection had been concisely and succinctly put, and not elaborated, but it was in our judgment entirely accurate and there was no reason why a jury should not have understood its import. It really did not call for any further elaboration. It was perfectly acceptable for the learned judge, having been corrected in that way, to point out to the jury that they should accept counsel's correction rather than his initial misdirection'.

Lord Justice Bridge gave very short shift to the defence point that:

'Although the said misdirection was pointed out at once to the learned trial judge by Counsel for the Crown, and although he accepted the criticism, the learned Judge failed to restate the proposition before allowing the jury to retire, and consequently it will be contended that they may have thereby been confused between the concept of unanimity and the burden of proof'.

As explained in the previous chapter, what had happened was that at 3.15 pm on Tuesday 21 July the jury had returned to the courtroom and the judge gave them a direction on reaching a majority verdict. As soon as he did so the foreman of the jury told him that they had reached a majority verdict. The judge insisted, and so directed the jury, that they should again try to reach a unanimous verdict. Clearly if they could not, then they should return a majority verdict. They retired again for a short time and then found Stefan guilty of murder by a majority of ten to two.

Lord Justice Bridge rejected this further ground of appeal as well. He did think however that the next ground of appeal that

'the verdict of the Jury was unsafe and unsatisfactory in that it involved the rejection of clear and uncontradicted medical evidence to the effect that the Appellant was, at the material time, suffering from such abnormality of mind as substantially impaired his mental responsibility for his acts in doing the killing',

It was accepted that this was a ground of the most substance in the appeal. This ground was advanced by defence counsel to invite the Appeal Court to exercise its power under Section 3 of the Criminal Appeal Act 1968 to substitute a verdict of guilty of manslaughter by reason of diminished responsibility for the verdict of guilty of murder returned by the jury. It has to be said again that at no time did Stefan ever admit that he had killed the little girl. He was adamant that he had not. David Waddington argued in his closing speech to the jury that the evidence did not prove that Stefan killed Lesley Molseed, but if it did, then his mental state established by the medical evidence justified a finding of guilty of manslaughter on the ground of diminished responsibility. The layman, the average man in the street, often described by lawyers as 'the man on the Clapham omnibus' might well be puzzled by the defence tactic that Stefan did not kill the child because his sworn alibi evidence showed he was elsewhere at the time, but if he was present at the crime scene and he did stab the little girl 12 times, then he was not guilty of murder but guilty of manslaughter because his mind was impaired at the time of the killing. As noted above, the jury rejected his defence and convicted him. The Appeal Court said that was a perfectly reasonable conclusion for them to reach and the conviction was neither unsafe nor unsatisfactory. `

It took the Appeal Court judges less than a day to dispose of the appeal and send Stefan back to Armley Gaol to serve a sentence of imprisonment for life. It was not that court's finest hour. Lord Justice Bridge had wrongly stated in the course of his judgment that Stefan had been 'arrested again' on 21 December 1975, and that he had been accused of indecent assault. That simply never happened. At no stage of the police investigation was Stefan arrested either for murder or indecent assault.

The use of the word 'again' in that context is meaningless. Mistakes of fact like this and mistakes of law impede the administration of justice for the innocent. No-one concerned with this case at that time raised the issue of illegally-obtained evidence from a person assisting the police with their inquiries, either believing, or pretending to believe, that Stefan was under arrest and in lawful custody all the time.

I consider that the Appeal Court ought to have exercised its powers under section 7 of the Criminal Appeal Act 1968 and ordered a new trial on the evidence relating to the juror point alone. The reason why the court refused to do so, I think, is that they could not envisage a police officer being so corrupt as to fabricate a written confession in the way it was done in Stefan's case. In doing what he did, Superintendent Holland acted wholly wrongly. In addition I wonder if the judges in the appeal court shared the view of the trial judge that Stefan had murdered Lesley Molseed.

I further consider that in order to conceal the fact that the woman juror had actually conversed with the prosecution representative who conveyed the information about the guilty plea to her and her companion, there was the pretence that she was eavesdropping on a conversation and knew nothing about either party to that conversation. It must surely be highly relevant that she was listening not to anyone who might be rehearsing someone else's gossip, but to the person who had every reason to know the full and entire content of the information.

Lord Justice Bridge disposed of the appeal by saying, 'We can find no grounds whatsoever to condemn the jury's verdict as in any way unsafe or unsatisfactory'. In my view, if David Waddington had asked, as I think he should have done, for the jury to be discharged and the trial started again in front of another jury, that application should and would have been granted by Mr Justice Park. The trial proceeded against Stefan when it should not have done so, to its inevitable conclusion. I believe that Stefan hoped, or more accurately expected, that he would be acquitted. He knew the truth all along but who, if anyone, believed him? He had not killed Lesley Molseed. We know now what he knew then. But did he really stand a chance of acquittal? Lord Justice Bridge recognised this when he said in the course of the appeal hearing '... for in truth the invitation to the jury to acquit him altogether was from the outset a perfectly hopeless prospect'. (See page 65 of the report at (1979) 68 Cr App. R).

Innocent clients can often be troublesome to their defence team (although I doubt if Stefan was, because he was so naïve and so trusting), especially when they believe, as almost all of them do, that the legal system convicts only the guilty and the innocent walk free.

The Appeal Court judgment was not reserved but given *ex tempore* on 28 May 1978. No-one from Stefan's firm of solicitors went to the prison to tell him in person that his appeal had been dismissed on that day. He received the news in writing. That was shameful, for it must have indicated to him that all hope was lost and he faced a life in prison.

Chapter Seventeen

The Fight Goes On

However despondent he may have felt after eventually receiving news of his unsuccessful appeal, Stefan continued to write letters. On 13 June 1978 he was on B Wing at Wakefield Prison in West Yorkshire. On that date he wrote to Sir Thomas Hetherington, the Director of Public Prosecutions at Queen Anne's Gate in London heading his letter, 'In the matter of: Regina v S. I. Kiszko (Mr).' He told the DPP that he was refused leave to appeal against his conviction for murder on 25 May 1978, but he said,

'I remain adamant about my "innocence"'. He was prompted to write, he said, because 'recently in my home town a young girl was sexually attacked by a man in a "white car" but initially when the investigations for the Rochdale girl were underway of which I have been convicted, the owner or occupant of a "white car" played a great prominence in the enquiries but was never traced. Yet he turns up again in this recent attack'.

It will be remembered that on the day that Lesley Molseed was abducted Mrs Emma Tong had seen a little girl sitting in a small white car outside her home in Rochdale. She was convinced that that little girl was Lesley. Was she right? And had Lesley's abductor and killer again sexually attacked another young girl in the same town, using the same car?

Stefan's recollection about the police inquires into a white car was totally correct as well. It is now known that a car of that colour had been high on the list of three cars deemed to be of interest to the police at the outset of the murder inquiry.

Stefan's letter shows that even after more than two years following his initial contact with the police, he could remember some of the detail of their inquiries and see their relevance to his case. He clearly had not yet descended into the deeply depressive state that enveloped him later in his prison sentence. What he wrote next however indicates his rather simple approach to life in general and his case in particular:

'Furthermore, I have many more qualms about my case, and I have learned that if this is the case a fresh Police enquiry by another force, can be made into one's case and grievances. Can you please let me know whether this is correct and what I have to do to get these fresh enquiries underway'.

Could he really have expected a fresh police inquiry into his case just because he had qualms about his own conviction?

His next sentence indicates his state of mind, and for the first time he expresses some unease about his legal team.

'I must in all fairness say that I never expected that one could suffer such "injustice" due to the fallacies of the police and the law Courts and those representing one'.

Which fallacies did he have in mind at the time he wrote that letter? He concluded by telling Sir Thomas Hetherington that he had never been in trouble with the police or the courts and

'as a Crown Servant in the Inland Revenue I am amazed at what can happen and how one's good name can be ruined … I await your reply on this matter at your earliest convenience and if you require any further details please let me know and I will supply them to you promptly. Thank You. I remain, Yours Faithfully, Stefan I Kiszko (Mr).'

Whatever reservations anyone may have had about the reference to the sexual offender in the white car in Stefan's letter of 13 June 1978, the letter was passed to the police and as far as is known nothing further resulted from it. The police reaction to the letter is not known. There was no fresh police enquiry until 1990 which led to the establishing of the long delayed truth.

Stefan's first attempt to appeal against conviction failed in May 1978. While the criminal justice system was sliding into disgrace, he was slowly going mad, labouring under the stigma of being a child killer for sexual purposes. He began also to fall into a delusional void, within which he imagined he was the victim of a State-sponsored plot to incarcerate an innocent tax office employee. Ultimately, he came to believe that even his devoted mother was a party to this complex conspiracy. He was sent first to Wakefield Prison, where for five years he was kept in isolation for 23 hours a day. He was violently attacked on two occasions by other prisoners.

The first assault was on 24 August 1976, when no fewer than six other inmates punched him and kicked him so violently in the face and on the knee that he was unable to walk properly for the following six weeks. On the second occasion, on 11 May 1977, the side of his head was caved in by the use of a blunt instrument. As always happens in these cases, nobody—neither the prison staff nor the inmates—saw anything.

Stefan's mother Charlotte believed in Stefan's innocence and would not give up the fight. She had the good fortune to encounter a solicitor, Campbell Malone, who took on Stefan's case with the resolution and courage that had been so demonstrably lacking previously. He was encouraged by the attitude and assistance of Philip Clegg, who had been junior defence counsel at the original trial. Clegg had serious misgivings about whether Stefan was guilty and he was prepared to say so.

A private detective, Peter Jackson, a former Royal Air Force police officer, was instructed to help. He was a superb objective seeker of truth, and his efforts in finding material witnesses paid off. At the very outset of his involvement he contacted Stefan's general practitioner, Dr D'Vaz, and took him to the lay-by on the A672 near to the spot where Lesley's body was found. The moment he saw the layout of the terrain the doctor immediately indicated that Stefan, labouring not just under his excess body weight but because of the fractured ankle and pin holding it in place, would never have been able to scale the hostile sloping ground as the killer must have done to take Lesley to her violent end. Why did no-one from the firm of solicitors instructed to defend Stefan do that same thing in December 1975, after Stefan was charged with murder?

Campbell Malone, by now deeply impressed by the passionate pleas for justice made to him by Charlotte Kiszko, worked long hours applying his experience and detailed legal knowledge and expertise with great attention to detail. He briefed another barrister, Jim Gregory, who is extremely able, greatly experienced and very hard working, and who became as committed as he was to establishing the truth (He took over from Philip Clegg following his appointment to the Circuit Bench). Their combined efforts led, after years of considerable effort, to a carefully drafted petition to the Home Office, asking that Stefan's case be referred back by the Home Secretary to the Criminal Division of the Court of Appeal (a function now dealt with by the Criminal Cases Review Commission and Ministry of Justice).

On 7 November 1990 an official in the Home Office Department C3, James McCarthy, sent the petition to the Chief Constable of the West Yorkshire Police. No-one could fail to be impressed by the force of the arguments set out in that petition.

The Home Secretary at that date was ironically David Waddington QC. He had been appointed by Margaret Thatcher, Prime Minister on 26 October 1989. He immediately passed the papers to Department C3 with instructions that when they had considered the matter the case should be put before a Minister of State at the Home Office, rather than himself. In fact Waddington left the Home Office on 28 November 1990. When the West Yorkshire Police eventually submitted their report he had been replaced as Home Secretary by Kenneth Baker. It was Baker who decided eventually to send the case back to the appeal court.

The 'Gregory petition' identified three areas of evidence from material witnesses and offered an extensive criticism of the way in which the defence had been conducted.

First he noted that there were three statements, apparently disclosed to the defence only on the morning of the first day of the trial, where witnesses saw a white car in the lay-by near to where the body of Lesley Molseed was found. These witnesses were not called at the trial before the jury. These three witnesses supported the evidence of another witness Mrs Tong, who believed she saw Lesley in a white car with a man earlier that Sunday at about 1.30 pm Her statement was not disclosed until the opening day of the trial also; she was called by the defence. Mr Gregory added later in the petition that 'The prosecuting authority had declined to explain the source of the information which caused the police to ask Kiszko if he had access to a white car and to televise a picture of a white car within two days of the murder'. What was there to hide in the provision of that information?

Second the petition also identified another witness who confirmed Stefan's alibi that he was in her shop at about 1 pm on the day of the murder. That supported the evidence of that witness's daughter.

The third area of important and relevant evidence was that of Dr D'Vaz who took the view that Stefan's physical difficulties were such that he would have been unable to climb the steep bank behind the lay-by on the A672. This led to the place where Lesley's body was found. Stefan had told the police in his description of the murder scene that '... it was a sort of grass banking, it wasn't very high and then it went flat ... I could see the road but I don't think anyone could see me'. He could not have climbed that embankment. Stefan was not the original source of this information. It was provided to him by Detective Superintendent Holland.

The petition noted the fact that the police were under great pressure to solve the murder and they were greatly influenced (as the jury must have been) by Stefan's strange medical history and the administration of the testosterone injections prior to 5 October 1975. Jim Gregory stressed the importance of the defence approach at the trial, which he described as 'bold' in seeking to show that the confession to murder was untrue by attempting to demonstrate that in confessing to offences of indecent exposure Stefan was obviously confessing to offences he did not commit. The direct result of this was that the prosecution were thereby allowed to call evidence to establish that those offences had taken place, thus, as noted previously, putting Stefan on trial for offences with which he had not been charged and to which he entered no plea.

The petition was also critical of the defence decision to lead evidence of Stefan's medical history for the purpose of putting the second limb of the defence before the jury, namely that he should not be convicted of murder on the ground of diminished responsibility. The evidence of

Dr Tarsh had a devastating effect on the course of the trial. Jim Gregory took the view that the defence attempt to run two defences at the same time was to destroy both. One elegant phrase used by him was, 'It is apparent from the judgment in the Court of Appeal and from the evidence called at the trial that while Kiszko himself was running the defence of alibi his Counsel were running the defence of diminished responsibility'. It could hardly be said that they were acting together in concert to achieve the same outcome. One sought an acquittal, the other a verdict of manslaughter.

As a result of that petition to the Home Secretary, the Assistant Chief Constable (Crime) of the West Yorkshire police, Tom Cook, nominated Detective Superintendent Trevor Wilkinson to carry out urgently a thorough investigation into the case. His report, some 94 pages in length, indicates the scale and extent of the murder enquiry. No less than 785 people were interviewed and a total of 6.131 statements were taken from them. The enquiry team concentrated their efforts on 1,335 men known to have convictions for sexual assault and/or offences involving masturbation. Wilkinson's heavily redacted 50 page report is undated. It can be accessed in Stefan's case files held at the National Archives in Kew (File reference DPP 2/6286).

It was the incident at the youth club in the grounds of Kingsway School on the Turf Hill Estate on Friday 3 October that particularly interested Wilkinson. More especially so where it was claimed that the man who exposed himself to children was armed with a knife. This was followed by another alleged incident of indecent exposure directed towards two girls on the following day, Saturday 4 October 1975. He needed to look at those allegations very carefully.

Wilkinson's report at paragraph 142 states, 'An examination of the evidence relating to the indecent exposure on Friday 3rd October 1975 revealed that a number of witnesses gave more than one statement concerning the incident. Some were taken at the time and others following the arrest of Kiszko'. (He too fell into the error of assuming that because Stefan went to the police station on 21 December 1975 he was taken there under arrest. He was not arrested, and in paragraph 49 of his report he acknowledges this by mentioning the series of police interviews at Rochdale Police Station with Stefan on both 21 and 22 December and adds the observation, 'In fact Kiszko remained at the police station overnight as a "guest" to facilitate those interviews'. For my part I have never encountered any suspect not under arrest being regarded as a 'guest' of the police who had invited him to assist in their inquiries and attend the police station in order to do so. It is an unusual word to use in this situation.

In his next four paragraphs, Trevor Wilkinson stated, 'Comparing the statements it is quite apparent that there have been as number of significant alterations'. He fails to say what those alterations are, what form they took, or how material they might be or even who made them. He adds 'not all of these statements were disclosed to the defence'. He fails to say why this occurred and does not indicate whether he and his team questioned those both in the police and the prosecuting authorities who were responsible for this non-disclosure of evidence that might undermine the case for the prosecution. If of course the alterations were substantial and material there would be very good reasons for suppressing the truth in order to convict an innocent man who had been induced by a police officer to make a false confession to murder.

> 'Each witness has now been re-interviewed. As a result it would appear that on the night of Friday 3 October 1975 there was much exaggeration and distortion of the truth by the girls involved'.

If by the expression 'distortion of the truth' he meant lies, why did he simply not say so? He then added, 'that night the police received reports of a man armed with a knife, exposing himself in the grounds of Kingsway School ... Kiszko admitted in his first voluntary statement to being that person'. So in truth and in fact Stefan had confessed to a crime that had not been committed.

To complete the destruction of the young girls' evidence Wilkinson added, at paragraph 147, 'the girls involved, on being re-interviewed, now say that they only saw the shape of a man. No-one will say that there was an indecent exposure, or that they saw a knife'. One if bound to ask, at whose behest did they exaggerate and distort the truth?

The two older girls, Catherine Burke and Pamela Hind, whose evidence was read to the jury did incalculable damage to Stefan. Did the jury ask themselves what kind of man uses such language to a 16-year-old and an 18-year-old? Did the jury look at the man in the dock and convince themselves that, by everything about him, his appearance and his lifestyle, he was entirely capable of saying such disgusting words? And very likely, going on from there, to be in the kind of person who would abduct, abuse and then murder a child?

Each of the two young women seemed to blame the other for their lies. Catherine Burke still claimed that there had been a man standing near to the clinic on that first Friday in October 1975 but he had not exposed himself to her. She said what she did only to go along with what Pamela Hind was saying. For her part, Pamela Hind now admitted that she had not seen the man's exposed penis and he never said the words, 'Come here, let me ram this up you.' Her explanation, which may be regarded as worthless, was that she 'must have got carried away… I must have gone along with what Kitty was saying… It was foolish but we were young and it was a confusing situation.' It was far more than foolish, it was criminal.

Each of these two young woman had signed a witness statement declaring it was true: they knew if it was given in evidence that they faced prosecution if what they deliberately said was false or they knew it was untrue. When it became apparent to the investigating police officers that Miss Burke and Miss Hinde had given false statements that had been read into evidence, they were interviewed after being cautioned and reminded of their right to stay silent. Notwithstanding that, they chose to answer questions and on this occasion to tell the truth. Superintendent Wilkinson records them as saying (at paragraph 152): 'They are now saying that their evidence was completely false. They were carried away with all the excitement'.

A decision was made by the prosecuting authorities for a senior police officer to caution them both for the criminal offence that each had undoubtedly committed. I do not agree with that decision. The discretion to issue an official caution was at that time vested in the police as an alternative to prosecution. This procedure can only be used if the person involved admits that what they did amounts in law to a criminal offence.

In my view, the interests of justice did require a prosecution against both Ms Burke and Ms Hind and the consequence of what they had done made it too serious a case for a caution to be administered. They may only have been aged 16 and 18 years at the time of the incident in 1975, but they were young adults and they must have known that their allegations would have far-reaching and devastating consequences for anyone charged with a crime as a result of what they said had happened. I consider that it should have been left to a criminal court to decide on the appropriate level of their sentence, since a guilty plea would have to be tendered in the light of what they both admitted to the police. It should be made plain to the public at large that calculated lies to the police, and thereafter to the jury, even in the form of a witness statement in the course of a criminal trial that endangers the liberty of another, will not go unpunished. As for Debbie Brown, who was only aged 13 at the time, I consider it would not have been possible to prosecute her in 1991, as there would have been no realistic prospect of convicting her. The prosecution could not show, in my view, that she had the mental capacity to form the *mens rea*, the mental element of the crime charged, and there existed a presumption in her favour that she could not do so. It would not be possible to adduce evidence to rebut that presumption.

Detective Superintendent Wilkinson's team must have been struck by the unusualness of the provision of the semen sample by Stefan Kiszko at the police station. They looked for the gathering of evidence after that. There should have been evidence of a comparison between the sample provided by Stefan and the stains found on Lesley's underclothing. They could not find it anywhere. The case was beginning to unravel.

On 21 February 1991, Detective Superintendent Wilkinson and Detective Inspector interviewed Ronald Outteridge at Wetherby Forensic Laboratory. He told the officers that he was unaware of Stefan Kiszko's medical background and placed no relevance on the absence of sperm heads in the sample he examined. He claimed (paragraph 204 of the report), that no reports were transmitted to the police which related to the presence or absence of sperm heads. All reports referred to semen.

No reports were ever prepared of the results of examination of the semen sample provided by Stefan Kiszko. The two officers considered that they should have been and on completion sent to the DPP.

Outteridge claimed not to know the purpose of the examination of the semen. He said there was nothing unusual in the making of no less than 14 slides of that semen, and five slides of semen taken from Lesley's clothing. He was unable to offer any explanation of why those five slides had gone missing at this point in time when Wilkinson sought access to them. It was highly convenient for someone that the five slides were now unaccounted for. All he knew was that they had been exhibits at Stefan's trial in 1976. Outteridge, of course, would have been entitled to rely on the appointed exhibits officer to account for their whereabouts during and after the trial. Their loss has never been explained by anyone.

The information set out in the preceding paragraph needs to be read in conjunction with the evidential issues canvassed when Ronald Outteridge and Richard Holland were subsequently served with summonses in July 1994 alleging that they had done acts tending to pervert the course of justice, following Stefan's release from custody by the Appeal Court.

One other matter disturbed Wilkinson also. When he interviewed Robin John Falconer of the Forensic Science Laboratory at Wetherby on 2 September 1991, the officer drew the attention of the scientist to the Laboratory's File in the Molseed Murder case, reference number C75/2444 at page 102A.

On that page was an entry stating that an interim report in relation to the examination of items taken from Stefan Kiszko's house had been passed by telephone to the murder incident room at 5.30 pm on 23 December 1975. The message made direct reference to the lack of sperm being found in the semen sample on the handkerchief that belonged to Stefan and taken from under the pillow in his bedroom. Paragraph 2.4 of Wilkinson's further report records,

'This message was passed by the laboratory to Detective Chief Superintendent Dibb and Dr Outteridge at the incident room, on the same day, but apparently before Kiszko provided a specimen of semen to Dr Tierney'.

The next paragraph explains the significance of this information.

'This contradicts Mr Outteridge's verbal statement to Superintendent Wilkinson that no information in relation to sperm count was passed to the incident room'

One is bound to ask, was this a lapse of memory on Mr Outteridge's part or was this a lie?

Robin Falconer made a witness statement on 8 February 1991 at the request of Detective Inspector O'Boyle from Wilkinson's team. It was later seen by Dr Paul E Belchetz, a Consultant Physician and Endocrinologist based at the General Infirmary in Leeds, referring to Wetherby laboratory notes

'concerning seminal stains on the skirt and panties of Lesley Molseed, on a handkerchief from Stefan Kiszko and a seminal specimen provided by Stefan Kiszko. The specimens on the girl's clothing showed the presence of spermatozoa ('sperm heads') but none were found in the handkerchief stains or the semen specimen provided by Stefan Kiszko.'

Those notes were made and retained at the laboratory. Who had concealed those notes for years and was that done in order to convict an innocent man? The comparison if disclosed as it should have been, would have seen the end of the case against Stefan Kiszko.

While Wilkinson and O'Boyle were dealing with the forensic aspects of the case, other officers in his team were looking at the evidence surrounding the fact that Stefan had admitted to an offence of indecent exposure on 3 October. They soon discovered, perhaps to their astonishment, that three of the girls involved were now prepared to admit they had lied in their witness statements regarding the alleged offence. The case against Stefan was gradually being demolished.

At the conclusion of his first report Detective Superintendent Wilkinson recommended that an independent examination be carried out into the circumstances surrounding Stefan's 'arrest' (again that error) and conviction and that the investigation into the murder of Lesley Molseed should be reopened and investigated further.

Chapter Eighteen

The Truth at Last?

On 10 May 1991, Assistant Chief Constable Tom Cook sent to the Home Office what he described as 'Mr Wilkinson's comprehensive report' into Stefan's case. Cook noted,

> 'It was not considered appropriate for the Force to either enquire into or comment upon the criticisms of the way in which the defence was conducted and Superintendent Wilkinson, therefore, confined his enquiries to the "new" evidence. This was a reference back to the substantial and perhaps scathing criticisms of the way in which the defence was conducted as set out in the Gregory petition lodged with the Home Office that led to the setting up of the police inquiry.'

Assistant Chief Constable Cook pointed out in clear and unequivocal language that there was a significant anomaly identified by Superintendent Wilkinson in the forensic samples in the case. He noted Ronald Outteridge had found that the seminal fluid on the victim's clothing did contain sperm heads. These were counted at the Forensic Science Laboratory by that scientist and written up in the notes as being of a low count, namely 1 on a scale of 1 to 4. (According to Robin Falconer it was the normal laboratory practice to assess the number of sperm heads found after staining of the extracts and microscopic examination. He said that this was a very crude and subjective assessment on a scale of 1 to 4, 1 being the small number of sperm heads and 4 meaning large numbers). So in this case the recorded level of sperm heads in the notes is put at 1, the lowest rating and this applied to the seminal staining on both pieces of clothing belonging to the little girl. Falconer was able to locate the original 18 slides of extracts from Stefan's handkerchief and the seminal sample provided by him, but he was unable to locate the slides relating to the extracts from either piece of Lesley's clothing. They had gone missing. (There are no prizes for guessing why. Lesley's clothes had been disposed of, but that was in accordance with the normal police practice, so there was nothing underhand about doing that. The slides are another matter altogether. They should have been retained and kept in safe custody. They constituted invaluable evidence and the beneficiary of their disappearance was the officer who wrote Stefan's confession, Superintendent Holland).

Cook pointed out the discrepancies between the samples from the victim that contained sperm heads and the samples from Stefan which did not. This discrepancy was not identified in any of the file documents or back-up papers, nor brought to the attention of the court or the defence. None of the five doctors in the original case, he noted, were made aware of this discrepancy and had they been, all five of them would have seized on its significance. When they examined Stefan all noted that he suffered from primary testicular failure and could not have produced sperm. In particular Dr Tierney indicated that he took the most unusual step of obtaining the semen sample from Stefan because he was aware of the seminal staining found on the victim's clothing and examination of the sample would either include Stefan Kiszko as a valid suspect or positively exclude him. Cook notes that Dr Tierney claimed that he had made this view known to senior officers from the West Yorkshire Police involved in investigating the case. As noted previously, those officers certainly included Detective Chief Superintendent Jack Dibb.

The Assistant Chief Constable goes on to record that when Ronald Outteridge was seen by the officers of Superintendent Wilkinson's team, he stated that he had never told the police of the anomaly between the seminal samples and he did not attach much significance to it anyway. This was an oral statement and apparently not put into writing (It is at odds with what the scientist told the police when they were interviewing him in connection with the proposed prosecution against him).

Cook canvassed three possible scenarios why the discrepancy between the samples was not identified. First, the senior officers informed by Dr

Tierney did not appreciate the relevance of the information and did not pursue it. (For my part I find this impossible to reconcile with the fact that on 23 December 1975 overtures were made by the police to Dr David Anderson (*Chapter Thirteen*) to try to get him to say that Stefan could, following the testosterone injections, produce sperm and thereby explain away the inexplicable).

Second, Outteridge did not appreciate the relevance of the discrepancy and did not identify it to the police or to the court (Again it should be noted that when it came to the police inquiry into whether he and Holland should face criminal charges he did maintain that he had told the police, as the district judge noted at the committal proceedings, 'that he had no doubt that he had told the investigating officers that the semen on the handkerchief and Kiszko's sample contained no sperm heads'). So he did appreciate the relevance, did pass on the information and that would explain why a detective inspector went to see Dr David Anderson on 23 December to take a statement from him. What is not explained is the failure of Outteridge to include this information in his witness statement, informing the DPP of this highly relevant evidence, and in his oral evidence to the court of trial that convicted Stefan Kiszko.

The third possible scenario was that individually or collusively police officer(s) and/or Ronald Outteridge did appreciate the significance of the difference in the sample and suppressed it as it did not support the prosecution of Stefan (In fact it so undermined it that no successful prosecution could ever have been launched).

Cook faced up to the possibility that if the jury had been told about the semen samples and the related medical evidence they would undoubtedly have looked at the confession evidence in an entirely different light. He told the Home Office that the judge had directed the jury that the main question for them to consider was whether the confession was true. There was no other evidence that established beyond reasonable doubt or otherwise that Stefan was the killer.

The Assistant Chief Constable emphasised that Wilkinson's inquiry showed that part of the confession relating to the alleged indecent exposure incident near the youth club on Friday 3 October 1975 must be wrong as clearly it never took place so that alone undermined the truth-fulness of the confession.

He further told the Home Office that Outteridge was seen briefly and interviewed verbally; there had been no formal interview, presumably under caution, and at length about the failure to identify the differences in the samples. He said that the officer in overall charge at the time, Superintendent Dibb, is now dead. The next step to be taken was the appointment of an outside police force to carry out an investigation into the case but the first priority was to place the facts before the Home Secretary and inform him that the report of Superintendent Wilkinson indicated that Stefan's conviction was unsafe and either his appeal should be allowed to proceed in the light of the forensic and medical evidence now available, or in the alternative that he be released from custody and either pardoned or his appeal to the court be allowed to proceed following his release.

After that information was sent to the Home Office no one could any longer claim that Stefan's 'delusions of innocence' were a manifestation of the symptoms of his paranoid schizophrenia. He was a completely innocent man.

On 19 December 1991 Stefan was granted technical bail. In truth, he was really too ill to be allowed to return home to his mother and he was taken to Prestwich Hospital, about ten miles from Rochdale.

Stefan's case was sent back to the Appeal Court and was listed for hearing on 17 February 1992 before the then Lord Chief Justice, Lord Lane, Mr Justice Rose and Mr Justice Potts. The prosecution had made extensive enquiries into the question of the forensic evidence and what it meant, and its use, or more accurately, non-use, at the original trial in 1976. Franz Muller QC for the prosecution did not apparently object to the defence counsel, Stephen Sedley QC, calling two former prosecution witnesses — the forensic scientist Peter Guise who, as was noted above, had analysed the semen found on Lesley's clothing, and Ronald Outteridge, who checked that analysis and also gave evidence at the appeal and made it clear that in the sample taken from the knickers and skirt there was traces of semen that contained sperm heads. Three doctors, Dr Alan Tawse Edwards, Dr Frederick Chung Wei Wu, and

Dr Paul Belchetz, probably the most eminent available in this branch of medicine, told the court that Stefan could not then, and never would be able to, produce sperm. On 18 February 1992, Lord Lane faced up to the inevitable. He said

> 'This man cannot have been the person responsible for ejaculating over the little girl's knickers and skirt, and consequently cannot have been the murderer. For those reasons, which we have endeavoured to express as concisely as possible, this appeal must be allowed and the conviction quashed as being unsafe and unsatisfactory.'

The Lord Chief Justice made no attempt to express the slightest regret for the wrongful conviction and long imprisonment of an innocent man. There was not one word of apology for the destruction of Stefan Kiszko from the most senior permanent judge in an uncaring State. I regard that as particularly regrettable. By this date, of course, Lord Lane knew almost better than anyone how quite routine it was in the English legal system for innocent people to be convicted and imprisoned while the guilty remained at liberty.

None of that meant anything to Stefan. He was free at last. Some of those who had vilified him (and his mother) after his conviction now wanted to make amends. The Molseed family publicly apologised for calling for Stefan's execution after his conviction and expressed their sorrow for things said to his mother immediately after the jury returned their verdict of guilty against him. Mr Justice Park took the exceptional step by writing to Stefan expressing his regret that he had been convicted. But he declined to shoulder any of the blame for the wrongful conviction of a totally innocent man. He said that the mistake in the case was dreadful, but he stressed that there was no criticism of how he conducted the case. He claimed that 'It is new evidence that cast very great doubt on the conviction'. I profoundly disagree with that statement. The evidence was not new, it was as old as the case itself. It had been concealed, and may have been suppressed for ever, as some hoped it would be.

Mr Justice Park may, however, have felt some regret for his post-trial remarks in 1976, when he praised the teenage girls who made the indecent exposure claims 'for their bravery and honesty' and 'sharp observations'. The learned judge was not easily deceived, but he had been deceived by the evidence of apparently honest witnesses who turned out to be anything but that. Catherine Burke, Pamela Hind and Debbie Brown seem never to have expressed any remorse for their lies. The original investigating police officers also stayed silent. They had been commended by the trial judge 'for their great skill in bringing to justice the person responsible for this dreadful crime and their expertise in sifting through masses of material'. Many officers had worked tenaciously to find Lesley's murderer, but others let them down when they suppressed vital evidence that exonerated Stefan Kiszko.

This judicial pronouncement is however seeming confirmation of Mr Justice Park's belief during the trial itself, however carefully he might have tried to shield it, that Stefan Kiszko murdered Lesley Molseed. Those who consider that criminal trials might be best conducted before a judge alone, sitting without a jury, might wish to bear that in mind.

It fell to Stephen Sedley QC to mention those who seemed overlooked and forgotten by the criminal justice system, namely Lesley's family. He said, 'We acknowledge their pain in having to listen to some of the details surrounding their daughter's death and the new pain of learning that her killer, after all, has not been caught'.

On 28 February 1992, ten days after the appeal was allowed and Stefan's conviction was quashed, Chris Mullen MP asked the Attorney-General in the House of Commons 'Why the results of the sperm test on Stefan Kiszko carried out by Dr Edward Tierney were not disclosed to the defence at the time of his trial'.

The Attorney-General replied in carefully drafted civil service speak. Is there anywhere in the free world a more latent ability to conceal the truth without actually telling lies than is to be found among the mandarins in Whitehall? The senior law officer's reply was:

'The sample of semen obtained by Dr Tierney from Stefan Kiszko was submitted to the forensic science laboratory for examination. The DPP was provided with a witness statement provided by the scientist concerned with the test and that statement was served as part of the committal documents.

The statement concluded with the assertion that the maker had found nothing else of evidential value and the DPP relied upon that assertion. As far as can be ascertained from the DPP's case file, no information was received by his staff to put them on notice that further evidential material was in fact available. The conduct of the original inquiry is currently under investigation by the Lancashire police.' (A request under the Freedom of Information Act to inspect the final inquiry report of the investigating officer was refused on grounds of time and cost).

I am unable to understand what is meant by the phrases 'nothing else of evidential value' and '… further evidential material was in fact available'. What that material was, who held it, and why it was not made available, are questions that arise from this answer.

When he was eventually able to return home from hospital, Stefan and his mother tried to lead some kind of a normal life, but the long years of imprisonment had taken their toll. On 23 December 1993 Stefan collapsed and died in his bedroom at his home. He was 41 years-of-age. Eighteen years previously, almost exactly to the day, he had left his home to become the victim of one of the most notorious miscarriages of justice in British legal history. His mother heard the sound of him falling and went upstairs to discover his lifeless body. She had fought ill-health for years, determined to see justice done for her beloved son. When he died, she really had little left to live for. She died 20 weeks after him, on 3 May 1994. She was 70-years-old. She had endured years of unimaginable suffering. So had Stefan. At his Requiem Mass on 5 January 1976, his parish priest Father William O'Connor spoke movingly first about Stefan's mother and aunt. He described them as women of fortitude, who made great sacrifices, showed great love and suffered great heartbreak. They must have found great consolation in those meaningful words, spoken with sincerity and compassion. Father O'Connor said that the world had failed Stefan, but there would be no more pain or suffering for him now. Stefan had told the BBC in an interview after his release that he was enjoying sleeping in in the mornings and catching-up with old friends. He and his mother had received hundreds of cards and letters from well-wishers all over the world. Stefan said he wished to make up for all those years in prison by 'going to Australia to enjoy myself, and maybe America as well, and have a good time'. Those were journeys he was destined never to take. After his conviction was quashed, Stefan had spoken of his faith in British justice and his confidence that one day he would be released from prison custody. Few shared that view.

Even at a time when he was extremely ill in 1998, the former Governor of Grendon Prison, Professor David Wilson, would later reveal, that while Stefan was an inmate there, he tried to persuade him to go on a sex offenders' treatment programme in which he would have to admit Lesley's murder and discuss the reasons for his offence. If he did, he would become eligible to apply for parole. Stefan refused. The penalty for his refusal was that he was almost certainly destined to stay in prison for the rest of his life because he refused to 'address his offending behaviour', a prerequisite normally for being granted parole. Before recommending release on licence, the Parole Board must consider whether the safety of the public would be placed at an unacceptable level by release. The board must also take into account, amongst other factors, when considering an application to be granted parole, whether the offender has such a willingness to address that issue by taking part in programmes or activities designed to address his risk, and whether the offender is likely to comply.

The one legal professional who was at the very centre of the drive to free an innocent man from the torture inflicted upon him by the full majesty of the law was Campbell Malone. He never gave up the fight to establish the truth.

The case of Stefan Ivan Kiszko demonstrates the glaring failures of the Criminal Justice System to subject evidence to a dispassionate and objective assessment no matter from whom and where it is to be found. Safeguards for suspects in police stations are more exact now than they were in 1975. But there should be no relaxation of the right of any suspect to fair treatment and due process in any criminal investigation or trial in England and Wales (or elsewhere). Failure to ensure this will result in another shameful miscarriage of justice to add to the long list of those wrongly convicted in the name of the law.

Stefan and his mother are buried in the same cemetery in Rochdale as little Lesley Molseed. Their names will always be associated together as an example of the frailties of an imperfect legal system which finds it difficult to embrace the truth.

Exhibit One — Stefan Kiszko's Draft Statement

STEFAN IVAN KISZKO — DRAFT STATEMENT

I was born in Rochdale on 24th March, 1952, and lived with my parents in the family home at 31 Crawford Street, Rochdale. My father was a Ukranian who came to Britain in 1949. My mother originates from Yugoslavia. My parents were extremely close, and very protective towards me throughout my formative years. From an early age I suffered from asthma and at 4 years of age I was taken to live with my maternal grandmother in Austria for several weeks. Because of my chest trouble I did not start school until I was 7.

I attended St Peter's and Newbold Infants' School and received a secondary education at Kingsway High School. I continued my education at Rochdale Technical College and obtained a Certificate in Office Studies. I have no other academic qualifications.

During my school years I didn't mix with the other children and did not form any friendships. At the age of seventeen I started work as a clerk at the Inland Revenue whose offices at that time were in Lonsdale House, John Street, Rochdale. My supervisor at work was Mr Higham. Initially I used public transport to get to work then in 1971, having passed my driving test, I bought a Hillman Avenger motor car, registered number VDK 157K. The car was new and was bronze in colour.

My route to work when travelling by car was to leave Crawford Street and drive down Oldham Road to the town centre where I parked my car on the staff car park. I usually went home for dinner. The only time I socialised with people at work was at Christmas time when we had an office party.

At the Inland Revenue we were provided with felt tip pens which were used to write names on file covers. From recollection these pens were marked to the effect that they were Government property.

My father died on 26th September, 1970; my mother and I continued to live in the family home.

In 1973 the Inland Revenue moved to office accommodation in Newgate House in Rochdale, which was a short walk from Bailey Street. I was happy at work but I still did not form any real friendships with anyone and I would very rarely go out in the evenings. My main source of pleasure was driving my car.

As far as my medical history is concerned, I have been very fat for many years. In my late teens I weighed some $17^1/_2$ stones. I currently weigh 20 stones. This is partly as a result of my medical condition and partly due to my dietary habits. I have also had a long standing skin complaint in that my skin is dry and scaly, for which I was prescribed ointment.

Early in 1974, I started bleeding internally and my doctor referred me to Rochdale Infirmary for kidney x-rays but nothing untoward was diagnosed.

In April 1974, I fell downstairs and fractured my left ankle. Two stainless steel pins were inserted into the ankle bone and my ankle remained in a plaster cast until September that year.

In August 1975, I was admitted to Birch Hill Hospital, Rochdale, suffering

from severe anaemia. At that time I was in the habit of drinking a lot of
cider, some three or four pints each day. Whilst I was in hospital the
doctors also found I was suffering from a condition known as hypogonadism.
I was given a blood transfusion to combat my anaemia. I was transferred
to Manchester Royal Infirmary where I was given injections to treat
the hypogonadism. As I understood it, the condition of hypogonadism
had retarded my physical development to the extent that I did not need to
start shaving until I was about 18 years old and even then I only found it
necessary to shave once a week. It also affected my sexual development.
From being about 17 years of age, I used to masturbate about once a week but
had difficulty in ejaculating. This situation eased once I had the
testosterone injections. I have never had a girlfriend, neither have I had
any form of sexual contact with any person, male or female, even whilst I
was in prison. To the best of my recollection, none of the doctors I saw at
that time raised the question of sterility with me and I was not, therefore,
aware that I was unable to produce spermatazoa. The injections had the
physical effect that I have described but they did not cause me to feel
hazy.

Sometime around April 1975, an incident occurred whilst I was driving my
car. Another vehicle owned by a man called Jimmy Gaughan tried to force me
off the road. Jimmy Gaughan at that time owned a plant hire business on
Moss Street, Rochdale. He had three vehicles that I knew of, a green van, a
Mercedes and a red Escort van. I had not come into conflict with Gaughan at
any time and do not know why this incident occurred. I later contacted the
Police at Rochdale and spoke to Police Constable Bell about this incident.
After some time elapsed, PC Bell contacted me and advised that should
anything similar happen in future, I was to write down the registered number

of the vehicle concerned and inform him as soon as possible.

I then got into the habit of writing down the registered numbers of cars that I thought were being driven badly.

At my trial at Leeds Crown Court in July 1976, one such car number, ADK 539L, was to play a significant role. I agree that I wrote down that car number on the piece of paper that was tendered in evidence at the trial but I could not then, nor can I now, recall when or why I made a note of that particular car number.

I can remember the events surrounding the disappearance of Lesley Molseed in October 1975, and the murder enquiry that was launched when her body was found a few days later. The matter received a lot of publicity but whatever knowledge I had of the murder was gained from reading the accounts published in the Rochdale Observer. This was a local newspaper published twice weekly and was the only newspaper I used to read. I also used to watch television and therefore could pick up any information from television reports.

The first time I was visited by Police Officers after Lesley's death was on 5th November, 1975. Two Police Officers, WPC Janet Shaw and PC Richard Oliver, came to my home address and spoke to me regarding an incident of indecent exposure. I cannot remember what time of day they came to see me but they remained for about half an hour. I cannot remember exactly what was said but the officers seemed to be satisfied with my explanation.

The following day, that is 6th November, 1975, my mother and I moved to our current address, 25 Kings Road, Rochdale.

My next contact with the Police was on 7th November, 1975. Sometime during that afternoon, a Police Officer in plain clothes came to my home address and spoke to me for about ³/₄ hour regarding another offence of indecent exposure. This was a completely different incident to that for which I had been interviewed two days earlier. Again the officers seemed to be satisfied with my explanation.

I heard nothing further about either of these matters until 21st December, 1975. About 10am that morning, two Police Officers called Whittle and Ackeroyd came to my home and made it clear that they wanted to talk to me about Lesley Molseed's murder. They quite abruptly asked me to go with them to Rochdale Police Station. I was quite happy to do this and drove my own car to the Police Station accompanied by Whittle, who sat in the front passenger seat.

When we arrived at the Police Station I was taken to an interview room. Present at that time were Whittle and Ackeroyd and two further Police Officers called MacFadzean and Steele. I remember Steele kept holding my right hand. He was quite pleasant with me. They spoke to me for quite a while, then some time later another Police Officer called Holland came into the interview room. He told me to empty my pockets which I did. At that time I was in the habit of carrying a penknife with me, which I used in the parcelling of packages at work and I produced this from one of my pockets. I was interviewed on and off for the rest of the day, and locked in a cell at the Police Station overnight.

The following day, I cannot remember the time the interview started again.

Holland was very aggressive and threatening in his manner. He kept poking me in the shoulder and kept saying, "I'LL GET THE FUCKING TRUTH OUT OF YOU ONE WAY OR THE OTHER". Shortly after this, Holland left the interview room.

I remember being very intimidated by what Holland had done and said to me, and I thought that I would get beaten up unless I made admissions which I thought was what he wanted me to do. I remember I did make some verbal admissions to Whittle, MacFadzean and Ackeroyd but I cannot remember exactly what I said to them. This admission consisted of a verbal statement that I had something to do with the murder, but I recollect it did not contain any detail.

I think two Police Officers called Steele and Mawson came into the interview room whilst the other officers left. With the benefit of hindsight, although I cannot recollect exactly what was said, the officers were questioning me about circumstances they thought were related to the murder.

I remember Holland coming back into the interview room and he just wrote out a statement without any discussion with me. When he had finished writing down the statement, he read the statement out to me and I just signed it. I did not read it.

I did not have a solicitor and I was never told that I could have one.

I later found out that my auntie, Mrs. Tosic, had contacted my supervisor at work, Mr Higham, and in turn a solicitor had been arranged for me. Sometime after making the statement, I spoke to Mr Albert Wright, a solicitor, and

told him that I was innocent and that I had admitted to something that I had
not done.

Because of this, a short time later I made a further statement to Holland
retracting what I had previously said. I cannot remember exactly when but I
was visited sometime later by Dr. Tierney whilst I was still at Rochdale
Police Station. I was taken into a medical room and the doctor gave me a
physical examination. A Police Officer was present throughout but I cannot
recollect who it was. It certainly was not Holland. I remember samples of
skin, pubic hair and nail scrapings being taken from me and I remember being
asked by the doctor to provide a sample of semen. I was not given any
explanation as to why the sample was required and I did not question the
necessity or relevance of it. I presumed that it was taken as a matter of
course. Because of this, I went behind a screen and ejaculated into a
bottle and handed it to Dr. Tierney who I did not see again.

I was then returned to the cells where I was left overnight and for much of
the following day.

Sometime later, in the evening, I left Rochdale Police Station and I
remember it was raining heavily. We stopped en route to Halifax at a place
that was allegedly the scene of the murder. I could not see properly
because of the conditions and because I was innocent it meant nothing to me.

I arrived at Halifax Police Station where I was fingerprinted and
photographed and charged with the murder of Lesley Molseed by Holland. I was
then left in the cells overnight, before appearing at the Magistrates'
Court. At no stage was I told I was under arrest. In the morning I was

8

represented at court by Albert Wright and I was remanded in custody and sent to Armley Jail, Leeds. At the prison I was isolated from other prisoners but not given any reason as to why this was done. After two weeks I was put in a ward in the prison hospital and I was treated alright by both the staff and other prisoners. I kept going back to Halifax Magistrates' Court for weekly remands.

At some stage whilst I was in prison, my solicitor gave me a number of depositions. Mr. Wright said there were over 6,000 other statements but I do not know how many I was given.

At some stage I told Mr. Wright that Holland had frightened me when he kept poking me and I thought that he would beat me up. I do not remember Mr. Wright giving me any advice on this matter at that time, neither did Mr. Wright comment on the fact that I had been asked to produce a semen sample. I did not realise at that time that I could have had a choice of solicitors.

Mr. Wright subsequently recommended that I engage Phillip Clegg to be my junior barrister at the eventual trial. I remember meeting Mr Clegg and talking about my case in general. I also recall Mr. Clegg mentioning the semen sample and the semen staining on the child's clothing, but I cannot remember in what context this discussion took place. I do remember that Mr Clegg appeared to place a lot of importance on the semen sample. I cannot remember when, although it was obviously prior to my trial, I was visited by both Mr. Clegg and Mr. Waddington who was to be my leading counsel. We just had a general discussion. I remember that I told Mr Clegg and Mr Waddington about my alibi that at lunchtime on the day in question I was in a shop on Tweedale Street and that Mrs Baran and her daughter could confirm this. I

remember telling them that Mrs Baran was on holiday in Italy but I thought
that she would be back in time for my trial. I also told Mr Waddington and
Mr Clegg that the carpets that were taken from my car were not the same
pieces of carpet that were inside the vehicle at the time the murder took
place. I told Mr Clegg and Mr Waddington that the reason I had admitted the
murder was because of what Holland had said to me and the fact that he had
poked me on the shoulder. Mr Waddington and Mr Clegg did not comment
about this.

Mr Waddington and Mr Clegg did go through the Police statements and I
reiterated to them that Holland had written the statement and I had just
signed it. Mr Waddington and Mr Clegg did not go through Mr Outteridge's
statement with me. At all times throughout this meeting I maintained my
innocence, and at no time was it suggested to me that I plead guilty to
murder or manslaughter. The whole meeting lasted some two hours and I had
full confidence in both men and left my defence with them.

I was later visited by Dr Tarsh and Dr Enoch. I understood Dr Tarsh to be a
psychiatrist and he asked me if I had had any side effects from the
injections I had been receiving. Dr Enoch gave me a medical examination and
told me I was hypogonadal. He did not explain what this meant and I did not
ask him. Dr Tarsh asked me about the effects of the injection but he did not
ask me specifically about feeling hazy.

I recollect on the first day of my trial, I was brought from prison around
9am and saw Mr Waddington, Mr Clegg and Mr Wright prior to court commencing.
For the first time Mr Waddington suggested that I plead guilty to
manslaughter. Because I knew that I was innocent, I did not agree to this

and I remember agreeing to Mr Waddington's suggestion that a dual defence could be run on my behalf. It is fair to say that I really did not grasp the significance of this, as I had total confidence in what my legal representatives were putting forward on my behalf. I cannot recollect why I was advised that this dual defence was appropriate. I did not really understand what was happening during the trial and I cannot remember a great deal of the evidence that was given. I remember that Dr Tarsh gave evidence and I remember thinking that his evidence was helpful.

Towards the end of the trial, but before the Judge summed up, Mr Waddington told me that things didn't look too good and again suggested that I change my plea to manslaughter. Because I was innocent, I did not take this option.

It was not until sometime after my conviction that I found out that a juror had come forward and suggested that she had heard that my defence counsel had been trying to get me to plead guilty, and despite this had been allowed to remain on the jury. Had I known about this at the time, I would have asked for a re-trial.

I was convicted of murder by a 10 - 2 majority and sentenced to life imprisonment.

I was taken to Armley Jail and again seen by Mr Albert Wright, who told me that I could appeal against my conviction. Shortly afterwards I saw Mr Waddington and Mr Clegg in Wakefield Prison with a view to arranging my appeal. Mr Clegg advised me that I could change barristers, but because I did not know anyone else, I settled for the same representation. Whilst in

Wakefield Prison, I was kept in isolation which involved remaining in a cell for 23 hours a day which lasted some 5 years. I have been attacked by other inmates on two occasions, the more serious of which involved the insertion of 17 stitches into a head wound.

I was informed of the outcome of my first appeal by letter and was not visited by any of my legal representatives.

On the 19th December, 1991, I was technically released on bail before returning home on the 17th March, 1992.

I have been shown two statements that are signed by me, and confirm that these statements are the statements produced at court relating to my confession and subsequent retraction.

Exhibit Two — Stefan's Confession Statement

FORM 75GF

GREATER MANCHESTER POLICE

STATEMENT FORM

Name of Person___STEFAN IVAN KISZKO

Address____25 Kings Road, Lower Place, Rochdale

Date _____3.20pm Monday 22nd December, 1975

CAUTION

I STEFAN IVAN KISZKO wish to make a statement. I want someone to write down what I say. I have been told that I need not say anything unless I wish to do so and that whatever I say may be given in evidence.

Signature of person making statement ___signed S.I.Kiszko

From the 5th August, 1975 I was in Hospital in Manchester for treatment for Haemoplastic Anaemia. That was Manchester Royal Infirmary and I was under Doctor English. I came out of hospital on the 15th September, and I went back to live with my mother at Crawford Street. I had to go back to hospital every three weeks for treatment for my lack of sex life. I had tablets from the hospital and injections both at the hospital and from my own doctor. When I had this treatment it made me go dizzy for three to four days after the injections and then I feel a lot better of myself and it helps me in my sex life. When I see a girl after I have had the treatment it makes me fancy her. A week or two after I came out of hospital, it was the beginning of October, a Friday or Saturday I was going from home to my aunties in Kingsway. I stopped my car on the left hand side of the road near a bus stop, facing towards Milnrow. I had come down Kings Road and turned left. It was fairly dark. There was a disco going on at the youth club and two girls came from down the road towards the disco. Something came over me and I got out of my car unzipped my trousers and got my penis out. I had a knife in my hand but that was a mere triviality. It was a small one with a black handle.

(GMP.59)

signed S.I.Kiszko

248

MM 756E

Continued Statement of... STEFAN IVAN KISZKO .... Check. .... Sheet No...2.....

The two girls went off towards the youth club and I got back into
my car and drove off towards my aunts. I didn't stop very long at
the house, as it isn't very safe parking near the bridge in the dark.
The following day about dinner time I had put an old carpet into my
car to take and dump on some spare ground near Vavasour Street. I
stopped my car in one of the side streets off Vavasour Street. I
got out, opened the boot up and took out the carpet, it was a pretty
hefty one. It was all rotten and we were getting a new one for Kings
Road. I unzipped myself and my shirt flap came out. I put that
back in and pulled my zip back up. There was an old lady and a fellow
in the street and I didn't deliberately expose myself that day. I drove
back home. For the rest of the day I sorted things out with my mum,
and packed crockery and took it up to the new house. I sometimes
went up to the new house at Kings Road in my own car. The next day
was Sunday and I got up about "Tenish". I had a drink and I went
out for a ride in my car on my own. I can't remember the time but
about dinner time I was driving down Broad Lane from Charlotte Street toward
Oldham Road. A girl was standing on the left near to a pub which is
on the right hand side and which stands back from the road. I mean to
say she was more or less opposite the pub. She was about nine years
old. I stopped the car and wound my window down. I can't remember
what I said to her but she got into the front of my car. I drove off
down Oldham Road and into Queensway down to the roundabouts and onto
the M62. She started shouting and I hit her with my hand. It was a
flat hand. I drove up the motorway towards the moors towards the
road that takes you down towards Ripponden. When I had first got
my car in 1972 I had been up there and I had got lost. I went right
down into Ripponden and then went over the other road through
Littleborough to Rochdale. That was the only time before this Sunday
that I had been on that road with the little girl in the car. I came
off the motorway and took the same road towards Ripponden, but not
very far. I stopped on the left hand side on a bit of a patch. I

(SIGNED)   S. I. Kiszko

RM-756E

Continued Statement of... STEFAN IVAN KISZKO .... Sheet No......3......

took her out of the car and up a sort of grass banking, it wasn't
very high, and then it went flat onto a flat piece. I could see
the road but I don't think anyone on the road could see me. The first
bit was the sex bit. She was standing up crying, I got my penis out.
I started playing with my self I can't remember if she said anything
I laid down by her, side by side, and held her with one hand and
used my left hand to wank with. She was laid facing me and I was
laid on my right side. I shot between her legs over her knickers.
I did not remove her knickers. I had a knife in my pocket and I
took it out and stabbed her in the throat she was still crying I got
a hazy feeling and I can't remember where or how I stabbed her.
She slumped over away from me and I don't remember what happened after
that. I left her where she was and I didn't bother to look. I
got back into the car and drove back home. I didn't tell my mother what
I had done I put my knife back into my pocket and I wiped it onto her
clothes or something. I can't remember what. I was a bit hazy then.
I didn't cut myself. I think I got to our house about "fourish"
that is about tea time. I always carry a lot of pens in my inside
jacket pocket for work because at work every amendment has to be in
a different colour. Some are issued at work and some are bought by me.
I have only been wanking since I had the hospital treatment. Before
the treatment I didn't ejaculate but after the treatment I have
done so every time except once. / signed S.I.Kiszko
I have read the above statement, and I have been told that I can
correct alter or add anything I wish. This statement is true. I have
made it of my own free will. signed S.I.Kiszko

Witness D. Wheater
concluded 5.35pm 22/12/75
signed Dick Holland Det. Supt.

(SIGNED)

Exhibit Three — Stefan's Retraction Statement

FORM 766F

GREATER MANCHESTER POLICE

STATEMENT FORM

Name of Person___STEFAN IVAN KISZKO_____

Address__25 Kings Road, Lower Place, Rochdale_____

Date ___6.30pm 22nd December, 1975_____

CAUTION

I STEFAN IVAN KISZKO wish to make a statement. I want someone to write down what I say I have been told that I need not say anything unless I wish to do so and whatever I say may be given in evidence.

Signature of person making statement ____S.I.KISZKO_____

I thought if I made a statement like the other one I would get home tonight. The first page and the top seven lines of page two are correct. From stopping my car in Kingsway what I said about the disco and the girls is not correct I did not show my penis and although I have a penknife with a black handle I had no reason to have it in my hand. I drove off towards my aunts. It's true that I didn't stop long there. What I have said about the carpet is correct. The business about the carpet and my shirt flap coming out as I got the carpet out of my car is true and I returned home after I had dumped the carpet. The account of the rest of the day is true. The following day my account of the time which I got up and of going out for a drive on my own is true but I didn't go to Broad Lane. I can't remember where I went or that particular day but I didn't go to Broad Lane. There was no little girl and no little girl got into the front of my car. I was nowhere near the M62 I didn't go on the M62 that day. I had no girl in my car to hit and I didn't go near to Ripponden. The part is true that I got lost and been over to Ripponden just after I had got my car. That is the only time I have ever been down that road. All the piece about

(GMP.59)   signed S.I.Kiszko

252

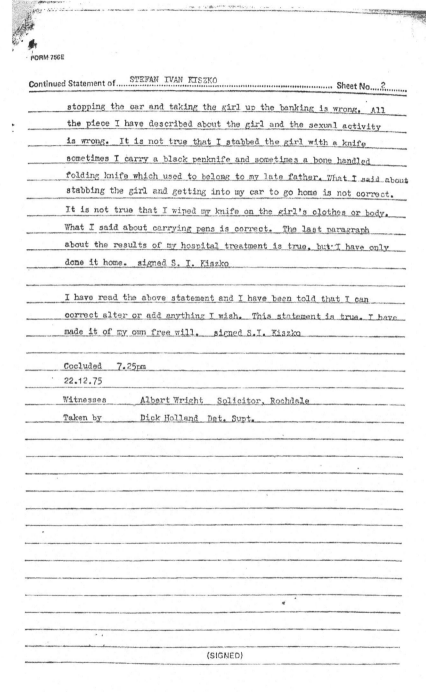

FORM 756E

Continued Statement of..... STEFAN IVAN KISZKO .... Sheet No.....2.........

stopping the car and taking the girl up the banking is wrong. All
the piece I have described about the girl and the sexual activity
is wrong. It is not true that I stabbed the girl with a knife
sometimes I carry a black penknife and sometimes a bone handled
folding knife which used to belong to my late father. What I said about
stabbing the girl and getting into my car to go home is not correct.
It is not true that I wiped my knife on the girl's clothes or body.
What I said about carrying pens is correct. The last paragraph
about the results of my hospital treatment is true, but I have only
done it home. signed S. I. Kiszko

I have read the above statement and I have been told that I can
correct alter or add anything I wish. This statement is true. I have
made it of my own free will. signed S.I. Kiszko

Cocluded   7.25pm
22.12.75

Witnesses   Albert Wright   Solicitor, Rochdale

Taken by   Dick Holland Det. Supt.

(SIGNED)

Further Documents Viewable at WatersidePress.co.uk

Richard Holland's Statement 22 December 1992

Criminal Proceedings Against Superintendent Holland and Ronald Outteridge

The Trial and Conviction of Ronald Castree

Dr David Anderson

Dr Edward Tierney

Index

Three False Convictions, Many Lessons:
The Psychopathology of Unjust Prosecutions
by David C Anderson and Nigel P Scott

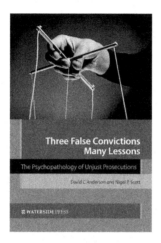

A new perspective on the roles of psychopathology, confirmation bias, false confessions, the media and internet (amongst other causes) of unjust accusations. Putting lack of empathy at the fore in terms of police, prosecutors and others, it considers a wide range of other psychopathological aspects of miscarriages of justice.

By looking at three high profile cases, those of Amanda Knox and Raffaele Sollecito (Italy), Stefan Kiszko (UK) and Darlie Routier (USA)—the authors show that motive forces are a mind-set in which psychopathy (what they term 'constitutional negative empathy') may be present and the need to reinforce existing supposition or lose face plays a large part.

Darlie Routier is still on Death Row in Texas despite overwhelming evidence that her conviction for killing her own child is false, whilst Knox, Sollecito and Kiszko have been vindicated by the highest judicial authorities and telling evidence. The authors show how and why unfounded rumours still persist in the Knox/Sollecito case and advance a new theory that the Routier killings were the work of a notorious serial killer.

Paperback & eBook | ISBN 978-1-909976-35-1 | 2016 | 280 pages

Fields, Fens and Felonies: Crime and Justice in Eighteenth-Century East Anglia
by Gregory J Durston

A new work on Crime and Punishment in East Anglia (and elsewhere) during the eighteenth century. It was a time of highwaymen, footpads and desperate petty offenders, draconian penalties, extremes of wealth and poverty, corruption and rough and emerging forms of justice.

The contents include justices of the peace, policing, crimes, courts and judges as well as such matters as summary trial and disposal, jury trial, execution (and reprieve), a variety of offences including murder (and other homicides), violence and sexual offences, smuggling, poaching, property crimes, riots and disturbances. The book also looks at the various hierarchies that existed whether social, legal, judicial, religious, military or otherwise so as to exert a variety of social controls at a time of relative lawlessness. A fascinating and statistically absorbing account of crimes, responses and penal outcomes of the era.

Paperback & eBook | ISBN 978-1-909976-11-5 | 2016 | 736 pages

www.WatersidePress.co.uk

The Monstering of Myra Hindley
by Nina Wilde
With a Foreword by Judith Jones and Beatrix Campbell

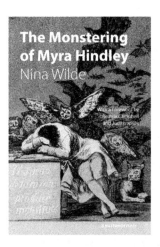

Fifty years after the Moors Murders and 15 years since Myra Hindley died in prison, after one of the longest sentences served by a woman, this book raises some delicate and searching questions. They include: "Why was Hindley treated differently?", "Why do we need to create demons?" and "What impact does this have on our whole notion of crime, punishment and justice?"

Set against the political backlash of one of the most notorious cases in English criminal history, *The Monstering of Myra Hindley* is a perceptive, first-hand portrayal of the most talked-about and maligned of women. Nina Wilde invites readers to hold back any adverse preconceptions as she seeks to show how the media selected Hindley as a monster and the politics at play around her de-humanising captivity. She compares how things are done in some other European countries and how the UK itself routinely releases others equally bad (arguably worse) quietly and away from the public gaze.

Paperback & eBook | ISBN 978-1-909976-34-4 | 2016 | 170 pages

www.WatersidePress.co.uk